ITALIAN FILM IN THE PRESENT TENSE

For observers of the European film scene, Federico Fellini's death in 1993 came to stand for the demise of Italian cinema as a whole. Exploring an eclectic sampling of works from the new millennium, *Italian Film in the Present Tense* confronts this narrative of decline with strong evidence to the contrary.

Millicent Marcus highlights Italian cinema's new sources of industrial strength, its re-placement of the Rome-centred studio system with regional film commissions, its contemporary breakthroughs on the aesthetic front, and its vital engagement with the changing economic and socio-political circumstances in twenty-first-century Italian life. Examining works that stand out for their formal brilliance and their moral urgency, the book presents a series of fourteen case studies, featuring analyses of such renowned films as *Il Divo, Gomorrah, The Great Beauty, We Have a Pope, The Mafia Only Kills in the Summer,* and *Fire at Sea,* along with lesser-known works deserving of serious critical scrutiny. In doing so, *Italian Film in the Present Tense* contests the widely held perception of a medium languishing in its "post-Fellini" moment, and instead acknowledges the ethical persistence and forward-looking currents of Italian cinema in the present tense.

(Toronto Italian Studies)

MILLICENT MARCUS is a professor of Italian studies and film & media studies at Yale University.

Italian Film in the Present Tense

MILLICENT MARCUS

UNIVERSITY OF TORONTO PRESS
Toronto Buffalo London

© University of Toronto Press 2023
Toronto Buffalo London
utorontopress.com

ISBN 978-1-4875-4618-2 (cloth)   ISBN 978-1-4875-4620-5 (EPUB)
ISBN 978-1-4875-4619-9 (paper)   ISBN 978-1-4875-4621-2 (PDF)

Toronto Italian Studies

Library and Archives Canada Cataloguing in Publication

Title: Italian film in the present tense / Millicent Marcus.
Names: Marcus, Millicent Joy, author.
Series: Toronto Italian studies.
Description: Series statement: Toronto Italian studies | Includes bibliographical references and index.
Identifiers: Canadiana (print) 20220447500 | Canadiana (ebook) 20220447527 | ISBN 9781487546182 (cloth) | ISBN 9781487546199 (paper) | ISBN 9781487546212 (PDF) | ISBN 9781487546205 (EPUB)
Subjects: LCSH: Motion pictures – Italy – History – 21st century.
Classification: LCC PN1993.5.I88 M37 2023 | DDC 791.43/750945 – dc23

We wish to acknowledge the land on which the University of Toronto Press operates. This land is the traditional territory of the Wendat, the Anishnaabeg, the Haudenosaunee, the Métis, and the Mississaugas of the Credit First Nation.

This book has been published with the assistance of the Frederick W. Hilles Publication Fund of Yale University.

University of Toronto Press acknowledges the financial support of the Government of Canada, the Canada Council for the Arts, and the Ontario Arts Council, an agency of the Government of Ontario, for its publishing activities.

To Vivian and Miles

our future

Contents

Acknowledgments ix

Introduction: Persistence of Vision, Vectors of Change 3

Part One: Mafias

1 Toward a New Language of Engagement for the New Millennium: Marco Tullio Giordana's *I cento passi* (The One Hundred Steps), 2000   19
2 The Anti-Mafia Martyr Film Takes an Unexpected Turn: Pierfrancesco Diliberto's *La Mafia uccide solo d'estate* (The Mafia Only Kills in the Summer), 2013   35
3 "This Is Not Just a Crime Film": Michele Placido's *Romanzo criminale* (Crime Novel), 2005   47
4 "The Unsustainable Normality of Devastation": Matteo Garrone's *Gomorra* (Gomorrah), 2008   60

Part Two: Neo-regionalism

5 "Per vacanza?" "No, per viverci!" (To vacation? No, to live here!): Giorgio Diritti's *Il vento fa il suo giro* (The Wind Blows Round), 2005   77
6 "What History Is This?": Giorgio Diritti's *L'uomo che verrà* (The Man Who Will Come), 2009   92

Part Three: Migrants

7 Channelling the Geographic Unconscious: Federico Bondi's *Mar nero* (Black Sea), 2008   109

8 "Your Position Please": Gianfranco Rosi's *Fuocoammare* (Fire at Sea), 2016   121

Part Four: Leadership

9 The Ironist and the Auteur: Paolo Sorrentino's *Il Divo: La vita spettacolare di Giulio Andreotti* (Il Divo: The Spectacular Life of Giulio Andreotti), 2008   137

10 Liberating the Left: Toward a Humanist Language of Engagement for a Post-political Age in Roberto Andò's *Viva la libertà* (Long Live Freedom), 2013   152

11 The Pontiff and the Shrink: Nanni Moretti's *Habemus Papam* (We Have a Pope), 2011   165

Part Five: Women

12 "It Ended the Way It Should Have Ended": Francesca Comencini's *Lo spazio bianco* (The White Space), 2009   179

13 Comic Relief: Riccardo Milani's *Ma cosa ci dice il cervello* (Don't Stop Me Now), 2019   193

Part Six: In a Category unto Itself

14 Hidden Beneath the "Blah Blah Blah": Paolo Sorrentino's *La grande bellezza* (The Great Beauty), 2013   209

Notes   225

Bibliography   255

Index   265

Acknowledgments

The writing of this book has taken place over "the long present tense" implied by my title – extending from the early 2000s until 2021. During this broad time span, the cast of characters supporting my work has multiplied beyond measure, so I apologize in advance for any omissions in acknowledging the generous help I've received throughout this decades-long research process.

Because the recent vintage of the films covered in my study means that the English-language scholarship on the subject is relatively scarce, I concentrated most of my efforts on the Italians' critical response to their nation's current cinematic output. In so doing, I've been inestimably helped by Cristina Dell'Orso, the wise, magnanimous, and energetic librarian of the Mediateca della regione Toscana in Florence. My annual summer pilgrimages to this mecca of cinematic knowledge (interrupted only by COVID) have sustained this project from start to finish. Without her help in tracking down the monographs, anthologies, journals, and other scholarly resources related to the new Italian cinema, I would have been lost.

On this side of the Atlantic, my project was nourished by events that brought this body of films to American shores as a way of focusing public attention, and academic scrutiny, on the Italian cinematic ferment of recent years. First and foremost has been the series of sessions titled "Italian Film in the Present Tense" at the annual meetings of the American Association of Italian Studies throughout the last two decades. To all the panelists who presented research on these occasions, thank you for your engagement with the new cinema and the eye-opening inroads you've made in the field. Among the enthusiastic supporters of these efforts has been a group of splendid women affectionately labelled *le fanciulle* – Deborah Amberson, Silvia Carlorosi, Fabiana Cecchini, Crystal Hall, Lina Insana, Giovanna Faleschini Lerner, Nicoletta Marini-Maio,

Elena Past, and Gabriella Romani – former graduate students at the University of Pennsylvania who have now become full-fledged colleagues in the profession, and who organized an entire conference entitled "Italian Cinema in the Present Tense" at Franklin & Marshall College in 2015, whose selected proceedings have been published in a special issue of the *Journal of Italian Cinema and Media Studies*, vol. 7, no. 2 (March 2019). A second initiative aimed at bringing contemporary films from Italy to public notice, this time directed toward lay viewing audiences as well as university faculty and students, has been the annual Yale Festival of New Italian Cinema. Made possible by the combined energies of Ann DeLauro, academic coordinator of the Department of Italian Studies, Anthony Sudol, the "perfectionist projectionist" of the Whitney Humanities Center, and the passionately engaged members of the various graduate student committees dedicated to planning and running the festivals over the course of years, this event has earned a devoted following on campus and in the New Haven community at large. The goal has been to create a culture of receptivity toward the new Italian cinema – to disprove, starting at the local level, the damaging and false impression that Italian cinema died with Fellini.

I would be remiss not to acknowledge the way in which teaching has fueled the writing of this book. The decades of input from undergraduates in my course "Italian Cinema from Post-war to Postmodern" have provided inspiration and proving-grounds for my critical approach to the films of the twenty-first century. And graduate seminars on new Italian cinema have been the venue for intellectual exchanges that have deepened and enriched my understanding of the subject.

Among scholars in the discipline I am immensely grateful to Gaetana Marrone for her generous, supportive, and profoundly insightful response to my work. I also deeply appreciate the colleagues who edited or co-edited the published essays that would become the basis of some of the chapters in this book: Joseph Luzzi, Giovanna Faleschini Lerner, M. Elena Damelio, Giancarlo Lombardi, Christian Uva, Emma Bond, Guido Bonsaver, Federico Faloppa, Patricia Bettella, Daniela De Pau, Georgina Torello, Laura E. Ruberto, Kristi M. Wilson, and Dana Renga.

On the institutional level, my work on this book has benefitted enormously from Yale's triennial leave policy, which made it possible for me to devote several semesters of full-time research to the project. In addition, an award by the Yale Hilles fund contributed generously to the book's publication.

I am profoundly indebted to members of the University of Toronto Press for their support on a number of fronts. Mark Thompson, acquisitions editor, has squired my manuscript through the vetting process with consummate skill, despite the delays and other road-blocks endemic to life in the era of COVID. His ongoing belief in the project has bolstered my morale throughout this dark time. Leah Connor, associate managing editor, has been extremely helpful in moving the manuscript toward publication and clarifying technical issues along the way. To my copy-editor, Terry Teskey, I offer heartfelt thanks. Her laser-sharp eye for inconsistencies, her receptive ear for the rhythms of my prose, and her light touch in questioning my choices have added much to the accuracy and legibility of this text.

To my ever-patient and supportive husband, Allan Hillman, I owe a debt of boundless gratitude. For him, relegation of this "present tense" book to the status of *fait accompli* could not come too soon.

ITALIAN FILM IN THE PRESENT TENSE

Introduction

Persistence of Vision, Vectors of Change

By a striking coincidence, two of the best films to emerge in 2000 were historically based accounts of the lives and premature deaths of little-known anti-Mafia crusaders, and in both cases the neorealist provenance of these works was critically acknowledged. Pasquale Scimeca's *Placido Rizzotto* was hailed as a latter-day example of "the best neorealism, that of Rossellini and of the authors who remained close to the facts, without embroidering on them,"[1] and Marco Tullio Giordana's *I cento passi* (The One Hundred Steps) was labelled "a neorealist film beyond neorealism, hovering between reality, revolt, and dream."[2] Though these statements show how elastic the attribution of a neorealist source can be – authorizing in the one case an unadorned, factually rigorous reportage and in the other a flight into utopian and even oneiric transfigurations of the historical record – such recourse to neorealism revealed its enduring hold over Italian filmmaking on the cusp of the new millennium.[3] Accordingly, recent scholarship has noted the renewed impulse to "dialogue with reality"[4] that has come to characterize current Italian cinema and has linked this trend to the great filmmaking tradition enshrined by Rossellini, De Sica, and Visconti in the immediate post-war years.

It is no mere accident of the calendar that the new millennium should be the venue for the reaffirmation of "the testimonial force of the image – its capacity for *truth-telling* ... by the filmmakers most aware of their political and social role."[5] If the entrance into the twenty-first

---

This chapter is a revised and expanded version of an essay entitled "Persistence of Vision: Realism and the Popular in Italian Cinema of the New Millennium," in *Italian Cinema: From the Silent Screen to the Digital Image*, ed. Joseph Luzzi (London: Bloomsbury Academic, 2020).

century brought with it the heavy symbolism of a rupture in time, that rupture was made literal just twenty-one months and eleven days later with the attack on the World Trade Center, when the ruling forces of nationalism and globalization gave way to something entirely alien, elusive, and seemingly impossible to combat.[6] But this watershed moment was preceded by one that had ushered in a less catastrophic, though no less momentous, reorganization of collective thought: the fall of the Berlin Wall in November 1989, with the subsequent collapse of the Soviet Union and the end of the Cold War. Within the Italian context these events spelled the death of the First Republic, with the splitting (and fatal weakening) of the once formidable Italian Communist Party, and the demise of the post-war governing coalition led by the Christian Democratic and Socialist parties, which had buckled under the weight of corruption charges brought by the judiciary in the so-called *mani pulite* (clean hands) campaign, leaving a power vacuum filled by Berlusconi and his media empire.

This moment of convulsive change in the Italian sociopolitical order coincided with a profoundly symbolic event in the history of Italian film: the 1993 death of Federico Fellini, the last of the great auteurs (De Sica, Visconti, Rossellini, and Pasolini had all died in the 1970s and Antonioni had suffered a debilitating stroke in 1985). It is of no small consequence that the year of Fellini's death also saw the release of a film that was to herald the advent of Italian cinematic rebirth: Nanni Moretti's *Caro diario* (Dear Diary), which sought a new form of *scrittura cinematografica* (cinematic language) in this period of abject "afterness." Moretti's search, both linguistic and existential in nature, would ultimately lead to a single human body, that of the filmmaker himself, which was revealed to be a cinematic sign pointing beyond its status as a mere signifier on-screen. In a shocking segment spliced into the flow of this otherwise meticulously staged cinematic text, Moretti included documentary footage of his own chemotherapy session, in a stark revelation of the fact that his on-screen image, his "body-language" as a cinematic sign, was underwritten by the death threat whose fulfilment he was able to defer.[7] The strong referential impulse embedded in *Caro diario* stands as a harbinger of what Christian Uva has called "a documentary idea that manifests itself directly in its way of looking at reality and in the ethical and aesthetic attitude by which it [reality] is given form."[8]

Such a claim runs counter to the general understanding of the postmodernist trend in contemporary culture as characterized by the withering of the referent and the triumph of simulacra,[9] a trend abetted in visual media by the onslaught of CGI technology. According to this commonly held view, postmodernism's penchant for parody, pastiche, citation, semiotic playfulness, imagistic saturation, and decorative exuberance stands in opposition to the referential seriousness and ethical urgency of realism. But this assumption has been vigorously challenged by Pierpaolo Antonello and Florian Mussgnug in their groundbreaking volume *Postmodern Impegno*, whose title announces its aim to align the post-war Italian tradition of committed art with contemporary cultural developments. To do so, they argue for an updated notion of *impegno* – one adapted to our post-ideological age, which replaces the monolithic, universalizing, absolutist prescriptions for social change rooted in Marxist thought with flexible, pluralistic, localized, ad hoc approaches to the concerns of the day.[10] Central to Antonello and Mussgnug's definition of postmodern *impegno* is the "turn to ethics" that has characterized recent advances in the humanities and the social sciences.[11] Where radical programs for the establishment of a more just social order have failed, a sense of responsibility for the well-being of others, enacted on individual and local community levels and based on a network of "thick relationships" defined by "passional and relational exchange rather than abstract norms,"[12] has come to replace the revolutionary projects that have run aground on the shoals of history.

The return of *impegno*, be it postmodern or aligned with more traditional neorealist practice, has been met with enthusiasm by contemporary Italian scholars who see it as an awakening from the torpor of the 1980s and early 1990s, when television gained ascendency over the cinema as the mass medium *per eccellenza*, and filmmakers followed the lead of their small-screen competitors, withdrawing from the arena of historical and civic engagement and retreating within "the confines of their own domestic walls."[13] Mario Sesti labelled this a cinema of "claustrophilia," while Lino Miccichè went even further, calling the result of such involution a veritable "cinecidio" in its production of "unexportable and often invisible little films, cute films, and trash."[14]

With the new millennium, Franco Montini notes that Italian filmmakers instead embraced a far bolder and more expansive cinematic vision, having "rediscovered the pleasure of narration and of the novelistic" and eager to confront "le grandi storie" (large stories/histories).[15] In a move crucial to the argument of this book, Montini links the turn toward a novelistic storytelling mode with the kind of protean creativity that defies the imposition of categories and hierarchies on Italy's recent output of films. "Italian cinema of the third millennium," Montini writes, "cannot be identified in a school or a movement, devoid as it is of any common denominator, [but] displays in the aggregate a renewed interest in the novel form, with a return to narration, to stories, to characters recounted in depth, in order to critically reflect the reality of the present."[16] It is the novel, as a literary mode broadly construed, and not just as a blueprint for adaptations, that provides the best analogy for the lively, amorphous, fluid, and evolving nature of new Italian cinema – a cinema that, like the novel, has resisted containment within canonical strictures and orders of importance and that, like its literary analogue, has not shied away from telling "the large stories" and engaging the urgencies of historical traumas, contemporary issues, and the complexities of the characters who confront them.

It is entirely appropriate that this novelistic "opening up" of the cinema, its turn toward the expansiveness of the novel form, should find its parallel in a contemporary movement of literary origin: that of the New Italian Epic or NIE, advocated by the Italian writers' collective whimsically named Wu Ming.[17] In their 2009 memorandum[18] the Wu Ming writers accord epic stature to works that are "large, ambitious, *a lunga gittata* [long range], and *di ampio respiro* [of ample breath]" (15), hailing these novels' liberation of new energies, in polemic reaction to Fukuyama's proclamation of the end of history and postmodernism's reduction to pure manner (19). Of particular interest to our present study, Wu Ming emphasizes the transmedial reach of the NIE, its invitation to "a cloud of spin-offs and 'lateral' narrations, web sites, songs, web games or board games, ... role playing of characters in the books and other grass roots contributions of an open nature" (45). Among the films included in this study, two are based on books deemed "new Italian epics" by Wu Ming: *Gomorra* (Gomorrah) and *Romanzo criminale* (Crime Novel), each of which spawned an enormously popular television series, along with copious amounts of fan fiction online.[19]

This fluid movement across media confines lends itself to the critical methods forged by scholars in the burgeoning fields of *intermediality* – "a way of understanding the relations between two media, such as writing and images, or the transgression of boundaries between them," and *transmedia storytelling* – "the expansion of narratives in media franchises such as Batman or Star Wars across multiple platforms including movies, TV, web video, comics, novels, and games."[20] While detailed inquiries into the workings of transmedial travel are beyond the scope of this book, the phenomenon itself is worthy of note for its bearing on film spectatorship as the vital link in the chain of transmission from book to televisual and eventual web-based spin-offs.[21] Though such popular manifestations as fan fiction may seem more aligned with postmodernism's aesthetics of playfulness than with its ethics of civil commitment, the creative impulses triggered by these stories have the power to engage their grass-roots "authors" in ethically charged reflection on the social issues underpinning their narratives, and in so doing to issue a call for activism in the public sphere.

This brings us back to the vision of engagé art proposed by Antonello and Mussgnug in *Postmodern Impegno*, and to its pluralistic, issue-based, open, and contingent nature in light of the evolving socio-historical context of the present age. And as Montini argued in positing the free-wheeling novelistic orientation of contemporary Italian cinema, such a body of work defies easy placement within the confines of a given school or movement. What emerges, instead, is a series of mini-trends, clusters of films that gravitate around thematic questions of the utmost relevance to the contemporary Italian condition. Noteworthy too is the ascension of fresh cinematic talents to public and critical acclaim, as well as the reappearance of established figures whose filmographies take surprising new turns in keeping with their own evolving authorial agendas and the pressures of cultural change. Such developments are the subjects of this introductory chapter, along with considerations of popular cinema, including such genres as horror, noir, and especially comedy, the mainstay of the Italian industry, whose relative inaccessibility to foreign audiences has to date excluded it from much Anglo-American scholarship.

Foremost among the auteurs who emerged in the new millennium are Matteo Garrone and Paolo Sorrentino, winners of top honours at Cannes in 2008 for *Gomorra* and *Il Divo* respectively. Though vastly different in formal terms, both films make strong claims to a realist heritage of *denuncia* (social critique), and in their disparate modes of pursuing that goal they reveal the multiple paths that contemporary film authors can take in fulfilling the mandate for civic engagement.[22] *Gomorra*, based on Roberto Saviano's sensational book about the workings of the Camorra (the Neapolitan mafia), adopts a technically "poor" style, whose unadorned visual imagery, spare musical soundtrack, settings of the most abject urban degradation, and frequent use of the Steadicam align the film with the documentary, anti-spectacular strain of post-war cinematic realism. Employing, for the most part, non-professional actors indigenous to the film's physical setting, allowing them to speak a local dialect that requires subtitles even for Italian audiences, and adopting a directorial style that privileges spontaneity, Garrone simulates a bottom-up approach to representation – as if the pro-filmic world under scrutiny were inventing its own sui generis form, devoid of authorial intervention. This is not to deny the workings of a powerful auteurship behind the film's pretence of stylistic transparency – on the contrary, Garrone's signature takes the paradoxical form of a self-concealing aesthetic that, by refusing to call attention to its constructedness, promotes the referential urgency of the film's message. "This world exists," the film asserts, "and it demands our attention."

In polar opposition to the immanence and transparency of Garrone's film language in *Gomorra* is the "extrinsic" and opaque quality of Sorrentino's style in *Il Divo*. The film's protagonist is Giulio Andreotti – Italy's most powerful post-war politician, whose bland, funereal persona would lead us to expect the most understated possible approach to representation. Instead Sorrentino treats us to an audiovisual extravaganza as he explores the paradox of the frenetic activity that this inert character seems to excite in others. Andreotti's personal inscrutability means that Sorrentino must entrust the signifying task to the film's formal properties. In particular, he makes *Il Divo* a series of stagings that foreground the prodigious effort of mounting this spectacle; hence the "primacy of style" and the "strong directing" that have become Sorrentino's authorial trademark.[23] But the filmmaker's stylistic virtuosity does not rule out an ethically charged approach to Andreotti's case. The film's focus on its protagonist's multiple criminal indictments (including the claim of Mafia collusion) and the location of its final scene in a courtroom place the viewing audience in the jury box, putting the onus on us to render judgment on this ambiguous and elusive pillar of post-war Italian political life.

While *Gomorra*, *Il Divo*, and Michele Placido's *Romanzo criminale*, along with other films such as Roberta Torre's *Angela* (2002), Sorrentino's *Le consequenze dell'amore* (The Consequences of Love, 2004), and Davide Barletti and Lorenzo Conte's *Fine pena mai* (Life Sentence, 2007), depict organized crime from a perspective internal to its workings, there is a significant mini-trend involving historically based portraits of young martyrs who stand up to injustice, in full awareness of the mortal price to be paid for their temerity. This cluster of films, whose most celebrated example is the above-mentioned *I cento passi*, features protagonists hailing from a variety of institutions and social categories: the judiciary, the church, the press, the labour movement, countercultural youth. The trend dates back to the early 1990s, as Mafia violence against legal authorities reached a fever pitch with the murders of trial judges Giovanni Falcone and Paolo Borsellino. In the wake of these atrocities, Alessandro di Robilant filmed *Il giudice ragazzino* (The Boy Judge, 1994) about the final years of Rosario Livatino, a young magistrate of impeccable virtue and intense investigative zeal who runs afoul of the Mafia and refuses to surrender to its tactics of intimidation. Six years later, Pasquale Scimeca's *Placido Rizzotto* recounted the life of his film's title character, a labour organizer whose activism culminates in a campaign, in defiance of Mafia threats, for the popular occupation of fields left uncultivated by the wealthy landowners of Corleone, leading to Rizzotto's violent end and the ignominious disposal of his remains. The church becomes the venue for a bold anti-Mafia crusade on the part of Don Puglisi in Roberto Faenza's *Alla luce del sole* (In Broad Daylight, 2005); Puglisi volunteers for a pulpit in the crime-infested Palermo neighbourhood of Brancacci, where his outspokenness and attempts to offer local youths an alternative to organized criminality earn him the inevitable assassin's bullet. Rita Atria, who was born into a Mafia family and who later turned state's evidence – a decision that required her to assume a false identity and live in hiding, and that finally drove her to suicide – is the subject of two films by Marco Amenta: the documentary *Diario di una siciliana ribelle* (Diary of a [female] Sicilian Rebel, 2002]) and *La ragazza siciliana* (The Sicilian Girl, 2008), a staged recreation of her life and its tragic denouement. A non-Sicilian instalment in the mini-trend of films dedicated to young martyrs in the struggle against organized crime is Marco Risi's *Fort'apasc* (Fort Apache, 2009), the story of Giancarlo Siani, an investigative journalist who would not be dissuaded from uncovering the saga of Camorra corruption and collusion in Torre Annunziata and later in Naples itself.

Among the most striking developments in twenty-first-century Italian cinema has been the pre-eminence of locality as a force that conditions both the narrative substance of the films and their modes of production. I have labelled this phenomenon "neo-regionalism" to explain the emergence of a film corpus rooted in a specific historical-cultural-physical landscape, characterized not only by dialogues in the local idiom but also by a cast of non-professional actors drawn from the region, by a narrative of broad, "choral" expanse, and by a synergistic relationship between humans and their natural environment. Especially noteworthy in this regard is the proliferation of regional film commissions – and here Italians use the English term:[24] Apulia Film Commission, Emilia-Romagna Film Commission, Film Commission Regione Campania, Film Commission Roma & Lazio, Film Commission Torino Piemonte, Toscana Film Commission, and many others[25] – whose emergence has been greeted enthusiastically by observers of the contemporary Italian film scene.[26] At a time when the support provided by the Rome-centred film industry has steeply declined, the regions have rushed in to fill the gap, offering financial incentives and procedural alternatives to a corrupt and bureaucratically burdensome cinematic establishment.[27] In addition to the economic and structural advantages of film administration that originates at the regional level (the power to attract new capital to the area, create local jobs, boost tourism, promote the distinct identity of a region or, in a word, its "brand"),[28] this trend has brought considerable innovation into the language of contemporary Italian cinema. Far-flung landscapes and townscapes, often unknown to audiences both domestically and abroad, are now debuting on Italian screens, where they are raised to levels of importance that far exceed mere background status. The setting thus becomes a prime determinant in the shaping of the film as a whole, acting as a protagonist of the conceptual process and the material realization of the work.[29] In this regard, it is worth quoting at length Vito Zagarrio's formulation of this movement's impact on the state of Italian cinema today. "The Film Commissions," he writes,

> have become the central motors of the national cinema's new identity in the third millennium ... If the cinema of the 90's was claustrophobic and claustrophilic, that of the new century and the new millennium breathes more deeply, revealing in its open areas, in its landscapes, and in its urban views, interesting strategies that attempt to obviate the long-lived, dramatic absence of a production apparatus of an industry and a system ever more in crisis.[30]

In light of the entrepreneurial strength generated by this grass-roots movement, and the resulting film corpus deeply tied to the pluralistic, regional nature of Italian life, the political implications of this development are far reaching. Above all, film commissions have helped rehabilitate the concept of regionalism after its abuse at the hands of the former Lega Nord (Northern League), which tethered local interests to the elitist, racist, and xenophobic values of a politics devoted to exclusionary ends. (In 2018, under the leadership of Matteo Salvini, the Lega dropped its modifier *Nord* in an opportunistic appeal to national unity, all the while maintaining its demagogic, populist, anti-immigrant agenda.) Neo-regionalism poses an alternative idea of what it means to identify with a subnational geography, arguing for a strong sense of local rootedness as the foundation on which to build engagement in ever-more-expansive spheres of political, social, and moral life. This line of thinking emerges with special clarity in the words of a character in Nicola Cirasola's *Focaccia Blues* (2009), a documentary about the failure of McDonald's to survive in the Pugliese town of Altamura, where a local bakery triumphed over the temporary allure of fast food and the more permanent economic pressures of globalization: "This is the great cultural theme of today – respect for local identities in the ambit of the great multinationals that by now govern the world. We are fully European, we are fully international, we are fully human, if we are truly *altamurani, pugliesi, italiani*."[31]

Food is no mere synecdoche for the triumph of the local in *Focaccia Blues*. As Carlo Petrini's Slow Food movement has made abundantly clear, gastronomy has served as the basis for a rethinking of our contemporary condition in natural and cultural terms, with its emphasis on indigenous culinary traditions, the use of ingredients locally grown, and the focus on sustainability and the general stewardship of the environment. In relation to Petrini's movement, the new culture of slowness emerges as a general category – a philosophical reaction against our obsession with velocity and all that it entails: feverish productivity, overstimulation of the senses and the mind, the hyper-connectedness of our technologically saturated existence, frenetic mobility aimed at the sheer accumulation of experience, and quantitative measures of value in all things. I therefore join scholars who have labelled films that partake of this cultural opposition to the reigning values of our globalized and digitized world "Slow Cinema."[32] By this I do not mean to suggest that all such films are slow moving in the literal sense (though some of them most decidedly are). The intent of "slow films" is first and foremost experiential – to immerse viewers in a world that challenges the primacy of technologically enhanced movement through time and across space, with all of the philosophical implications this entails. Michelangelo Frammartino's *Le quattro volte* (The Four Times, 2010), for example, is so devoid of the usual mechanisms for spectator engagement that it exacts from us an entirely new mode of attention, resulting in a pure phenomenology that places us before the raw spectacle of existence without the filters necessary to contain its mystery.

Related to the category of slow cinema is the trend toward environmentally conscious filmmaking – the emergence of works that elevate to the foreground interactions between the human and natural worlds. In extreme cases, such as that of *Le quattro volte*, *homo sapiens* is banished to the margins of the story so that landscape, animal, and mineral spheres no longer occupy mere background status within the material setting of the film. This decentring of the human and concomitant privileging of the environment places such slow films in an overlapping relationship to "eco-cinema," a field that is just now coming into its own within the American academy.[33]

A film that shares important features with *Le quattro volte* – a leisurely pace, a de-dramatized plot, a visual fixation on landscape as both object of contemplation and source of an independent subjectivity, a reverence for the primordial human condition, and a fascination with goats (!) – is Giorgio Diritti's *Il vento fa il suo giro* (The Wind Blows Round, 2005). Set in the remote recesses of north-eastern Piedmont, *Il vento fa il suo giro* gives hyperbolic expression to the neo-regionalist impulse in Italian film. But it is important to note that Diritti's work is hardly an unequivocal paean to provincial life, delivering instead a balanced and at times caustic view of the human fauna that inhabit this spectacular natural landscape. The ideal of a progressive, welcoming, all-embracing collective identity that flows from a firm sense of local rootedness and spreads to ever broader spheres of civic engagement in *Focaccia Blues* meets its negative counterpart in Diritti's film. When Philippe Héraud, a French goatherd, chooses a village to settle his family and ply his trade as a cheese maker, the local populace is taken by surprise. While the municipal leaders embrace this young family as an infusion of new life into the languishing community, deeply entrenched suspicions soon surface among a growing number of residents, and the family is eventually expelled from their midst.

Though the Hérauds' French roots exempt them from the virulence with which non-European immigrants are greeted, their difficult adjustment to Italian soil results from factors common to the migratory experience as a whole. Indeed, it should come as no surprise that the influx of migrants would occupy a growing sector of cinematic production in today's Italy.[34] Documentarist Gianfranco Rosi takes on this development in the award-winning *Fuocoammare*, a film set on the tiny island of Lampedusa, accidental port of entry for African migrants shipwrecked on the way to Europe. Rosi's film belongs not only to the body of work that addresses the most searing issue facing Italian collective identity in recent times, but is also part of the wave of documentary filmmaking that has surged since the turn of the new millennium, thanks to the democratizing power of digital technology and the "urge to go and see things, there, where they are, the events where they occur, to document them," writes Roberto De Gaetano, "even if no guarantee is granted to the documentary image, beyond that of being the trace of this need, and of the search for the meaning [that emerges] when encountering the real."[35] Statistics speak eloquently of the millennial spike in documentary filmmaking, as reported by Daniele Dottorini, who cites the rise from 170 works in 2006 to 572 in 2011 (an increase of 345% over 2005) and to 607 in 2012, as confirmation of this upward trend.[36] To complicate and enrich the study of recent production in this sector, a number of disparate categories fall under the documentary rubric, including but not limited to ethnographic cinema, the memoir, the mockumentary, the *commedia documentaria*, the film-essay, the I-film, the found-footage film, the documentary of animation, the guerilla documentary, in addition to the numerous other cinematic exercises that linger on the border between reportage and fiction.[37] Given the energy behind this development, and its experimental nature, the documentary has been deemed "a laboratory pulsating with expressive urgencies far from the 'normality of the media'"[38] – a status that accords this mode a place of privilege in debates about the definition of realism itself in the twenty-first century.

Cinema al femminile has also undergone a welcome increase in recent years, after taking off in the 1970s with Lina Wertmuller's and Liliana Cavani's rise to auteurship, followed by the entrances of Francesca Archibugi, Christina and Francesca Comencini, Susanna Nicchiarelli, Wilma Labate, Roberta Torre, Costanza Quatriglio, Alice Rohracher, Alina Marazzi, and Sabrina Guzzanti into the ranks of Italian women filmmakers. It should come as no surprise that the theme of motherhood would hold a place of prominence among the films of *cinema al femminile*. Francesca Comencini's *Lo spazio bianco* (The White Space) is a prominent case in point, dealing not only with the personal trauma of premature birth but of societal failures with respect to single motherhood. Though the *cinema al femminile* label refers specifically to films made by women, I broaden the category to include works that foreground female subjectivities, regardless of authorial gender, such as *Mar nero* (Black Sea), focused on the rich and complex interaction between an elderly Florentine widow and her Romanian caregiver, or *Ma cosa ci dice il cervello* (Don't Stop Me Now), about a self-effacing mother/office worker who radically (and hilariously) overturns all of the stereotypes associated with her drab public persona.

Although to this point I have focused on trends and specific examples that have characterized the changing complexion of Italian cinema since 2000, it is important to acknowledge an element of continuity that has underpinned the health and viability of the industry over the years. I am referring to the popular genres that make up the great bulk of domestic production and constitute the main diet of Italian film-goers (aside from the inevitable Hollywood fare that takes up a significant share of the menu). Among the genres that flourish in Italian soil are, according to Christian Uva, "il noir, il thriller, l'horror, the detective story"[39] (note the international provenance of these labels, revealing perhaps the frisson of the foreign that underwrites their appeal?). Above all, it is the comic genre that might well be considered the "macro-genre," "the mode of being of our 'industry,'" in the words of Vito Zagarrio.[40] The spectacular success of Italian film comedy from the very outset of the industry speaks to the genre's deep roots in national culture, harking back to the Renaissance *commedia dell'arte* and to the other rich comedic traditions native to the country's literary and theatrical history. It is the quintessential *italianità* of this mode, its ability to hold up the mirror to the Italian national self and to reflect that image back as the object of therapeutic laughter, that explains the genre's perennial hold on the collective imagination. "Italian film comedy represents the identity of the Country – one ... associated with 'national character,'" writes Vito Zagarrio.[41] The critic goes on to label *la commedia italiana* a "macro-genre" embracing "a panorama of typologies with different nuances" including carry-overs from the 1980s and 1990s, auteur works by the likes of Carlo Verdone and Leonardo Pieraccioni, generational comedies that appeal to the youth imaginary and feature the casting of new sex symbols (Riccardo Scamarcio among them), and eccentric comedies that adapt old Hollywood models to Italian modernity.[42] Foremost in the sub-categories of Italian film comedies, according to Christian Uva, is the *cinepanettone* (Christmas-cake film), "whose release is ... rigidly programmed for the winter holidays and whose primary artificer has been, for approximately twenty years, the director Neri Parenti" in collaboration with the "actor-fetish Christian De Sica."[43] The summer equivalent of this phenomenon is the *cinecocomero* (watermelon film), or beach movie – a mini-genre that overlaps with another popular genre, the "teen movie," crowned by the smash hit *La notte prima degli esami* (The Night Before the Exams, 2006, by Fausto Brizzi) and the sequel that it spawned. Seriality, or in Hollywood terms the "franchise," is key to the success of such popular cinema, contributing to its ritual appeal, often tied to seasonal celebrations and promising the assured pleasures of the familiar with enough novelty to keep it from becoming stale and passé.[44] Of considerable critical interest in this regard is the elevation of the popular to the level of serious and sustained study by recent scholars who argue convincingly for the importance of genre films as manifestations of the ideological and psychological issues confronting the Italian collective self.[45] Thus Mary Wood interprets "the continuing narrative and visual tensions in popular cinema, characterized by its emotional and visual excess," as symptoms of the "impossibility of constructing a completely modern consensus of Italian values."[46]

"Books often aspire to order things," Gianni Canova remarked in his 2010 volume *Cinemania: 10 anni, 100 film: Il cinema italiano del nuovo millennio*. "One writes them to categorize, to forge hierarchies, to define, to catalogue. This book ... has no such ambition. It does not want to *ingabbiare* [enclose in a cage] the multiform dynamism of contemporary Italian cinema within a rigid, constrictive taxonomy."[47] Over a decade later, I have found myself in full accord with Canova's position – his refusal to confine the exuberant eclecticism of twenty-first-century Italian film production to a fixed set of labels or prescriptive schemes. This book celebrates the triumphant impurity of the contemporary screen, its resistance to strict measures of ideological orthodoxy or aesthetic norms. It also celebrates the vibrant energy and experimental vision of a cinema that has defied the grim forecast of inexorable decline with the passing of the great generation of post-war Italian auteurs. In assessing cinematic developments over the first two decades of the new century, Alessia Cervini insists on affirming, first and foremost, "the vitality of an expressive form that does not cease to remodel languages and instruments in the light of impulses as variable as the world that produces them," and while her study has an international scope, the applicability of these remarks to the Italian case will be among the pre-eminent concerns of the pages to follow.[48]

Needless to say, full coverage of twenty-first-century Italian film production would be neither possible nor desirable within the bounds of a single volume, but in this work I hope to make up in depth and detail what it may lack in expanse. Fourteen case studies will form the content of my chapters, organized in groupings that reflect shared thematic concerns rather than chronology or genre. "Mafias" is the first and largest unit, demonstrating both filmmakers' and the public's preoccupation and fascination with the workings of organized crime. As previously mentioned, this cluster of films displays a dual perspective on criminality: the anti-Mafia focus of both Marco Tullio Giordana's *I cento passi* and Pierfrancesco Diliberto's *La Mafia uccide solo d'estate* (The Mafia Only Kills in the Summer), and the depiction from within of Michele Placido's *Romanzo criminale* and Matteo Garrone's *Gomorra*. In the second unit, "Neo-regionalism," the name I have given to the recent outpouring of works resulting from the decentralization of the film industry and the new entrepreneurship emerging from the provinces, finds among its most accomplished practitioners Giorgio Diritti, two of whose films, *Il vento fa il suo giro* and *L'uomo che verrà* (The Man Who Will Come), make up this unit. Diritti enacts their "situatedness" in strikingly linguistic terms through the use of dialects specific to these narrowest of localities: Occitan (a vestige of the medieval *lang d'oc*) in the first film and the peasant dialect of the countryside adjacent to Modena in the second. The phenomenon of immigration, which has attracted urgent and wide-spread cinematic attention ever since the tidal wave of fugitives from poverty and/or persecution began arriving in Italy from Africa and Eastern Europe in the early 1990s, provides the subject of the third unit, "Migrants." The pair of titles in this unit span geographic and generic distances – Federico Bondi's *Mar nero* is a fiction film set in Tuscany and Romania featuring the intimate story of Angela, a young Romanian caregiver, and Emma, an elderly widow resentful of her need for care, while Gianfranco Rosi's *Fuocoammare* (Fire at Sea) is a documentary about the inhabitants of Lampedusa, an island in the Pelagian archipelago, site of heroic and sometimes failed attempts to rescue victims of the unseaworthy vessels that set sail from Libyan shores in hopes of reaching the European mainland. The fourth unit is "Leadership," a chronic concern of a country whose memory of Mussolini still haunts the collective consciousness and whose quick rotation of governments in the post-war period has favoured the ironic longevity of such figures as Giulio Andreotti and, more recently, of Silvio Berlusconi. Actor Toni Servillo stars in two of the films included in this grouping, both dealing with politics: as Andreotti in Paolo Sorrentino's *Il Divo* and as identical twin brothers who take turns leading the party of the opposition in Roberto Andò's *Viva la libertà* (Long Live Freedom). Outside the political arena, but hardly devoid of political implications, is the leadership vacuum in the church that occurred after the death of John Paul II. Although Nanni Moretti could not have known that Pope Benedict XVI would abdicate the papacy two years after the release of *Habemus Papam* (We Have a Pope), the filmmaker must have intuited the crisis at the heart of the Vatican and the formidable challenge that it posed to whoever was appointed John Paul's successor. Cinema *al femminile* is the subject of the penultimate unit of the book, which includes two films of vastly different registers and production values. Francesca Comencini's *Lo spazio bianco* is based on Valeria Parrella's eponymous novel about a mother's vigil beside the incubator of the baby born to her in the sixth month of pregnancy and whose fate wavers between viability and death. Comencini transposes this story into a film of considerable psychological nuance through an understated technique capable of activating viewers' most powerful impulses of identification and angst. Riccardo Milani's *Ma cosa ci dice il cervello* (Don't Stop Me Now), by contrast, is an over-the-top comedy featuring a female lead with Marvel Comic strength, versatility, and brains. This slick, cleverly plotted, big-budget production exemplifies the best of the *commedia italiana* genre – the mainstay of domestic film production – with a neat feminist twist.

"In a category unto itself," the final unit, sets Sorrentino's *La grande bellezza* (The Great Beauty) apart from the rest of the works considered in this volume for its unabashed aestheticism. The film becomes its own privileged object of contemplation, but manages to deflect charges of self-indulgence by probing deeply into the protagonist's creative crisis, and his emergence from it. Whether Sorrentino's aesthetic turn is a harbinger of a general trend within new Italian cinema remains to be seen. But even if *La grande bellezza* is an isolated case, Sorrentino's achievement stands as a vital contribution to the "multiform dynamism" that resides at the heart of this book.

PART ONE

Mafias

Chapter One

Toward a New Language of Engagement for the New Millennium: Marco Tullio Giordana's *I cento passi* (The One Hundred Steps), 2000

Direction: Marco Tullio Giordana. *Screenplay*: Claudio Fava, Monica Zapelli, Marco Tullio Giordana, Vanda Vaz. *Cinematography*: Roberto Forza, Stefano Paradiso. *Editing*: Roberto Missiroli. *Sets*: Franco Ceraolo. *Costumes*: Elisabetta Montaldo. *Music*: Giovanni Sollima. *Cast*: Luigi Lo Cascio (Peppino Impastato), Lorenzo Randazzo (Peppino as a boy), Luigi Maria Burruano (Luigi Impastato), Lucia Sardo (Felicia Impastato), Paolo Briguglia (Giovanni Impastato), Toni Sperandeo (Tano Badalamenti), Andrea Tidona (Stefano Venuti), Claudio Gioè (Salvo Vitale), Pippo Montalbano (Cesare Manzella), Ninni Bruschetta (Cousin Anthony), Paola Pace (Cosima).

Synopsis: Set in Cinisi, a province of Palermo, the film begins with a luncheon at the home of the family patriarch, Cesare Manzella (uncle of the ten-year-old Peppino Impastato) to celebrate the engagement of cousin Anthony, from New York, who has returned to Sicily to find a bride. Tensions between Manzella and Tano Badalamenti, a member of the extended family and obvious contender for Mafia power, flare up at the gathering. When the former is killed by a car bomb, Tano takes his place as local boss. In homage to his uncle, Peppino seeks to have a portrait of the slain man painted by Stefano Venuti, a staunch communist who becomes the young boy's mentor. Peppino grows up to become a militant activist – a position that puts him into

---

This chapter is a revised version of an essay entitled "In Memoriam: The Neorealist Legacy in the Contemporary Sicilian Anti-Mafia Film," in *Italian Neorealism and Global Cinema*, ed. Laura E. Ruberto and Kristi M. Wilson (Detroit: Wayne State University Press, 2007). © 2007 Wayne State University Press, with the permission of Wayne State University Press.

open Oedipal confrontation with his father, Luigi, who is beholden to Mafia patronage for his livelihood. After a particularly violent family confrontation, Peppino takes his younger brother Giovanni on a walk from their house to that of Tano Badalamenti, separated by the one hundred steps of the film's title, and rails against the corruption and injustice of Mafia rule. As Peppino's political and cultural activism increases in intensity, he takes to the airwaves to transmit his message, establishing an independent radio station, Radio Aut, and surrounding himself with a devoted circle of followers. A hippie commune takes root on the outskirts of the town, bringing an infusion of liberated young women to the area, along with a guru who wants to collaborate with Peppino to "deprovincialize" Radio Aut. In time, Peppino decides to run for office, choosing the Democrazia Proletaria party (to the left of the Partito Comunista Italiano), but just before the election he is kidnapped and murdered by Tano's henchmen. Though Peppino's tragedy is overshadowed by terrorist developments on the national level, in Cinisi the funeral procession of the young anti-Mafia martyr turns into a political protest of powerful and massive proportions.

"They haven't forgotten Peppino." These are the words uttered by Felicia, Peppino's mother, as she looks down from her window at the vast demonstration against the Mafia murder of her son. In so stating, she gives voice to the impetus behind the making of *I cento passi* – to memorialize the anti-Mafia activism of one whose martyrdom was upstaged by the concurrent discovery of Premier Aldo Moro's tragic end on 9 May 1978, after his kidnapping and execution by the Red Brigades. The film's profound memorialist impulse harks back to a little-noted legacy of the neorealist tradition, embedded in Roberto Rossellini's first post-war works: *Rome Open City*, which eulogized the populist heroics of Pina, Manfredi, and Don Pietro; and *Paisan*, which commemorated characters whose mortal sacrifices would otherwise have gone unrecorded – those of Carmela (Sicilian episode), of the anonymous partisan who dies in Harriet's arms (Florentine episode), and of Cigolani, Dale, and their co-combatants (Po River episode). It could well be argued that the makeshift sign used to mark the grave of the executed partisan retrieved from the waters of the Po in *Paisan* reveals, retroactively, the identity of Rossellini's first neorealist films as epitaphs, literally understood as writings on tombs.

In keeping with the memorialist strain of neorealism, *I cento passi* presents itself as epitaphic, as a cinematic tomb inscription designed to transmit the legacy of moral engagement and social justice for which its protagonist gave his life. Needless to say, the neorealist ancestry of *I cento passi* requires considerable updating before it can give rise to an adequate account of the film's memorialist achievement. In fact, Giordana's work bears the imprint of several film-historical developments since the neorealist era, including the *cinema politico* genre of the 1960s and early to middle 1970s along with the more poetic, nuanced treatments of politically charged issues in the subsequent decades.[1] Giordana's own explicit citing of Francesco Rosi's *Le mani sulla città* (Hands on the City, 1963) is of great interest in this regard: Rosi's ground-breaking exposé of corruption in the Neapolitan building industry is featured prominently in the striking episode of a post-screening debate led by Peppino in *I cento passi*, set in a local youth club devoted to the enjoyment of "cinema e musica." As the final frames of *Le mani sulla città* flicker on the screen-within-the-screen and the lights go up, Peppino rises to initiate a discussion of Rosi's film but is interrupted twice by the DJ, who is eager to begin the "musica" part of the evening's entertainment.[2] Yielding to the crowd's preference for rock 'n' roll over a learned debate on the film's intellectual and formal attributes, Peppino good-naturedly joins his peers on the dance floor, gyrating as unrestrainedly as the rest of them. In this meta-cinematic moment so fraught with meaning for Giordana's film, the message is clear – the harsh militancy of *cinema politico* must give way to a more accessible style that will promote identification among new generations of viewers, for whom the orthodoxy of 1960s political art could hardly produce "imitable models" for a later, less ideologically disposed demographic.[3] In other words, Giordana must "humanize" Peppino, and he does so by offering a psychological portrait that roots the character's public activism in a profoundly personal microcosm of family entanglements and deep moral convictions.

As the scion of a man beholden to the Mafia for his livelihood and a mother deeply attuned to her son's unconventional leanings, Peppino occupies a place rife with Oedipal implications within the family circle.[4] Two episodes bring these psychoanalytic mechanisms to the fore, and in both cases it is the physicality of the mise-en-scène that tells the story. The most raw and primitive of these encounters occurs after Luigi Impastato learns that his son has used the airwaves to mount a campaign of public ridicule against the local Mafia boss, Tano Badalamenti, and his minions. Luigi begins by complimenting Peppino on his radio show, but he punctuates this pleasantry with a blow to his son's stomach that sends the young man sprawling on the floor. The older man falls upon his son and locks him in a tight embrace, while repeatedly invoking the biblical commandment to "honour thy father" and insisting that his son recite it in turn. The struggle is shot from a suffocatingly close distance, which confines the viewer to the intimate space between the two: Luigi's face is nestled in the crook of Peppino's neck for some seconds and inches away from the young man's mouth in others, implicating us in this emotionally disconcerting embrace. Luigi's appeal to Peppino's training in catechism and his recourse to the sovereignty of the church to bolster his own claims for patriarchal authority only infuriate his son, who literally flips over his father to assume the uppermost position in their physical struggle as the scene draws to a close.

Appropriately, the next installment in this Oedipal scenario presents the maternal side of the equation.[5] Felicia is shown lugging a suitcase toward the squalid den where Peppino is living after his expulsion from home. When she enters this cave-like domain, the young man's physical appearance displays the unkempt and run-down state of his solitary confinement: he sports a scruffy beard and is dressed only in jockey shorts, displaying an emaciated torso.[6] His bare chest, and the vulnerability that it reveals, presents a stark contrast to the obvious brute strength that he displayed during his brawl with his father in the immediately preceding scene. But his physical undernourishment in the scene with his mother has been offset by a diet of reading, and the heavy suitcase that Felicia has brought him is laden with books. Chief among them is a volume of Pasolini's poetry, which Peppino immediately opens to the verses of "Supplica a mia madre" (Plea to my mother, 1962). "E` difficile dire con parole di figlio" (It is difficult to say with words of a son), he recites:

> ciò a cui nel cuore ben poco assomiglio.
> Tu sei la sola al mondo che sa, del mio cuore
> ciò che è stato sempre, prima d'ogni altro amore.
>
> (what in my heart I so little resemble.
> You are the only one in the world who knows, what has always
> been in my heart, before every other love.)

At this point, Peppino hands the volume to his mother, who continues:

> Per questo devo dirti ciò che è orrendo conoscere:
> è dentro la tua grazia che nasce la mia angoscia.
> Sei insostituibile. Per questo è dannata

alla solitudine la vita che mi hai data.
E non voglio esser solo. Ho un'infinita fame
d'amore, dell'amore di corpi senza anima.
Perché l'anima è in te, sei tu, ma tu
sei mia madre e il tuo amore è la mia schiavitù.[7]

(For this, I must tell you what is horrendous to know:
it is within your grace that my anguish is born.
You are irreplaceable. For this reason,
the life you gave me is condemned to solitude.
And I don't want to be alone. I have an infinite
hunger for love, love of bodies without a soul.
For the soul is inside you, it is you, but
you are my mother and your love is my enslavement.)

Though Pasolini's poem continues for another eight lines, Felicia stops her recitation here, turns to her son with a stricken look, and holds that expression as the scene slowly fades to black.

Giordana's decision to write and direct this scene as a dialogue – to have Peppino and his mother share in the reading of a single-voiced poem – is rich with dramatic implications. It means that not only does Pasolini's verse serve as a vehicle for expressing Peppino's Oedipal attachment, but that his mother is given an active, culturally engaged role in the process. She need not remain the passive object of filial adoration but can acknowledge, by vocalizing these verses, her part in this reciprocally binding and enslaving rapport. The poetic performance becomes an intervention, a way for Peppino to suture into the text of his own life the epiphanic power of Pasolini's art.[8]

This recourse to Pasolini is but one of many instances in which Giordana highlights a given art form or medium as a potent expressive tool for the contemporary filmmaker in search of a new language of engagement, beyond the austerities of the *cinema politico* model. The art of portraiture occupies pride of place in the palette of aesthetic options available to such a filmmaker. It is therefore no accident that Peppino's political mentor, the communist activist Stefano Venuti, happens to be a painter, and that the young boy's political coming-of-age begins in the latter's studio. Earlier, Stefano had spotted Peppino in the piazza while delivering his stump speech, and had noted that the boy was possessed of a face both "beautiful" and "clean" and graced with "intelligent eyes." This reading of the face according to a typology that equates physical features with moral attributes, as enshrined in the ancient science of physiognomy, underwrites the dramaturgy of Peppino's fateful

24   Italian Film in the Present Tense

Peppino's diametrically opposed relationships to his father and mother emerge clearly in these juxtaposed stills. Commanding Peppino to "honour his father" by quoting scripture, Luigi physically enacts the power he seeks to exert over his son. Felicia instead, at Peppino's gentle urging, recites lines from Pasolini that enable her to fathom the sanctity and entrapment of their mother-son bond.

visit to Stefano's studio. The pretext for the visit is the boy's request for a portrait of his slain uncle, Mafioso boss Cesare Manzella, but Stefano refuses on grounds that are rooted in his own ethically engaged theory of representation. "A face can be a garden, a forest, an isolated land where nothing grows. I only paint the landscapes that I like."[9] With this response, Stefano expresses not only his artistic freedom of choice but also his belief in the transformational power of his craft, which turns faces into symbolic landscapes based on the moral attributes of the sitter. Peppino, who is immediately drawn to the portrait of the poet Vladimir Mayakovsky, cheerfully enters into Stefano's metaphoric system, asking not who the subject is but what landscape he evokes. The answer, "a river, a great river in flood," reveals Stefano's belief in the revolutionary power unleashed by the poet's art. Peppino, eager to hear more, is told "it's a long story," followed by a grave look that Stefano casts upon the boy to convey the moral weight of the testimony that he is about to receive. The child answers, "raccontala" (literally, recount it) with the gravity that accompanies the sealing of a solemn pact. Giordana chooses to represent on screen neither the story of Mayakovsky nor Stefano's telling of it, opting instead to jump ahead some ten years to show Peppino as a committed communist engaging in a campaign to occupy farmlands expropriated by the government for the expansion of the local airport. The cut from the scene of childhood storytelling to adult activism implies a causal relationship between the two events, so that the tale of Mayakovsky becomes the catalyst, the exemplum that replicates itself in the life of the listener. Presented elliptically, the Mayakovsky account invites the active collaboration of the film viewer in the making of meaning, so that we too are invested in the interpretive process by which exemplary art can intervene to change the course of human life. As receivers of the paradigmatic story of Peppino Impastato, we in turn form the next link in the chain of artistically inspired social action.

The episode in Stefano's studio is not the only instance in which portraiture features prominently in the film's plot. Toward the end of *I cento passi*, the adult Peppino will return to that same studio, where a surprise awaits: Stefano shows him a portrait he sketched during Peppino's childhood visit to the place. We retrospectively come to realize that the painter had all along intended to insert this portrait into the gallery of political activists whose images had populated the space of his studio on the day that was to determine the young boy's political future.

Among the other art forms and media incorporated in Giordana's film as he seeks to broaden the linguistic repertoire of *cinema politico* are literature (cited already in the examples of Mayakovsky and Pasolini); music, both popular and classical; and, of central importance to Peppino's biography, radio. The station established by Peppino and his friends, Radio Aut, grew out of the *radio libera* movement, reflecting the widespread impulse in Italy to use the airwaves for the spread of an alternative, countercultural voice. Umberto Eco estimates that there were over one thousand such independent stations in Italy by 1978,[10] including Radio Alice of Bologna, Onda Rossa of Rome, and the fictitious Radiofreccia of Reggio Emilia, subject of Ligabue's nostalgic 1998 film of that same title. Having been banned from performing political theatre in the streets of Cinisi and ousted from the pages of the radical newspaper *Idea Socialista*, Peppino resorted to the airwaves to exercise the free-speech prerogative denied him in other public forums. "When they don't give us permission to hold a rally, when they close our club house, when they confiscate our material," Peppino explains to Barbablu, his equipment supplier, "they can't confiscate the air."

Of utmost importance is the fact that Peppino's revolutionary project is strictly regional in scope. He has no pretensions to reaching an audience beyond the limited confines of Cinisi. When Barbablù boasts that "today a tape player and a little antenna are enough to set up a radio. There must be a thousand of them in Italy," Peppino responds succinctly: "For me, it's enough for them to hear it in Cinisi." Later, in choosing to occupy the radio station to shake his supporters out of their complacency, Peppino defines their political mission as follows: "We're not in Paris, or Berkeley. We're not in Goa, in Woodstock, or the Island of Wight. We're in Cinisi, Sicily, where all they expect is our disengagement, our withdrawal into private life ... For this I wanted to symbolically occupy the radio station: to reclaim your attention." In the many scenes involving the installation and operation of the broadcast studio, the film bears witness to the rise of a utopian community of young male idealists orbiting around a charismatic leader who embodies a transcendent social idea. Here, as elsewhere, Pasolini comes to mind, with his celebration of the sub-proletarian community of *Accattone*, or the more constructive, culturally prestigious one of Jesus's disciples in *The Gospel According to Matthew*, or of Giotto's workshop in the *Decameron*.[11]

Though anti-cinematic in its confinement to the small recording studio, the style of the scenes shot during radio broadcasting is of great visual interest, for it establishes an iconography of communicative power and revolutionary zeal. Sporting the elaborate headset of the radio announcer, hunching over the microphone, and delivering impromptu speeches of varying degrees of intensity, these "talking heads" become visual icons of a counterculture that has found its voice and revels in the freedom to use it. These are ecstatic images of the media outreach that even a limited technology can support, and as such they provide a model for an anti-spectacular yet cogent cinematic ideal. But the energy and excitement that radiates from these scenes is tinged with the knowledge of their evanescence, and the music – so redolent of 1970s tastes – lends an air of finality to their evocation, which marks this period as irrevocably past.

The austerity of means that underwrites Radio Aut's success does not, however, translate into an anti-aesthetic stance on the part of Peppino (or, by extrapolation, Giordana). Instead, Peppino exhibits a longing for beauty that reaches the level of doctrine. "So perhaps more than politics, the class struggle, consciousness and all these silly things ... we need to remind people of what is beauty. Teach them to recognize it. To defend it," Peppino tells his friend Salvo after admiring the panorama from a hilltop above Cinisi "Beauty is important," he continues. "From that everything else takes second place." In classical terms, Peppino is advocating a Platonic concept of beauty that cannot be divorced from goodness or truth, and that when recognized will hasten the soul's journey to enlightenment. In practice it means the quest for a pedagogy that will reach a mass public through the appeal of the beautiful, or, in less exalted terms, the pleasurable and the entertaining. According to Gianni Quilici, Peppino's task is to invent "a language which connects politics with aesthetics, in a poetically spectacular dimension. Impastato understands that politics, the facts and understanding of them are the center on which to structure a communication that unites politics and poetry, radio and theatre, low with high, direct messages with mediated ones, farce with morality."[12] In his ability to reach mass audiences with his politically progressive message, Peppino becomes the organic intellectual heralded by Antonio Gramsci, able to penetrate the humus of popular culture to bring about a political awakening.

Among the arts that Giordana appropriates to enrich his film language of *impegno* is pop music, given the prominence of Radio Aut in Peppino's arsenal of communicative tools. Though recourse to period songs in films has been critically demeaned as a short cut to evoking an era, extorting reactions of nostalgia and longing for lost youth that foreclose more nuanced thinking about the past, Emanuele D'Onofrio has offered a meticulous and convincing defence of Giordana's musical choices in *I cento passi*.[13] From the film's very earliest glimpses into Peppino's boyhood, pop music provides rich cultural contextualization and psychological insights into his character. When Peppino and his younger brother Giovanni sing the lyrics to Domenico Modugno's

Volare (To Fly, 1958), they give voice to post-war Italy's new-found optimism on the threshold of the Economic Miracle. In personal and metaphorical terms, Peppino will enact the flight announced in the song's exuberant lyrics by soaring above his society's provincial limits, thanks to the humanist values imparted by his education and his inborn moral revulsion against Mafia rule.

It should come as no surprise that the scene of Peppino's boyhood political conversion in Stefano's studio would be accompanied by appropriate diegetic music issuing from the painter's own record player: Django Reinhardt's "Minor Swing" (1937). Delving into the history of this piece, D'Onofrio proclaims its subversiveness on multiple counts: Reinhardt was of gypsy origin (hence ethnically "other" in Paris, where he lived and worked before and during the Nazi occupation), and his musical medium was jazz – always in an oppositional relationship to the cultural mainstream.[14] When the adult Peppino revisits Stefano's studio toward the end of the film, diegetic music is still issuing from the record player, but now it is Mahler's Symphony No. 2, *Resurrection*.[15] In this later scene, Peppino announces to his former communist mentor that he is running for office under the aegis of the more radical, extra-parliamentary party Democrazia Proletaria. The title of Mahler's symphony is thus doubly ironic in that Peppino has indeed resurrected himself, but under a banner quite different from that of his previous political incarnation. Far from presaging a triumph over death, Peppino's new party affiliation and his public campaign to promote it will only intensify the Mafia's determination to deal him a fatal blow.

Of the pop music featured in the segment of the film devoted to the 1970s, D'Onofrio points out an anomaly: all of the songs, with one exception, hail from the previous decade. This choice, according to the critic, reflects Giordana's inclination to associate Peppino with the revolutionary enthusiasm of 1968, rather than with the violence and terrorism of the late 1970s.[16] In so doing, the filmmaker seeks to idealize the youth culture that Peppino had come to embody, softening the hard edges of the militant left of the "Years of Lead" by eliding it with the utopian movement of the previous decade.[17]

Other songs whose lyrics and sonorities yield deepened understandings of Giordana's musical choices include Leonard Cohen's exaltation of his lady love in "Suzanne," the non-diegetic accompaniment for the radio broadcast of a feminist comuniqué; Janis Joplin's raw and hallucinated performance of Gershwin's tender lullaby "Summertime," the background to Peppino's capture, beating, and execution; and of course Procol Harum's "A Whiter Shade of Pale," accompaniment to Peppino's funeral procession-turned-protest rally.[18]

Of all the cultural forms surveyed by Giordana in constructing his cinematic language of *impegno*, it is literature that offers the most sustained and convincing argument for the power of the arts to intervene in the course of human life. Above, references to Mayakovsky and Pasolini have been interpreted as catalysts for change in the relationship between Peppino and Stefano, in the first case, and between Peppino and Felicia, in the second. Significantly, Giordana's opening gambit, in fact, is to set up poetry as the basis of Peppino's distinctive claim to an identity that will lead him to "Volare" above his culture's limits and to spearhead a social movement fraught with revolutionary potential.[19] The setting is a luncheon in honour of the family's cousin Anthony, who has travelled from New York to Cinisi to find a bride. The young Peppino delivers his family's toast to the prospective bride and groom, and he does so in the form of an iconic poem, Giacomo Leopardi's "L'infinito," introduced *in English* as follows: "Dear Anthony and dear Cosima, my family offers you this poem to remember our language and our land."

> Sempre caro mi fu quest'ermo colle,
> e questa siepe, che da tanta parte
> Dell'ultimo orrizzonte il guardo esclude.
> Ma sedendo e mirando, interminati
> Spazi di là da quella, e sovrumani
> Silenzi, e profondissima quiete
> Io nel pensier mi fingo; ove per poco
> Il cor non si spaura. E come il vento
> Odo stormir tra queste piante, io quello
> Infinito silenzio a questa voce
> Vo comparando: e mi sovvien l'eterno,
> E le morte stagioni, e la presente
> E viva, e il suon di lei. Così tra questa
> Immensità s'annega il pensier mio:
> E il naufragar m'è dolce in questo mare.

> (Dear to me always was this lonely hill,
> And this hedge that excludes so large a part
> of the ultimate horizon from my view.
> But as I sit and gaze, my thought conceives
> Interminable vastnesses of space
> Beyond it, and unearthly silences,
> And profoundest calm; whereat my heart almost
> Becomes dismayed. And as I hear the wind

Rustling through these branches, I find myself
Comparing with this sound that infinite silence:
And I call to mind eternity,
And the ages that are dead, and this that now
Is living, and the noise of it. And so
In this immensity my thought sinks drowned:
And sweet it seems to shipwreck in this sea.)[20]

For Anthony, who emigrated as a child and whose Italian is therefore halting, dialectal, and forced, the recitation of the Leopardian verses represents the opposite of the path that he has chosen – that of Mafioso stardom in the underworld of New York. But Giordana's choice of "L'infinito" goes beyond its status as literary monument, to signify Peppino's capacity to leap over the constraints of his Mafia-controlled environment and to conjure up a utopian alternative to a stultifying status quo. While Anthony may have overcome limits of a mere geographic sort in his relocation overseas, Peppino's foray into the "interminati spazi di là" (interminable spaces on the other side) is of an imaginative nature, granting him a world of inner resources that will be continually nurtured by a humanist education.

The ten-year-old child's recitation of this hallowed text is a theatrical performance fraught with significance for his status within this micro-community of listeners. The camera cuts back and forth between the earnest young deliverer of Leopardi's lines and the audience's rapt attention to them. For most of these listeners, whose limited literacy keeps them on the far side of comprehension, Peppino's mere mastery of the verses gives him the cultural prestige that leads his uncle Cesare to anoint the child his successor. For Felicia, who silently mouths the words as Peppino utters them, this scene foreshadows the later one in which mother and son will recite the Pasolini poem in dialogue form. And in another charged literary reference, this time to *Don Quixote*, Peppino reads aloud the passage about the knight's tilting at windmills when Luigi erupts into the bedroom to initiate the climactic father-son confrontation. The protagonist's anti-Mafia campaign may well be seen as the latter-day equivalent of the Hidalgo's efforts to fight battles in the name of a behavioural code at variance with the social realities of his age.

The centrality of literature to Peppino's political mission is nowhere more evident than in his wickedly parodic rewriting of Dante's *Inferno*, to be read over the airwaves of Radio Aut. Though verging on travesty, this scene invites comparison with the film's opening sequence in which the ten-year-old Peppino had recited the verses of Leopardi's "L'infinito." Both scenes depend, for their dramatic effect, on knowledge of the literary canon, and both scenes include extensive intercuts to the faces of the listeners, who recognize the sanctity of the textual sources. In both cases, Peppino is bolstered by the authority that mastery of Italian literature confers upon him. In the film's earlier scene, it is he who has the privilege of bestowing upon the newlyweds Anthony and Cosima the cultural heritage for which the Leopardi poem stands, by antonomasia. And it is through Peppino's Dantesque parody, in the later scene, that Italian high culture will pronounce its condemnation of Mafia rule.

As in the earlier sequence, here too the camera cuts to reaction shots of Peppino's listening audience, increased exponentially by the medium of radio. Those awestruck by the young boy's recitation of Leopardi are now fragmented into a number of varying response groups, from the men listening collectively in a cafe, to the aged few gathered to hear the broadcast in communist party headquarters, to the patrol car of the local carabinieri, to the solitary Felicia ensconced in her living room at home, and finally to Don Tano himself, enthroned in a barber's chair, as the razor glides across the surface of his well-lathered face. In the series of poetry readings that punctuate the film, Peppino assumes a progressively more active and creative role. He begins as a passive vessel, merely parroting the Leopardian lyrics in a monotone indifferent to the text's gradations of meaning, but by mid-film he has advanced to the level of stage director who turns Pasolini's love poem to his mother into an anguished duet. This progression from passive recitation to active co-authorship culminates in the long and brilliant radio broadcast of Peppino's spoof on *Inferno*. Here, Peppino reinvents Dante's journey to the underworld in terms relevant to his contemporary anti-Mafia crusade, so that the City of Dis becomes Mafiapoli, the giants guarding the ninth circle become the town worthies of Cinisi, and the sinners of Malebolge become the local Mafia bosses.

Peppino's use of Dante belongs to a broadened category of parody whereby the original text functions not as the target of ridicule but as its delivery system.[21] This means that the dignity and authority of the medieval poem serve to indict the contemporary world for its failure to live up to its magisterial cultural heritage. Peppino's parody reveals him to be a profoundly engaged reader of the *Commedia*, attuned to the prophetic fury and satiric bite of Dante's own social critique. In his creation of the Dante-inspired Mafiapoli, peopled with caricatures of Cinisi's ruling elite, Peppino is recapitulating the medieval poet's own transposition of local power politics onto an infernal landscape, and in so doing brings Dante's formidable moral and ideological apparatus – this gigantic judgment machine that is the *Commedia* – to bear on his indictment of Mafia rule. It would be no exaggeration to say that in making Dante an "ally" in his campaign, this anti-Mafia crusader is stocking his arsenal with all the weapons of literary high culture in his war against the powers that be.

Peppino's recitation of his "Cretina Commedia" over the airwaves of Cinisi begins as a brilliant spoof of the medieval source, but as the performance proceeds the tight structure of his stanzas begins to unravel, and disciplined parody gives way to a talking jag verging on hysteria. Impervious to his friends' signals that he bring his diatribe to an end, Peppino babbles on, fueled by the generative force of Dante's example. It is this textual model that inspires Peppino to engage in his own courageous and provocative act of *poesis*, to channel his righteous indignation into the composing of an imaginative dystopia whose bitterness, like that of Dante, is a measure of the utopian disappointment it hides. Dantesque, too, is Peppino's outsider's status, or rather his position as *internal* exile, whose alienated, oppositional role banishes him from the realm of normal familial relations, from party politics, from romantic attachments, and finally from life itself. If Dante, in giving voice to his exilic state, had to find a new medium, the *vulgare illustre* to replace Latin as the vehicle of his culture's most serious philosophical and spiritual concerns, for Peppino that venue was of course the *radio libera*, unencumbered by an institutional past, yet possessed of the oracular authority that Italians had traditionally accorded this medium of pure voice.

Perhaps most important for Peppino's recourse to Dante is the *Commedia*'s status as a motivational text, bearing witness to the poet's conversion experience in the hope of igniting the reader's own ardour for redemption. Throughout the *Commedia*, Dante incorporates examples of literary texts that serve as incentives to act – damnably in the case of Paolo and Francesca, but blessedly in the cases of Statius and the many others who found spiritual inspiration in the pages of Virgil. In *I cento passi* Peppino's references to Dante function for the listeners of Radio Aut as Stefano Venuti's story of Mayakovsky had for Peppino himself – as an exemplum, an attempt to awaken the public to the need for revolutionary action.

I would be remiss to conclude without acknowledging Giordana's own farewell gesture to Peppino. For it is here that the film achieves its full measure of epitaphic remembrance. Among the many noteworthy techniques in Giordana's final sequence are the still photographs and "home video" clips that he edits together to compile an album of memory, outside the film's narrative flow, for his viewers. The funeral procession that turns into protest march traces the famous one hundred steps of the title from Peppino's house to Tano's, echoing and re-enacting the protagonist's earlier warning to his brother Giovanni not to end up "looking like them" in defiance of the temptation posed by proximity. As colour imagery gives way to back and white, the finale assumes the trappings of a documentary with all the immediacy of an eyewitness account as the camera moves unsteadily like a member of the crowd mourning for Peppino and accepting his call to arms. In a visually shocking and emotionally destabilizing move, Giordana intercuts amidst the footage of this solemn, monochromatic sequence a series of brightly coloured home movie clips of Peppino stuffing his mouth with potato chips, mugging for the camera, and basically acting silly. Though we haven't seen precisely this footage before, it recalls earlier moments that we *have* seen – Peppino clowning around in the radio station, slathering his buddies with paint or mooning the girls as they deliver their feminist manifesto. This penultimate footage, shot in super-8, contrasts with the slick filming of Giordana's camera, suggesting the presence of other, amateur perspectives on Peppino's plight – specifically the perspectives of his family and friends for whom Peppino could be, and often was, just a goofy kid. The effect of such super-8 shots – so grainy and garish in their image quality – is to conjure up our own memories of home movies (it's significant that my students labelled these "home videos") – our own recall of the moments when we held or appeared on camera in scenes of unstaged domesticity. In *I cento passi*, these clips create a repository of visual memory that reminds us that inside the coffin lies the shattered body of someone who was once very much alive, an ordinary kid whose goofiness meant that he was not necessarily destined for martyrdom. Only at this point does the screen fade to black and the lettering appear that reports on Peppino's murder and its judicial aftermath. The succinctness of this inscription serves to highlight the glacial slowness with which Peppino's case made its way through the Italian legal system (over the course of two decades!) so that any sense of closure that a final written text may confer on the preceding narration is derailed. But Giordana's epitaphic strategy only reaches its culmination in the film's postscript – a succession of still photographs of the historic Peppino Impastato. The effect is striking on many levels, not least of which is the uncanny resemblance of the actor Luigi Lo Cascio to his real-life counterpart. But the photo montage enacts a paradox – it both authenticates the film and alerts us to its artifice. It reminds us that what we've just seen is a reconstruction, the work of an auteur (or at this point, a bricoleur), and yet at the same time it insists that the representation points beyond itself to a referent in historical reality, a referent who lived and died, whose remains lie encased in a coffin like that shown on screen and whose story has a truth-value as unquestionable as it is uncomfortable for us. Earlier in the film Peppino was warned by his friend Mauro not to be too strident, not to "fare la voce grossa" (raise your voice). But at the end, during the funeral march-turned-protest rally, a banner reads "La Mafia kills, and so does your silence." This film is the "voce grossa." It is the epitaph that memorializes a strong life in order to inspire strong deeds in the living.[22]

I will end with a scene in which Peppino seems to step outside the story of his life to deliver a meta-commentary on the very film that we are watching. It is a moment we've considered before: Peppino's attempt to lead a discussion after the screening of Rosi's *Le mani sulla città*. In the hope of spurring an exchange of ideas, Peppino offers the following reflection: "A film is always a work of art. It never reproduces reality as it is, but by means of a certain interpretive gaze, a certain slant, it reinvents this reality, transfigures it and fills it with meaning." No great effort is required to read into these words Giordana's own mission in filming *I cento passi* – to reinvent and transfigure the story of Peppino Impastato, and to infuse it with meaning for a contemporary social context notoriously deficient in the kind of revolutionary fervour that animated the 1970s liberation movements and that drove this young man to martyrdom. "The moment has come," Chiara Modonesi had written, "to tell how every social and cultural conquest is born from the initiative and courage of a minority, if not from one single individiual. Not to engage in facile rhetoric but, on the contrary, to indicate the path of an imitable model."[23] *I cento passi* offers a double fulfilment of that charge, as both a spur to civic activism for new generations of viewers and an impetus to filmmakers in search of the path to an ethically and politically engaged cinema on the cusp of the new millennium.

Chapter Two

The Anti-Mafia Martyr Film Takes an Unexpected Turn: Pierfrancesco Diliberto's *La Mafia uccide solo d'estate* (The Mafia Only Kills in the Summer), 2013

Direction: Pierfrancesco Diliberto (Pif). *Screenplay*: Pierfrancesco Diliberto, Michele Astori, Marco Martani. *Cinematography*: Roberto Forza. *Editing*: Cristiano Travaglioli. *Music*: Santi Pulvirenti. *Sets*: Luciano Cammerieri. *Costumes*: Cristiana Ricceri. *Cast*: Pierfrancesco Diliberto (Arturo Giammaresi), Alex Bisconti (Arturo as a child), Cristiana Capotondi (Flora Guarnieri), Ginevra Antona (Flora as a child), Claudio Gioè (Francesco), Barbara Tabita (Arturo's mother), Rosario Lisma (Arturo's father), Maurizio Marchetti (Giampierr), Antonio Alveario (Totò Riina), Antonino Bruschetta (Fra Giacinto), Enzo Salomone (Rocco Chinnici), Roberto Burgio (Boris Giuliano), Totò Borgese (Salvo Lima), Turi Giuffrida (Generale Dalla Chiesa).

Synopsis: Set in Palermo from the early 1970s to the present, Diliberto's film recounts the story of Arturo Giammaresi, whose childhood coincides with the Mafia's most intense war against the Italian state. As a young boy, Arturo falls hopelessly in love with his classmate, Flora Guarnieri, but events in the public sphere constantly thwart his efforts to win her affections: attempts to woo her are disrupted by the assassinations of the Carabinieri chief Carlo Alberto Dalla Chiesa, head of Palermo's crime unit Boris Giuliano, anti-Mafia lawmaker Pio La Torre, and prosecuting magistrate Rocco Chinnici. Leading the Mafia scourge of these years is Totò Riina, presented in the film as a comic character whose cluelessness in no way blunts the force of the evil he

---

This chapter is an amplified version of the essay "From Comedy to Commemoration: Pierfrancesco Diliberto's *La Mafia uccide solo d'estate*," in *Mafia Movies: A Reader*, 2nd ed., ed. Dana Renga (Toronto: University of Toronto Press, 2019). Reprinted with the permission of the publisher.

unleashes on the life of the city. Despite the Mafia's spectacular assaults on anti-criminal forces, Palermo remains in a state of denial, and Arturo is himself lulled into disbelief by the politics of Christian Democratic leader Giulio Andreotti, whom the child has come to venerate. Francesco, a young journalist who befriends Arturo, challenges the boy's Andreottian allegiances, and the assassination of Dalla Chiesa further opens the child's eyes to the hypocrisy of his idol and the reality of Mafia rule. After a hiatus of some ten years, Flora and Arturo reunite, this time under the joint employ of Salvo Lima, a local Christian Democratic leader with Mafia sympathies. But the assassinations of two heroic anti-Mafia magistrates, Giovanni Falcone and Paolo Borsellino, within months of each other in 1992 bring about a political awaking, and in the midst of a massive street demonstration Flora and Arturo meet and fall into each other's arms, leading to the film's finale with the birth of their son, whom they are quick to induct into the ranks of future activists against the Mafia scourge.

Though Marco Tullio Giordana's *I cento passi* (2000) was the first film to gain visibility in the genre dedicated to memorializing martyrs for the anti-Mafia cause, several other works had preceded it during the years of Cosa Nostra's most concentrated assault on the Italian state. The assassinations of Carabiniere general Carlo Alberto Dalla Chiesa and magistrates Giovanni Falcone and Rosario Livatino prompted cinematic renderings of their stories in 1984, 1993, and 1994 respectively, but not until the new millennium did a full-fledged genre of films emerge to commemorate activists who stood up to the Mafia and paid for it with their lives. The years between 2000 and 2013 saw an outpouring of such films, based on historical figures who opposed the crime syndicate through a variety of institutional means: the court system, the labour movement, the clergy, the youth counterculture, the press, and even the family.[1] Structured biographically, these films followed a predictable path, detailing the twists and turns of the protagonists' anti-Mafia campaigns that were conducted in full knowledge of the mortal risks incurred by their actions.

While the Hollywood term term "bio-pic" would seem best to describe this body of work, I prefer to characterize it less by narrative structure than by its debt to the tradition of neorealism and its offshoot in the *cinema politico* genre of the 1960s and 1970s – a claim I developed in chapter 1. In analysing *I cento passi* I argued for its link to the commemorative impulse of Rossellini's first neorealist films – their insistence on the construction of a monumental history to celebrate heroic intervention in the course of events and to instil the desire for intervention in new generations of viewers. These films could be considered "epitaphs," writings on tombs, designed to recommend the heroic dead to the living as models of engagement in the public sphere and to perpetuate the ideals for which they died. In keeping with this epitaphic drive, the anti-Mafia martyr film often ends with a written inscription on-screen regarding the protagonist's death and its judicial aftermath as a way of tethering the film's fictional re-creation to its referent in the historical record, and to inspire an ethically charged response to the burning questions raised by this history within the public arena of today.

Pierfrancesco Diliberto's *La Mafia uccide solo d'estate* may appear to be an unlikely candidate for inclusion in this venerable genealogy of films. Its narrative focuses on an ordinary citizen/witness, Arturo Giammarresi, who undertakes no heroic action and who remains a spectator as the painful history of the anti-Mafia struggle unfolds. More importantly, the film belongs to the genre of romantic comedy, foregrounding the love story between the protagonist and Flora Guarnieri – a relationship that begins in childhood and culminates in marriage. And finally, the film's director, who also plays the role of the adult protagonist, hails from the world of Italian television. Exploiting his prefabricated celebrity, he both imports into the film his televisual persona (known as "Pif," a pseudo-acronym for his given name) and stages a highly charged encounter between the languages of the small and large screen.

It is the very deviations from the norms of the anti-Mafia martyr tradition – the movement away from the heroic to the ordinary, the foray into romantic comedy, the intrusion of a TV aesthetic – that make *La Mafia uccide solo d'estate* such a striking effort to update and reactivate the monumental history of the struggle against the Sicilian crime syndicate. In fact, I would argue that the film foregrounds, in very explicit terms, the tension between its pull toward entertainment and its solemn testimonial imperative. The framing of *La Mafia uccide solo d'estate* – its written dedication "to the officers of the Palermo police squad, to the members of the Quarto Savona 15 [Giovanni Falcone's escort], to all of the police escorts fallen in the line of duty" – gives way to Diliberto's narration in voice-over – "see that girl … I have been in love with her since we were kids." The clash of registers between the solemnity of the paratext and the frothy lightness of the narration could not be more evident, leaving the spectator in a state of generic uncertainty. To complicate matters, the camerawork strikes an incongruous note within the norms of romantic comedy by pointing out a plaque on the wall of Flora's apartment building, whose text recounts the martyrdom of Judge Rocco Chinnici in the anti-Mafia struggle. The interplay between Mafia chronicle and the course of love is explicitly announced in the protagonist's next quip: "I didn't have the courage or the occasion to declare myself to her because [at this point there is a pause in the narrator's commentary as the camera pans left to reveal that the voice we've been hearing belongs to the television star Pif, speaking in the role of the adult Arturo] we're in Palermo. And here, the Mafia has always influenced the life of everyone [now the camera cuts to a pan of the city, nestled between mountains and sea coast], especially mine." This opening sequence functions as a kind of overture, sounding the themes and forecasting the narrative mechanisms that will govern the film as a whole: its commemorative thrust, its characterization of Palermo as both physical setting and social order in thrall to organized crime, and its storyline of Mafia-thwarted romance.

The bulk of the film is characterized by its upbeat tenor, product of the witty voice-over narration, the bouncy musical score, the good-natured relationships between adults and children, and the ingenuity of the plot's Mafia-based impediments to Arturo's pursuit of Flora. But in a tonal shift of the utmost ethical consequence, the film ends on a deeply solemn note – one that departs from the canons of romantic comedy and retroactively aligns the film with the testimonial and commemorative tradition of the anti-Mafia genre. In its final seven minutes, the register changes drastically, as breeziness and irony give way to urgency tinged with anger. The murders of prosecuting magistrates Giovanni Falcone and Paolo Borsellino finally compel all those living under the reign of silence and denial to acknowledge the Mafia scourge. "Lo capì Fofò Cassina" (Fofo Cassina understood it), the voice-over announces, concerning Arturo's erstwhile school friend, now adult eye-witness to the Falcone assassination. "Lo capì Gianpiero," (Gian Piero understood it), the voice-over continues, referring to Arturo's employer and host of a TV show, who rushes to his mother's apartment damaged by the bomb that killed Borsellino. "Lo capirono tutti i palermitani" (all the Palermitans understood it), he summarizes, adding "e lo capii anch'io" (and I understood it too). These repetitions and variations on preterite forms of the verb *capire* verbally enact the sudden and widespread awakening that followed the spectacular murders of Palermo's most celebrated anti-Mafia prosecution team.

But the film's most powerful testimonial frames come next. Arturo and Flora have become parents of a baby boy, and this child, in a succession of eight clips that trace his growth from infancy to school age, is shown being taken on a tour by his father to monuments for fallen

Diliberto's *La Mafia uccide solo d'estate* 39

Arturo, together with Flora, leads their son on the first of their visits to memorials honouring slain anti-Mafia activists throughout Palermo.

anti-Mafia heroes throughout the city.[2] This montage is ingeniously constructed along three parallel lines. The first is Arturo's dogged determination to reverse his own upbringing, shrouded in parental denial of the Mafia scourge. To counter this program of mis-education, Arturo begins exposing his own son to Mafia history by focusing on the possibility of its resistance. Their pilgrimage to various memorial sites is accompanied by Arturo's capsule summaries of the heroes' positive accomplishments – his "translation," for the sake of his child, of the lugubrious rhetoric of the actual inscriptions on the commemorative plaques. The camerawork reinforces Arturo's constructive pedagogy, zooming in on an individual name (often heading a list of collateral victims – the driver and bodyguards of the Mafia's designated target) as Arturo recites his achievements. Each stop in this tour of remembrance offers its own suggestion of a life story that could spin off into an entire film in its own right – another full-blown biographical entry into the archive of films dedicated to the struggle against organized crime.

The second development tracked by the "pilgrimage" montage is that of the child's development from infantile oblivion to his burgeoning grasp of Arturo's teaching. In three of the clips at the mid-point of the montage, the child is figured as a toddler who clearly begrudges this exercise, walking dyspeptically beside his father, emitting sounds of annoyance, and obviously unreceptive to his parent's pedagogy. Flora, who had been present in the earliest clips, but absent in those of the toddler phase, joins the father-son pilgrimage for the final three visits. The child is now school age, and ready to absorb Arturo's lessons, which become personal and anecdotal as the family stands before the monument to Boris Giuliano ("a man with a mustache [who] offered me an iris [pastry]"), to Carlo Alberto Dalla Chiesa ("granted me my first interview"), and to Rocco Chinnici ("your mother and I even met him"). Throughout these final clips, the camera has cut to the boy's face, now listening with rapt attention to his father's commentary, or gazing thoughtfully at the memorial plaque before him. Arturo's persistence has paid off – his ongoing determination to convey the urgency of anti-Mafia *impegno* (civil commitment) has created a new secondary witness, preparing to take up the task of remembrance, and to shoulder the ethical burdens of a historical chapter still playing itself out in the present day. The paradoxical yet pressing impulse to induct a small child into the annals of history connects the ending of *La Mafia uccide solo d'estate* to that of the Taviani brothers' *La notte di San Lorenzo* (Night of the Shooting Stars, 1982), in which the audience of the narrator's account is revealed to be a sleeping baby. Diliberto's film takes the Tavianis's ending a step further, leading the oblivious infant to a state of boyhood understanding that can then be projected onto a future of adult activism, the creation of a new family committed to the pursuit of social justice, and to transmitting this inheritance to the next generation.

The third development tracked by the "pilgrimage" montage is municipal in nature.[3] It concerns the city's efforts to remind its residents that in the spaces of everyday urban life – its roadsides, sidewalks, shop fronts, parking places – men have been shot down or pulverized by explosives for their opposition to Mafia control. While most of the memorials are conventional in style – marble plaques with rhetorical inscriptions – some exhibit a variety of materials, and in one case sculptural effects, indicating a desire to add variety to this collection of commemorative markers. (The camerawork makes a special effort to warn viewers against becoming inured to such hallowed sites by panning to a sign that reads "Don't leave trash under the plaque of Generale Dalla Chiesa.")[4] In spatial terms, Arturo's father-son tour thus becomes a tour of Palermo itself, as if the city map were studded with assassination markers, as if its topography were defined by this pointillist collection of sites of Mafia bloodshed.

The film does not conclude, however, with this climactic pilgrimage scenario. Instead, Diliberto moves beyond the limits of the family saga and the borders of Palermo to embrace the national consciousness of Mafia violence as conveyed by its journalistic accounts. The film's final frames are thus devoted to newspaper clippings featuring photographs and texts about twelve slain anti-Mafia activists, several of whom were characters within the fictional action of the preceding plot. The clippings appear one at a time and remain in place until the entire screen is filled. So congested is this space that the articles must overlap to fit within the frame, creating a collage effect that gives depth as well as expanse to this archive of anti-Mafia martyrs. What the father-son visits to the memorial plaques revealed sequentially, across time, is now displayed spatially in a single shot, crowded with obituaries in this seemingly endless gallery of fallen heroes.

From the perspective of this finale, the film becomes a means for reigniting collective memory, bringing life and movement to the official reports that languish in state archives and to the frozen plaques that adorn the city walls. This process of reanimation does not take the form of heroic biography, but emerges from the testimony of an ordinary citizen-witness whose own life story intersects with the annals of Mafia violence from the 1970s to 1992. The plot therefore serves as a fictionalized and often satirical enactment of the truth announced in the film's opening voice-over – "we're in Palermo. And here the Mafia has always influenced the life of everyone."

In Arturo's case, Mafia influence begins at conception. The film traces the child's physiological origin to the event that marked Totò Riina's rise to power when the aspiring Mafia boss staged a successful assault on his rival Michele Cavataio, in the very same apartment building where Arturo's parents were consummating their marriage on an upper floor. The scene of fertilization is represented as a cartoon encounter between an egg and a flotilla of sperm that withdraw in fear as the building trembles under the impact of the Mafia eruption below. A single sperm cell, oblivious to the mayhem, arrives belatedly to pierce the egg. "That spermatozoa," the voice-over explains "was me."

In his analysis of the "causal" relationship between the act of Mafia violence and the physiology of Arturo's conception, Massimiliano Delfino sees the protagonist's very being as "biologically determined by the Mafia,"[5] signifying on the micro level the organization's power over the body politic as a whole. The uncanny awareness of the Mafia's presence that the young Arturo displays throughout the film's early scenes amounts to a form of "imprinting," endowing him with special powers that align his childhood story with the genre of the superhero.[6] Concerned that their toddler has not yet begun to talk, his parents try desperately to extract at least a "mamma" from the reticent child, whose first word, instead, is "Mafia" uttered in the wake of a visit by the parish priest, known to have underworld ties. Later, on a visit to see his newborn brother at the hospital, Arturo notices another baby's father, Riina himself, cooing at his own infant daughter. "That man scares me," the boy confesses – a remark that Arturo's father dismisses as utterly baseless, given the mob boss's tender effusions over his newborn offspring. In the light of such denials, the boy comes to mistrust his hypersensitivity to Mafia presence, and falls prey to the euphemisms required by the communal pact of *omertà*, taking literally the reassuring explanations for a spate of killings as crimes of passion: "it's a question of women," rationalizes the butcher; "a problem concerning another woman," concurs the barber; "he was a skirt chaser," opines the barista. This popular impulse to deny the Mafia threat is enshrined in the film's very title, which echoes the father's nonsensical, self-cancelling reassurance to his son when asked if the organization kills people. "Now we're in winter. The Mafia only kills in the summer," he explains, as if the adverb "only," implying that three out of four seasons per year were exempt from mob violence, could put his son's anxieties to rest.[7] The ludicrous nature of this evasion casts a satiric light on all of the discourses of denial that have facilitated public coexistence with Mafia rule up to this point in the film.

The most dangerous and consequential of these discourses comes from Giulio Andreotti, who claims that "the emerging criminality is in Campania and Calabria," putting the entire onus for the surge in violence on two other crime syndicates, the Camorra and the 'Ndrangheta, native to those respective regions. Because the young boy has developed a reverence for Andreotti bordering on cult worship, climaxing in the child's masquerade as the Christian Democratic leader for *Carnevale*, he is particularly vulnerable to his idol's strategy for explaining away the Mafia threat. But the incongruity of Arturo's childish veneration for this dry, austere, aloof public figure – a figure who lends himself easily to the grotesque, as Sorrentino's *Il Divo* so flamboyantly demonstrates – is not a mere pretext for humour. There is a pointed social commentary in Arturo's puerile fandom, which casts the Italian public itself in the role of credulous followers, naive consumers of the Christian Democratic leader's deceptively pious facade.

Events will eventually conspire to break the spell that Andreotti has cast over this impressionable child. Most important in this regard is the Christian Democratic leader's absence from the funeral of Generale Carlo Alberto Dalla Chiesa, felled by Mafia hitmen. Against the backdrop of collective grieving, Arturo's voice-over account grows increasingly bitter as he asks why Andreotti would downplay the Mafia menace and why he had not joined the ranks of mourners, which included all other top government officials. Especially noteworthy is the fact that this turning point in Arturo's development coincides with a jarring technological effect within the language of *La Mafia uccide solo d'estate*. The scene of Dalla Chiesa's funeral is composed of archival footage – its imagery is blurred and the colours are garish, in striking contrast to the sharp resolution and chromatic sobriety of the rest of the film. The eye experiences the shift from the fictional footage to this documentary clip as a radical change in texture, as if vision had given way to touch. At this point, the film gains a degree of thickness and layeredness that draws the spectator into an ethically charged relationship to the action portrayed. Most obviously, the documentary footage anchors the entire film, no matter how unabashedly fictional, to a verifiable referent in the realm of historical experience. The newsreel clip releases the full indexical power of the image to commandeer belief in the mind of the viewer, or, to borrow the terminology of Marco Dinoi, it serves as a "prelievo" (specimen) – a "document of the past, an archaeological trace or residue that links the text to an historic situation."[8]

The archival footage serves to authenticate and validate the referential thrust of the film – it is the gold standard of representational truth. At the same time, it calls attention to the constructedness of the fiction film within which the clip is embedded. The aesthetic shock of encountering the documentary image, a "foreign body" in Christian Uva's terms,[9] within the fiction film triggers a metalinguistic awareness on the part of viewers, prompting them to actively engage with the history to which it points. In other words, the use of the archival image as a springboard for artifice announces to the viewers that the film is exhibiting "a manner of reasoning about the facts that comes from the exegesis and interpretation of a rich documentation."[10] It serves not only as an impetus for viewers to judge the validity of the filmmaker's interpretive "take" on historical events, but also as a stimulus for them to elaborate their own acts of historical re-creation, to embark on imaginative and personal recastings of the factual record as a form of liberation from the received, officially sanctioned readings of history.

The ethical nature of the viewer's relationship to the "prelievo" hinges importantly on the issue of time. It is impossible to ignore the temporal journey along which older technologies lead us. Just as sepia-toned photography immediately catapults us back to the dawn of the 1900s or super-8 home movies to the 1950s, the newsreel clips of Dalla Chiesa's funeral have the power to transport us to the moment of their filming in 1982. This documentary insert replicates how Italians experienced public events in the immediacy of their reportage, sitting in living rooms or watching collectively in bars or other televisually equipped spaces.[11] Because mass media imagery serves to reveal how an era represented itself to itself, we are temporarily invited to occupy a 1980s Italian subject position not only in the immediate processing of a given news item but in the total cultural immersion that this older technology makes available. As spectators of *La Mafia uccide solo d'estate* we are invited to take responsibility for the course of historical injustice and to acknowledge its traces in the contemporary status quo.

To complicate our reading of this richly stratified moment in the film, Diliberto executes a technological sleight of hand that crosses the border between fiction and documentary, between outer film and embedded video clip. At a certain point in the funeral footage, Francesco, Arturo's journalist friend and mentor, makes his way through the crowd, his figure blurred and chromatically coordinated with that of the individuals who surround him. Soon after, Arturo himself makes an appearance amidst the documentary throng, desperately searching for the absent Andreotti. At the end of the sequence, a grim-faced Chinnici materializes, looking into the camera, as if contemplating the similar doom that awaits him in his anti-Mafia crusade.

This insertion of frames including fictional characters amidst documentary footage heightens our awareness of the artifice and gimmickry of the film while at the same time raising the scene's ethical stakes. By means of this technique, Arturo has been able to "enter" the historical arena – a witness, via video simulation, of the communal grieving that will serve as a preliminary step in mobilizing the anti-Mafia movement of Palermo. His simulated presence within this documentary space prefigures his adult debut as an anti-Mafia activist in the protest rally by Palermo residents blocked from attending the funeral of the five bodyguards killed along with Borsellino toward the end of the film.[12] Not coincidentally, this later scene marks the moment when Arturo can finally declare himself to Flora, who is also at the rally and is more than willing to fulfil the young man's amorous hopes.

It is of the utmost significance that the ritual of mourning stands at the centre of the film's "happy" ending, at the level of both the love plot and that of the political awakening experienced by the populace of Palermo. If mourning is the appropriate therapeutic response to traumatic shock,[13] and if, as Dana Renga has argued,[14] Mafia violence is experienced as trauma in the collective Italian psyche, then Diliberto's scene of the funeral-turned-protest-rally enacts that therapeutic function. The cathartic release of repressed energy in this mass gathering enables Arturo to overcome his inhibitions with regard to Flora, just as Palermo is able to emerge from its fatalism, fear, and paralysis and

With the help of twenty-first-century computer effects, Arturo joins the throng of mourners within the frames of the 1982 video of Carlo Alberto Dalla Chiesa's funeral in Palermo's Chiesa di San Domenico.

publicly denounce Mafia rule. For both our protagonists and the Palermitani, the result is the birth of a new order: a burgeoning family unit for the young couple, and "an idea [born from mass mourning] of a civil society capable of elaborating a collective commitment and strategy in which new generations still too uninformed and disillusioned, assume a role in the foreground as an antidote"[15] to the Mafia hold on public life.

La Mafia uccide solo d'estate is not Diliberto's first cinematic involvement in memorializing the martyrs of the struggle against organized crime. Significantly, he served as apprentice to Marco Tullio Giordana in the making of *I cento passi* (2000), an experience that surely contributed to his technical mastery of the cinematic art[16] as well as his determination to use the medium to revive historical memory and instil activist fervour in a public notoriously deficient in it. Diliberto's most explicit homage to Giordana's film emerges in the climactic scene of the funeral-turned-rally, echoing the analogous moment at the end of *I cento passi* when Peppino's mourners erupt into spontaneous chant, raise their fists in defiance, and manifest their will to resist Mafia rule. Giordana's film does not resort to archival footage in this scene – it contents itself with a fictional re-creation, making recourse to documentary images only at the end with a series of still photographs of the historical Peppino Impastato. Diliberto's frequent recourse to newsreel clips, instead, testifies to his abiding interest in transmediality, with a particular focus on the conflictive montage effects produced by the inclusion of TV footage within the body of the fiction film, as analysed in the scene of Dalla Chiesa's funeral.

This technical interest in televisual vs. cinematic imagery speaks to the larger issue of Diliberto's awareness that he is importing his small-screen celebrity into the large-screen medium, with all of the cultural implications of such a move. Conscious of the venerable film history into which he is entering, thanks to his experience with Giordana, Diliberto stages the transformation of his TV persona from the frivolity of his "candid camera" character in the show "Le iene" (The Hyenas) to his MTV interviews in "Il testimone" (The Witness) to the eventual *gravitas* of the father who transmits anti-Mafia history to his son at the end of La Mafia uccide solo d'estate.[17] In other words, Diliberto has opted to exploit his celebrity status as a TV star, with particular appeal to a young demographic, in the service of *impegno civile*. Leveraging his popular allure, Diliberto entices a new generation of viewers to La Mafia uccide solo d'estate with the promise of hip entertainment, but in the process manages to transform "the comic into the tragic, reminding us that it is possible to rebel."[18]

Indeed, the very act of making La Mafia uccide solo d'estate was a form of resistance, both in its content and in its mode of production, which involved the refusal to pay the *pizzo* – protection money expected of every business venture that takes place in Palermo. In so doing, Diliberto joins the movement known as "Addio [farewell] pizzo" organized by a small group of young anti-Mafia business owners, featured in one of the episodes of Pif's TV show back in 2007. It may be pure coincidence, but I cannot help but connect the title of his television series, "Il testimone," to the testimonial function of La Mafia uccide solo d'estate, where the true meaning of bearing witness – the forging of an ethically charged relationship between a representation and its audience – becomes a call to judgment and a summons to act.

Chapter Three

"This Is Not Just a Crime Film": Michele Placido's *Romanzo criminale* (Crime Novel), 2005

Direction: Michele Placido. *Subject and screenplay*: Stefano Rulli, Sandro Petraglia, Giancarlo De Cataldo, in collaboration with Michele Placido (based on the eponymous novel by Giancarlo De Cataldo). *Cinematography*: Luca Bigazzi. *Editing*: Esmeraldo Calabria. *Music*: Paolo Buonvino. *Sets*: Paola Comencini. *Costumes*: Nicoletta Taranta. *Cast*: Kim Rossi Stuart (Freddo), Pierfrancesco Favino (Libanese/Libano), Claudio Santamaria (Dandi), Stefano Accorsi (Nicola Scialoja), Riccardo Scamarcio (Il Nero), Jasmine Trinca (Roberta), Anna Mouglalis (Patrizia).

Synopsis: Set in Rome during the 1970s and 1980s, the film offers a fictionally embroidered account of the Banda della Magliana, the most powerful criminal group to ever operate in Rome. Led by Libano, Freddo, and Dandi, three friends with strong ties since childhood, the gang achieves its long-cherished dream of "Roman conquest" by pooling the ransom money earned in the kidnapping and murder of Barone Valdemaro Rosellini, and using it to fund a kind of criminal cooperative. Such resources, along with the merciless treatment of competitors, enable them to seize absolute control of the city's drug trade and to develop lucrative forays into prostitution and gambling. The gang's escapades bring them into collusion not only with the Mafia but also with right-wing extremist elements within the government itself, and despite the fact that the film's criminals seem to live in a parallel universe, they become tangentially involved with some of the most searing historical

---

This chapter is a revised version of an essay entitled "*Romanzo criminale*: The Novel and the Film through the Prism of Pasolini," which appeared in *Watching Pages, Reading Pictures: Cinema and Modern Literature in Italy*, ed. Daniela De Pau and Georgina Torello (Newcastle upon Tyne: Cambridge Scholars Publishing, 2008).

events of their times. One law enforcement officer, Commissioner Scialoja, intuits early on the power of this syndicate and doggedly follows the members' trails, but it is the effect of internal vendettas and the Secret Service that finally spell the organization's demise: Libano and later Dandi are killed in a settling of scores, and Freddo will be felled by an anonymous gunman, most likely an agent of the state. Women play only a secondary role in this chronicle of male bonding and the jockeying for power – the glamorous prostitute Patrizia serves as both Dandi's mistress and Scialoja's occasional love interest, while Roberta's wholesome femininity leads Freddo to question and ultimately reject his criminal vocation. Roberta is killed in reprisal for Freddo's liquidation of a double-dealing gang member, and he himself is gunned down on the eve of his meeting with Scialoja to turn state's evidence.

"This is not just a crime film," Michele Placido remarked of *Romanzo criminale*. "It is also a film of tragedies, of sufferings, of sentiments, of love, of people who are trying, in the end, to survive the life that had been implanted in them in their adolescent years."[1] With this description, Placido acknowledges the place of his film within a generic context – its depiction of the criminal underworld from an internal point of view – and the dangers he faces in the process. While American filmmakers had travelled this path to great advantage, most notably Coppola in the *Godfather* trilogy, De Palma in *Scarface*, and Scorsese in *Goodfellas*,[2] Placido was well aware of the ethical pitfalls of humanizing and romanticizing gangsters whose exploits, in his case, were based on those of Rome's infamous Banda della Magliana. "I tried not to make mistakes," he conceded, "but it's inevitable that ... rendering them human, there's the risk that one could grow fond of these characters."[3] Not surprisingly, critics charged the film with fascist sympathies, given its exaltation of violence and its inclusion of Il Nero, a particularly swash-buckling gangster with a fondness for the philo-Nazi Italian intellectual Julius Evola. Further ideological criticism was aimed at the film's neglect of the student-worker revolution of 1968 and other progressive currents within the decades of the gang's operation. Such detractors declined to acknowledge the film's penetrating critique of right-wing extremism within the Italian state – a critique with ongoing implications for the twenty-first-century body politic. It is this element that prompted Placido to coin the label "gangsteristico-civile" (loosely translated as "a crime film with a social conscience") to describe the hybridity of his filmmaking intentions.[4]

Beyond considerations of ideology, the film's critics were also fixated on genre. Dazzled by the star-studded cast, the hip glamour of the performances, the fascination of the criminal underworld, the nostalgic re-evocation of 1970s style, reviewers mistrusted the film's popular appeal and therefore failed to accord it serious and nuanced efforts at interpretation.[5] Though detractors were able to concede the film's surface brilliance in generic terms, they begrudged Placido his intent to couch his work within the broader context of Italian history during the emotionally traumatic and politically destabilizing Years of Lead.[6] For such critics, the film could not be at once *gangsteristico* and *civile*, simultaneously bound to a point of view internal to the *malavita* while levelling a critique of the Italian condition during those turbulent years.

The public response to *Romanzo criminale* proved otherwise. Such a rigid, genre-oriented approach refused to countenance the viewers' freedom to move fluidly across the dividing lines between genres and thereby to find a personal space for reflection and interpretation. This summons to active viewer involvement in the making of meaning and the rendering of judgment emerged nowhere more clearly than in the transmedia life of the story itself, which began within the pages of the eponymous bestselling 2002 novel by Giancarlo De Cataldo before its adaptation in Placido's 2005 film, followed by an enormously successful twenty-two-episode TV series in 2008–2010. So powerful was the hold of this saga on the public imaginary that it prompted an explosion of spin-offs, "in the form of grassroots textuality such as fan-fiction, parodic videos, homages and artifacts of a heterogeneous nature [that] build up *Romanzo criminale* as a culture and as a world."[7] By inspiring such playful and imaginative appropriations, the film's afterlife served to advance one of the cherished goals of ethically committed filmmaking – that of confronting audiences with historical conflicts whose troubling causes have remained unresolved to the present day.

The invitation for viewers to move freely and creatively across genre categories and ideological divides owes much to the film's source, De Cataldo's above-mentioned book, whose very title (borrowed verbatim by the filmmaker) authorized the generic freedom that the novelistic form ushered into the annals of literary history. The Italian term for the novel, *romanzo*, carries with it a storied past, evolving from Greek and Latin antecedents, through medieval and Renaissance chivalric romance, to the eighteenth- and nineteenth-century novel of manners, to later-nineteenth-century experiments in realism, and up to the most recent flowering of extended prose fiction in a wide variety of subgenres.[8] Even today, the historic association between the novel and the saga of serial adventures persists, and for the *romanzo cavalleresco* (chivalric romance) to become *romanzo criminale* no great leap of imagination is required – the violent *gesta* (exploits) of the paladins of yore, with their loyalties, betrayals, quests, and vendettas are easily translatable into the escapades of De Cataldo's and Placido's criminals, themselves obedient to behavioural rules as codified and ritualized as those of their feudal forebears. But while the characters of medieval and Renaissance romance may have been restricted to a rigid set of norms, the *romanzo* as genre came to embrace unruliness, hybridity, and a general indifference to any formal constraints during the course of its evolution. Mikhail Bakhtin defines the novel as a literary mode in continual transformation, "the sole genre that continues to develop," "a genre-in-the-making, one in the vanguard of all modern literary development," chafing against any conventional limits and unbeholden to traditional categories or strict hierarchies in its exaltation of eclecticism, hybridity, and impurity of style.[9] It would be no exaggeration to argue that De Cataldo (seconded by Placido) chose this title, which foregrounds the formal openness embodied by the novel form, as a liberating gesture, one that licensed him to incorporate a number of extramural discourses into his prose, including archival passages from the Banda's notebooks, official documents from police and trial records, words of period pop songs, and verses from Dante's *Inferno*.

In the case of the film, Placido took the *romanzo*'s licence to generic freedom a step further, reaching beyond the limits of both his immediate textual source and the cinematic category within which the film was working – that of the *poliziesco*, or crime movie. Placido's most daring step in his own pursuit of freedom from generic restraints was to reach out to a powerful, alternative literary and cinematic prototype, that offered by Pasolini, whose novels *Ragazzi di vita* (1955) and *Una vita violenta* (1959), and above all the films *Accattone* (1961) and *Mamma Roma* (1962), served as precedents for a poetic rather than a genre-bound evocation of socially marginalized lives. In conceding his awareness of the dangers entailed by sensationalized and glamorized renderings of underworld characters, Placido explained that this was his motivation for adopting "a gaze closely bound to the films, or the culture, labelled 'Pasolinian' ... the boys of *Romanzo criminale* are the grandchildren of the slum-dwellers magnificently portrayed both by Pasolini and Sergio Citti.[10] It's really for this reason that at the beginning and the end [of the film] there is an homage, even in the stylistic sense, to Pasolini."[11]

Romanzo criminale opens with an on-screen inscription, announcing both the film's grounding in historical fact and its freedom to indulge in the fictional embroidery that will lead to the Pasolinian lyricism of its first scene.

> A metà degli anni '70 una banda di delinquenti di strada partì dalle periferie per conquistare Roma. Per inseguire il loro sogno ingenuo e terribile, travolsero ogni ostacolo. Strinsero alleanze pericolose. Si credevano immortali. La nostra storia è ispirata a quei fatti reali. I personaggi sono frutto dell'immaginazione degli autori.
>
> (In the mid-1970s, a band of street hoodlums left the outskirts of the city to conquer Rome. In order to pursue their naive and terrible dream, they overcame every obstacle. They formed dangerous alliances. They believed that they were immortal. Our story is inspired by those real facts. The characters are the fruit of the authors' imaginations.)

This written passage sets the stage for an enactment of recent historical events that will confer upon them the status of epic.[12] The prose itself performs a series of journeys: from periphery to centre, from petty criminality to imperial conquest, from factuality to imaginative reinvention. But this heroic beginning gives way to a very different narrative register in the following sequence, which recounts the childhood origins of the criminal band whose adult exploits will consume the rest of the film. It is here that the Pasolinian influence emerges in a *ragazzi di vita* episode of adolescent high jinks gone terribly wrong, marking the film's three main characters for life. Set in the late 1960s, the scene opens with a joyride in a stolen car by four boys, filmed to the music of the pop hit "Io ho in mente te."[13] Singing along with this irresistibly catchy and seemingly wholesome sound track, the boys win our sympathy for what appears to be an innocent though somewhat risky endeavour – we cannot help but be caught up in the beat of the music, the synchronized and fast-paced editing, and the sense that we are witnessing a "boys will be boys" nocturnal adventure. But when they run a police blockade, having plowed down the officer standing guard, the sequence takes a dire turn, and we follow the boys to their secret hideout, a broken-down trailer in Ostia where the most innocent-looking of them all, Andrea, slowly succumbs to the injury he has sustained in their rampage. Against this fatal backdrop, an initiation rite takes place, linking the origin of the gang with violence and death, and introducing the theme of destiny that will shadow the three surviving characters throughout the entirety of the film.[14] It is the dying Andrea who proposes that they each assume new names, and he does so in reaction to his friend's report that "la polizia s'è bevuta il Bavoso"[15] (the police put the Drooler in the drink).

52 Italian Film in the Present Tense

The boy's response to this news is whimsical: "un nome del cazzo si porta appresso una vita del cazzo" (you carry a shitty name throughout a shitty life) – as if the moniker were the cause of its bearer's plight: *nomen omen*. "Per questo," he continues, "noi il nome dobbiamo scegliere da soli" (This is why we need to choose our names by ourselves), and with this announcement Andrea becomes Adam – he appropriates for himself and his cohorts the biblical right to exert power over the things that are named, in this case their newly minted, socially marginalized selves. Or, to put it more bluntly, the freely chosen nomenclature will liberate them from the "shitty life" prescribed by their underclass lot. No sooner is this self-christening complete than the police erupt onto the scene, forcing all the boys to flee except Andrea, who is held back by his injury. Scattered about the sand dunes, the other three boys cry out for help using their nicknames – a sign that their new identities have taken root so quickly and so firmly as to resist the trauma of the chase. This then has been the true baptism, amidst the dunes[16] of Ostia where the characters will enact, in embryonic form, their plot function in the full-fledged narrative to come.

A brief return to the dying Andrea filmed against foreboding background music gives way to a temporal leap, heralded by the intrusion of rock drumbeats and the appearance of the film's title in large red letters. The lyrics of "Ballroom Blitz" (Sweet, 1975) take over the soundtrack in the second example of period rock that will punctuate the film, serving as a potent means for linking characters' lives to their moment in culture, and for transporting us viewers back to that time (even if we did not directly live it – such is the power of song to conjure up an entire era). Against this musical backdrop, the story's second naming ceremony takes place. Through a series of editing moves, the films suture us into an emotionally charged exchange of gazes between Libano and Freddo as their nicknames emerge in captions during their first adult appearances on screen. A man overlooks a prison entrance from which a newly released inmate emerges. A reverse shot reveals the face of the swarthy, unshaven observer, underneath which appears the caption "Libanese" (also referred to as "Libano"). When this man whistles, the camera cross-cuts to the first man, who makes eye contact with Libanese and receives the caption "Freddo," as if the very act of recognition and reconnection had given rise to the naming process.

Our own visual collusion in the men's interlocking gazes and our simultaneous reading of their names draws us into a closed, highly codified world, subscribers to the rule of *omertà* that pits the criminal subculture against the society of officially given names, and against the laws that put their bearers in prison. In a lightning-fast montage,

Libano's whistle and gaze in the previous shot give way to this portrait of Freddo as he exits prison to re-enter the world of organized crime.

Placido introduces a series of additional characters with vignettes of each, complete with written names and, in most cases, their vocations: "Dandi" zooms onto the scene on a flashy motorcycle, followed by shots of "Ciro Buffoni, second-hand dealer; Scrocchiazeppi, mechanic; Ricotta, car wrecker; Fierolocchio, unemployed; Bufalo, a restless kid;" ending with "Il Nero, a Nazi."

With this slick, fast-paced parade of characters, accompanied by "Ballroom Blitz" and edited according to the rhythms of our contemporary MTV age, Placido seems to align the body of his film with the conventions of the above-mentioned *poliziesco*, a 1970s genre made up of low-budget, high-adrenalin, mass-produced works aimed at exploiting the anxieties of The Years of Lead.[17] But it is the previous childhood episode, the rite of naming and baptism in blood (Andrea's), which serves as the gang's *scena madre*, establishing the inviolate bond that will link the lives of its three core members, Libano, Freddo, and Dandi, despite the rival claims of romantic love, individual greed, and suspicion that will conspire to drive them apart. Patterns of behaviour will emerge in their adult lives that can be traced back to this rite of initiation and its immediate aftermath. During the police onslaught on the boys' hideout, Dandi had raced ahead through the dunes onto the beach, abandoning Libano and Freddo to their pursuers. While the two who are left behind repeatedly call out to the third, the camera focuses on this fugitive, so that the sound of his name and the image of his flight converge to seal the identity of this character as one who chooses escape over risk, self-preservation over fellow feeling. In what follows, Dandi will exploit the wealth and power afforded by gang membership to feed his own insatiable appetite for luxury cars, showy real estate, flashy dresswear, and exclusive claim to the favours of Patrizia, the high-class prostitute "who makes men dream." Instead, the paths of Libano and Freddo will be more closely intertwined. A fact of utmost significance that will only emerge later is the broken leg that Libano suffered during the chase. In adulthood, his body "remembers" the injury in the form of a persistent limp, but the implication is that he is far more damaged than this minor impairment would suggest. Unlike Freddo and Dandi, he is indifferent to women, and not even homosocial pressures induce him to make a show of sexual interest, or just engage in salacious banter. While the film stops short of imputing a homoerotic edge to his bond with Freddo, it does hint that Libano experiences his injury as a blight on his manhood. The result is a penchant for solitude, highlighted in scenes of painful self-isolation set in the nouveau riche mansion-cum-swimming pool where Libano is shown either desperately pacing or drinking shots of whisky between hits of cocaine. Strikingly, the first of such scenes follows immediately upon the delicate and tender consummation of Freddo's romance with Roberta, a woman who hails from a world alien to the criminal underground and who will eventually inspire him to abandon life outside the law.

But Freddo's decision to sever his ties with Libano and leave the Banda behind cannot be ascribed exclusively to the influence of Roberta. An underlying ideological conflict had long characterized the two men's understandings of the radical freedom to which the Banda had vowed allegiance in the aftermath of their first successful heist. For Libano, this freedom could be achieved by following the imperial models of Augustus, Titus, Hadrian, and their modern counterparts Mussolini, Hitler, and Stalin. For Freddo, who is "not cool with dictators" (con i dittatori non mi si trovo proprio), the choice to live outside the law is anarchist in nature, radically opposed to authoritarian (or any other kind of) rule.

Parodoxically, it will be Libano who sharply limits the gang's freedom of operations by forming misguided alliances with the Mafia and the Secret Service, making him a pawn of forces within the "deep state" when an undercover operative engineers his release from prison. This character, Carenza, henchman of a sinister, nameless figure (called "Il Vecchio" in De Cataldo's novel), will embroil the gang in some of the most dramatic events in Italian history of the 1970s and early 1980s, in particular the kidnapping of Aldo Moro and the bombing of the Bologna train station. Dandi too will fall prey to external pressures, leaving Freddo alone to tread the path of free agency. That path will take its most desperate and radical form in his decision to exchange a prison term for a hospital stay (easily escapable) by willingly contracting a mortal illness through the injection of contaminated blood.[18] In so doing, Freddo is able to win the right to live his last days in the way he sees fit, as a free man, in the company of Roberta, and in full control of his own death. Ironically, that prerogative is denied him when a sniper attack, ordered by the state, cuts him down before he can succumb to the mortal scenario of his own devising.

It should come as no surprise that the film itself would replicate Freddo's pursuit of existential freedom at the level of style, just as it had in its recourse to a Pasolinian model in the film's opening scene. In this later portion of the film, when Freddo's character begins to imagine an alternative to the *malavita*, the film undergoes a marked shift away from the stylistic conventions of the *poliziesco* – those of fast action, glorified violence, obtrusive musical score, and conspicuous editing. Throughout *Romanzo criminale* the technique of the montage sequence had displayed those crime genre elements in their most acute form, signaling distinct stages in the rise and fall of the gang's fortunes, from the initial massacre to take control of the streets, to the processing of narcotics heralding their dominance of the drug trade, to the series of reprisals led by Freddo to avenge the death of Libano, and finally to the arrests of gang members after one of them, Sorcio, turns state's evidence.

In aesthetic terms, no scene could depart more radically from these generic conventions than the visit of Roberta and Freddo to the Basilica di Sant'Agostino. In the lead up to this scene, Freddo sets the stage for a conventional seduction – a ride in his spiffy sports car, destination the beach. But it is Roberta who ends up determining the course of their first outing when she asks Freddo to reverse direction and return to the city because she wants to take him to "a place." The scene begins in darkness, interrupted by the sound of a coin dropping into the box that will shed electrical light on the *Madonna of the Pilgrims* altarpiece by Caravaggio. What follows is a virtuoso example of ecphrasis in which the film's medium-specific tribute to the painting enacts Roberta's own reverence for it, as conveyed to Freddo through dialogue. The couple's spectatorship is foregrounded by lighting effects enhanced by a bank of votive candles, while the figures of Roberta and Freddo are presented in shadow, from behind. A cut to their faces in close-up gives way to a slow pan down the canvas as Roberta describes the Madonna's display

Roberta leads Freddo to Caravaggio's *Madonna of the Pilgrims* in the Basilica di Sant'Agostino, creating a bond between the two that serves to separate their couple's plot from the surrounding film in aesthetic as well as generic terms.

of her child to the pilgrims positioned below. Though her commentary does not explicitly mention Caravaggio's use of chiaroscuro, which bathes the mother's face and the baby's flesh in a crystalline light, her words explain the figurative import of these effects – the Madonna's gesture is a "sign of grace," the child is a "symbol of salvation." In a second pan shot, this time moving from bottom to top, Roberta remarks that Caravaggio added a white sheet to this iconography in "un segno premonitore" (a foreshadowing) of Christ's shroud.

Needless to say, the impact of Roberta's lesson is not lost on Freddo, whose transport in the presence of Caravaggio's masterwork is directed to the flesh-and-blood woman at his side. "If he saw you, he would have put you in his painting, Caravaggio, instead of the Madonna." Out of context, this could easily be taken for a cheap pick-up line, but what gives it the ring of sincerity is the sense of awe that the actors and the aesthetic values of the cinematography impart to the scene. Throughout the visit, Freddo's gaze has shifted from the painted Madonna to Roberta and back, pointing out the shared aura of sanctity with which he, and the camera, invest them. This leisurely paced, highly aestheticized, classically edited, emotionally tender scene serves as a counterpoint to the rest of this hard-hitting film, just as the Freddo-Roberta relationship functions as an exception to all the other relationships within the world of crime.

Overlooked in our analysis until now is Nicola Scialoja, the police commissioner assigned to investigate the workings of the gang. This young, attractive, and earnest crime-fighter must contend with some troubling impulses, including his obsession with Patrizia, the prostitute who "makes men dream" and is in league with the Banda, along with the hint that in some dark corner of his mind there resides a tinge of envy for the luxury and comity of gangster life. Spying on Patrizia, for example, as she exits from her apartment gorgeously attired for a night on the town and dances into Dandi's arms to the rock soundtrack of "Shake Your Booty," Scialoja is clearly aroused. But for all his ambivalence, the commissioner steadfastly pursues the struggle against criminality, and he addresses this scourge in its two virulent forms – that of the streets and that of the "deep state" that colludes with the *malavita* when it serves the interests of a corrupt, authoritarian status quo. In fact, Scialoia is poised to win this battle when he prepares to meet with Freddo to receive the dying man's confession. But the deep state intervenes to thwart the commissioner's efforts by ordering a sniper attack on Freddo to protect against the incriminating intelligence that this would-be informant could so easily provide. At the site of the assassination, as Scialoia is surveying the carnage, Carenza appears to offer his condolences, and congratulations – the former for the loss of Freddo, "he could have explained many things to us," indicating the state agent's own insider knowledge; the latter for Scialoia's promotion to chief of police.

This brings us back to the controversial label "gangeristico-civile" with which Placido had described his intentions in filming *Romanzo criminale*. While this description most obviously applies to the gang's involvement in historical events, its deepest relevance surfaces in Scialoia's climactic confrontation with Il Vecchio. The scenography of this encounter is of paramount importance, for it takes place in the latter's office, whose windows give onto a monument to Victor Emmanuel II, with a focus on the equestrian statue of Garibaldi. This view literalizes the character's powers of oversight, and it subsumes all of the film's monumental settings that have been featured up to this point: Trajan's market, the Torre delle Milizie, the forum of Largo Argentina, the Spanish steps, Santa Maria di Trastevere, Castel Sant'Angelo, the Basilica di Sant'Agostino.[19] The film's discourse on Roman history, from the imperial past to its election as the capital of the modern Italian state, finds its cynical embodiment in this dark and mysterious character – the contemporary, underground incarnation of the emperors applauded by Libano in his exchange with Freddo on the beach. Il Vecchio's association with criminality, which he openly admits ("I interact with the bad") is what leads Scialoia to threaten an investigation against him. But the old man heads off that threat by announcing his own imminent retirement, and his reasons are what constitute the basis of the film's "denuncia civile" (civic condemnation). This self-proclaimed "servant of the state" interprets the approaching fall of the Berlin wall and the end of the Cold War as the death knell of the political class that has ruled until now. It becomes clear that Il Vecchio stands for the deep state's will to use any means at its disposal to preserve its hegemony. Hence his desire to bow out in the face of the unstoppable historical forces that have rendered the old order obsolete. Yet this is not the last vestige of deep state control that the film brings to light, given the continued ability of the secret service to wield power, as evidenced in the silencing of Freddo on the eve of his meeting with Scialoja. Il Vecchio may have made a show of packing up his office and leaving the scene, but the deep state has clearly survived the end of the old order and continues to exert its covert influence beyond the end of the First Republic.

This is "not just a crime film," Placido had said, signaling his ambition to reach beyond the confines of genre in *Romanzo criminale*. There is no better place to take the measure of Placido's achievement than at its ending, which brings together not only the *gangsteristico* and *civile* elements, but also the Pasolinian and aesthetic strands that complicate and enrich the film's generic identity. Scialoja's final words in the film, "cover this corpse," lead to the convergence of all of those strands. He had just been congratulated by Carenza for his promotion to chief of police, but for this investigator Freddo's death is a defeat, a recognition of the limits of his authority in the face of the state's power to obstruct justice. Heeding Scialoja's order, an attendant covers Freddo with a white sheet in fulfilment of Caravaggio's "segno premonitore" as his corpse lies with arms spreadeagled in cruciform position, sprawled on the steps of the Basilica di Sant'Agostino (which, significantly, houses the *Madonna of the Pilgrims* altarpiece). The whole of the Roberta-Freddo love story is conjured up in this desolate mise-en-scène, which reduces all of the emotional and aesthetic promise of their relationship to the level of a body bound for the morgue.

But the film leaves the spectator with a final impression strikingly at odds with the spectacle of Freddo's squalid demise. In a stunning move, Placido inserts a flashback to the boyhood scene in Ostia just as the sheet is being lowered over the dead man's face. This final flashback stands as the culmination of the web of recalls that have punctuated the film, revealing that the foundational scene is being constantly rewritten, according to the needs and obsessions of the characters within whose subjectivity the memory is couched (Libano's and Dandi's in previous instances). The conclusive return to the foundational scene rewrites it with a happy ending, a counterfactual chronicle of the childhood escapade in which Andrea does not die, Libano does not break his leg, and Dandi does not abandon his friends to the tender mercies of the police. In this revised flashback, Andrea emerges from the trailer oblivious to the impending police onslaught, and is met by his friends who urge him to join them in flight. The children are filmed in an exuberant sprint through the dunes and onto the beach – the kinetic enactment of the total freedom from restraints that they long for in adulthood but will never achieve. Once on the beach, they continue to run single file, with Dandi in the lead, while Freddo grabs the hand of Andrea, who brings up the rear. It is here that the film soars into the realm of Pasolinian *poesia* as the reverie concludes with a mise-en-scène of the boys pictured in silhouette, racing against a marine background illuminated by the shimmering rays of the setting sun. Following behind them is a parade of jogging policemen, unable to catch up with their prey. This supremely lyrical sequence, so sharply at variance with what happened after the death of the boy Andrea in the film's opening moments, could be read as the deferred representation of the dying child's reverie, or as Freddo's "posthumous" wish-fulfilment fantasy.

But the flashback's final frames fade to a crane shot of Freddo's shrouded corpse, and the result is a vertiginous plunge from the lyrical "high" of the reimagined childhood scene to the stark image of mortal defeat. In so doing, the conclusion opens up the widest of interpretive spaces, drawing the spectator into the gap between the flashback's celebration of imaginative transcendence and the finale's surrender to the impossibility of redemption and the finality of death. It is in this breach that the viewer is called upon to fully experience the complexity of this genre-defying achievement, and in the process to exercise the interpretive freedom that the film has licensed all along. In the end, Freddo's bold but deeply flawed quest for freedom finds its positive counterpart in the viewer's freedom of interpretation and the filmmaker's freedom to claim the mantel of auteur.

Chapter Four

"The Unsustainable Normality of Devastation": Matteo Garrone's *Gomorra* (Gomorrah), 2008

Direction: Matteo Garrone. *Subject*: Roberto Saviano, based on his 2006 novel of the same title. *Screenplay*: Maurizio Braucci, Ugo Chiti, Gianni Di Gregorio, Massimo Gaudioso, Matteo Garrone, Roberto Saviano. *Cinematography*: Marco Onorato. *Editing*: Marco Spoletini, *Sets*: Paolo Bonfini. *Costumes*: Alessandra Cardini. *Cast*: Toni Servillo (Franco), Gianfelice Imparato (Don Ciro), Maria Nazionale (Maria), Salvatore Cantalupo (Pasquale), Salvatore Abruzzese, (Totò), Marco Macor (Marco), Ciro Petrone (Ciro/"Pisellino"), Carmine Paternoster (Roberto).

Synopsis: Set in the outskirts of Naples, the film is made up of five discrete stories about characters whose lives are entangled with the Camorra, the crime syndicate based in the region of Campania. These stories unfold against the background of a war between the dominant clan in the area and a break-away faction of "secessionists." *Gomorra* begins with a massacre in a tanning salon, before launching into the stories of (1) Don Ciro, who delivers payments to families of relatives jailed or killed in clan warfare, and who is eventually coerced into helping the secessionists by inadvertently luring his comrades into a trap, leading to a blood bath that leaves him unscathed; (2) Totò, a thirteen-year-old who longs to enter the junior ranks of the clan and whose membership "dues" involve betraying an adult friend whom he dearly loves; (3) Marco and Ciro ("Pisellino"), young hoodlums in thrall to the mystique of *Scarface*'s Tony Montana, who refuse to submit

---

This chapter is a revised version of an essay entitled *"Gomorra* by Matteo Garrone: 'La normalità dello sfacelo,'" which appeared in *Italian Political Cinema: Public Life, Imaginary, and Identity in Contemporary Italian Film*, ed. Giancarlo Lombardi and Christian Uva (Peter Lang, 2016).

to the authority of the local boss but finally surrender to a lucrative clan-sponsored mission that leads to their gruesome demise; (4) Roberto, a university graduate who is hired by Franco, manager of a toxic waste management firm, and who eventually resigns once his eyes are opened to the unscrupulous and poisonous aspects of his employer's practice; and (5) Pasquale, a gifted tailor who directs a sweatshop under the aegis of an exploitative owner, and who agrees to work undercover for a secretive Asian garment operation that, once discovered by the clan, leads to the assassination of the Chinese project manager and to Pasquale's departure from the world of fashion.

Amidst the many scenes of carnage that punctuate Garrone's film, the one that physically assaults the body of the viewer, causing a kinetic reaction of astonishing intensity, is ironically a scene of simulated violence. I am referring to the moment in which the adolescent Totò allows himself to be shot in the chest (albeit protected by a bulletproof vest) as a form of initiation into the junior ranks of the Camorra. It is impossible not to flinch when Totò falls back from the force of the bullet's impact. This is the film's most acute example of Garrone's expressive strategy throughout *Gomorra* – to immerse us in the brute materiality of *la malavita campana* (the criminal life of the Campania region) without the buffers of familiar iconographies, conventional dramaturgies, or obvious stylistic filters to protect us from the raw force of its blows. "I wanted there to be nothing to mediate between the spectator and the reality within the frame," Garrone remarked in a 2008 interview with Emilio Cozzi.[1]

> I reduced to the minimum the camera movements, zooms, dolly shots, musical interventions, availing myself only when I couldn't avoid them. The objective is that those who watch the film smell the odours that surround them. The spectators must be immersed in what they see, without being conditioned by anything else.[2]

With this statement, the filmmaker makes explicit the somatic intent of his film, its synesthetic ambitions to bring all of the viewer's senses to bear on the experience of entering Camorra territory. Adding to the obvious visual power of the film is a soundtrack emanating strictly from the diegesis, whose sonorities are so layered and dense as to "project us into a hallucinatory drift in which we even seem to smell the odours, inhaled by virtue of the sensation of finding ourselves truly there"[3] where olfactory perception is invoked as shorthand for all the senses not usually associated with cinema. The film's address to us as embodied spectators means that we become fully present to the world of the *malavita campana*, through a phenomenology that catapults us into its midst in an existential way, inhabiting its spaces, absorbing its sensations, and ultimately assuming the ethical consequences of the "charge of the real," to echo Vivian Sobchack's resonant phrase.[4]

Needless to say, such a seemingly unobstructed relationship between "the spectator" and "the reality within the frame" requires the workings of a powerful auteurship – one fully schooled in the techniques of self-concealing artifice. To that end, Garrone takes the documentary, anti-spectacular strain of post-war cinematic realism to its extreme, endowing the camera with an eye-witness intrusiveness and ductility that aligns the film with the reigning "reality TV" aesthetic of our current age.[5] Using a shoulder-mounted camera that he personally wields 60 per cent of the time, and affecting a naive, tabula rasa curiosity that borders on the meddlesome, Garrone clings to the faces and bodily gestures of his characters with a maniacal closeness that precludes the distance necessary for judgment or even understanding. For the most part, Garrone's documentary claims are rooted in the casting of non-professional actors who speak a local dialect that requires subtitles even for Italian audiences and the decision to film in the degraded housing projects of suburban Naples, prime real estate for the Camorra's workings.[6] Such was the authenticity of Garrone's approach that it attracted the willing participation of local gangsters as consultants, and his free-wheeling directorial style created a collaborative relationship with actors that made them veritable co-authors of the film.[7] Working without a storyboard, depending heavily on his actors' spontaneous artistry and the stimuli provided by the location settings, Garrone's process recalls that of Rossellini, who put a premium on his own receptivity to the cues emanating from the atmosphere on set. Like Rossellini in his neorealist phase, Garrone simulates a grass-roots orientation, as if the world before the camera lens were demanding its own custom-made technique, free from authorial contrivance.[8]

Strikingly, Garrone had to forego his *own* highly mediated view of organized crime: "I had Scorsese-type faces in my head," he confessed, "and instead I had to acknowledge a strong anthropologic change."[9] That Garrone attributed his shift in approach to factors of a social-scientific rather than a stylistic nature is telling. It suggests an acknowledgment of the profound otherness of the Camorra world, and of the ways in which cinematic stereotyping has masked and tamed that anthropological division. In this light, Garrone may be seen to have made an ethnographic film – one that accepts the chasm separating our realm of experience from that of the *malavita* but that nonetheless undertakes the challenge of its representation.

Accordingly, the film's opening scene may be read as a "user's manual" – a set of instructions as to what viewing habits must be left behind and what new ones must take their place as we enter an alien, "anthropologically other" realm of experience. The scene begins in utter darkness, accompanied by a motorized sound of unknown origin. Dim blue lights begin to emerge behind the black silhouette of a man whose contours gradually take shape in the reflected glow of mechanical illumination. In his stillness and the mineral shine of his skin, he could be the metalized man of the Futurist imaginary, until he scratches his nose and we realize that there is a living, breathing human being within this eerie epidermis, and it soon dawns on us that he is undergoing neither torture nor the ordeal of some ghoulish scientific experiment, but only the mundane workings of a *centro estetico* (spa).[10] Outside the tanning booth, there is much activity and banter among customers who await their turns, while another of them solemnly undergoes a manicure. This frivolity and bonhomie come to an abrupt halt when the most gregarious of them all pulls out his gun to unleash a shooting spree, abetted by a pair of other comrades in arms, leaving four victims lifeless in various gruesome poses throughout the premises.

This prologue scene is rife with interpretive leads for the film to follow. At the cognitive level, it plunges us, without preparation or explanation, into a nightmare world whose inner workings will remain forever closed to us. If *Gomorra* were a conventional crime film, later plot developments would shed a retroactive light on the horrific events of the opening scene. Eventually, we will indeed come to understand that this massacre is an episode in the war among rival factions of the Camorra, but no specifics about who or why will ever be divulged. Garrone's genre-bending dramaturgy refuses such concessions, leaving us in a prolonged and unrelieved state of disorientation.[11] At the thematic level, the scene demonstrates "the cult of beauty and fashion,"[12] which astonished Garrone upon his first encounter with the world of the Camorra. Significantly, this scene was not envisioned in the original screenplay,[13] and by adding it Garrone invites us to relish the irony that the mobsters' obsession with physical appearance is what leads to their physical undoing, rendering them vulnerable to attack from within. Utterly defenceless as they relax under the shower of artificial sunlight or the delicate ministrations of the manicurist, these assiduous cultivators of the body beautiful cannot possibly conceive of the fact that their soon-to-be-killers could enter the premises for any other reason than to enhance their looks. As Garrone leaves the tanning salon-turned-slaughterhouse for the wretched housing projects and scorched earth of suburban Naples and Casal di Principe, he announces his film's radical iconoclasm, his determination to debunk the mass media image of the mobster, to divest it of the allure and mystique that popular culture has conferred upon this abject figure.[14]

In terms of dramaturgy, Garrone achieves this aim by a levelling process that refuses to set up a conventional narrative arc of events, and that focuses instead on the quotidian nature of Camorra operations – the day-to-day business of working and surviving in the closed universe of organized crime. In this, Garrone displays a Zavattinian attentiveness to the mundane detail, but he does so to the opposite effect of his neorealist predecessor.[15] Whereas Zavattini sought to render the condition of ordinariness – for example "a woman buys a pair of shoes" – the object of surpassing curiosity and ethical concern, vowing to make the event "spectacular, not through its exceptional, but through its *normal* qualities,"[16] Garrone focuses on the quotidian to demythologize the iconic figure of the mobster enshrined in the popular imaginary. Accordingly, *Gomorra*'s cast of characters includes none of the charismatic dons, none of the upper echelon holders of power and wealth featured in mass media coverage of organized crime, limiting itself instead to the low-level functionaries of the Camorra rank and file.[17]

Of the utmost importance in this debunking operation is Garrone's decision to dedicate one of *Gomorra*'s storylines to the seductive power of Hollywood's gangster genre over the minds of naive young consumers who aspire to criminal stardom. Its protagonists are Marco and Ciro, who imagine themselves as characters in *Scarface* (that is, Brian De Palma's 1983 remake). These young viewers experience De Palma's film as an unproblematic endorsement of Tony Montana's criminal heroics. It is Scarface's swagger, his unapologetic flaunting of ignorance and vulgarity, his insatiable appetite for power, money, and glitz that have inspired the young hoodlums' cult of emulation. In their rampage through a hollowed-out structure that Marco and Ciro imagine to be their hero's villa, Garrone displays the mechanisms that make these fans such artless and self-destructive consumers of De Palma's film. The scene is set strategically in the actual ruins of a residence belonging to Camorra boss Walter Schiavone, who had ordered his architect to reconstruct the Miami villa of *Scarface* as gleaned from repeated viewings of the film on VHS. By the time Marco and Ciro stage their own replay of *Scarface*, Schiavone's villa is in shambles because the boss ordered its demolition from prison, marking the denouement of a "real-life" criminal saga that could not have been more anti-climactic when compared to the paroxysm of violent death and destruction of his Hollywood counterpart.

In the scene that provided the still for the Criterion Collection's DVD of *Gomorra*, Marco and Ciro's euphoria over their discovery of a weapons cache takes *Scarface*-inspired form. Wielding assault rifles, standing by the banks of a waterway, clad only in their tennis shoes and jockey briefs (which add a bizarre erotic dimension to their brandishing of these potent arms), Marco and Ciro shoot a round of ammunition across to the other shore, spewing forth triumphant bits of imagined film dialogue. Marco's posture in particular as he pivots expertly to fire in a 180-degree arc recalls Tony Montana's moves as he guns down a horde of enemies during his climactic last stand.

Through Marco and Ciro's literal mimesis of their filmic idol, Garrone comments on the pernicious power of spectacularized crime, and reaffirms his film's demystifying intent. Whereas De Palma complicates his portrait of underworld glamour through irony and the workings of "poetic justice," for consumers like Marco and Ciro such layered and sophisticated representation collapses into a monolithic paean to criminal celebrity. Garrone, instead, will dispense with the veneer of spectacle that requires viewers to penetrate the seductive formal surface of a film in order to uncover its hidden critique. In other words, Garrone's film language functions like the ruins of Schiavone's villa – the indexical traces of a Camorra fantasy-turned-historical fiasco.[18]

But Garrone's demystifying operation never involves an overt authorial judgment on the Camorra world. In this, his film differs markedly from its source text – Roberto Saviano's best-selling account of the Camorra's workings, narrated by a strong moralizing voice with an obtrusive tendency toward self-inscription.[19] Saviano constantly stages his subjectivity, calling attention to the witnessing process itself through the saga of his first-person encounter with the Camorra world and the report of his reactions, both physical and moral, to its horror.[20] Garrone's phenomenology precludes such explicit interventions. Withholding the impulse to condemn this social illness, in its place the filmmaker offers a "thick description"[21] of the Camorra world, displaying, rather than denouncing, its pathology. Garrone has repeatedly claimed that *impegno sociale* is not the primary concern of his work, that his impulse is first and foremost aesthetic in nature, that "the strongest aspect for me has always been the image."[22] "My objective is to lower the spectator into the interior of certain dynamics, to immerse him within places and mechanisms of criminality without allowing the appearance of any judgment on what has been described."[23] Thus Garrone's phenomenology neutralizes Saviano's overt didacticism, entrusting that task to the visual language and storytelling structures of his film. "Without a thesis," Garrone explains, "I am aware of not doing anything other than following my characters along the unforeseen deviations of their pathways,"[24] in a formulation that conjures up the Zavattinian ideal of "*pedinamento*" – the trailing or stalking of characters through space and, metaphorically, through deviant narrative trajectories. It is by means of this two-tiered *pedinamento* that *Gomorra* builds to its powerful denunciation of Camorra rule, reversing Saviano's thesis-driven, investigative approach through what I would call a process of indictment by induction, leaving it to the viewer to work from the ground up to arrive at the kinds of conclusions that the literary text imposes from above.

One of the crucial ways in which Garrone's film foreswears the unified/moral approach of Saviano's book is by spreading its inquiry across five separate stories, focalized through as many characters (considering Marco and Ciro as a single *dramatis persona*) whose narratives provide a pluralistic, anti-totalizing view of the Camorra underworld. In a further fragmentation of narrative perspective, each plot is broken down into a series of modular units whose forward movement is constantly interrupted by the insertion of units from the four other plots. Along with the film's attention to Camorra *quotidianità*, this editing technique blunts the momentum of conventional dramatic structure – the build-up of tension and expectation is offset by cross-cutting among separate plot lines. Unlike the great choral films of Robert Altman, *Nashville* and *Short Cuts*, or such composite works as *Babel*, *Crash*, and *Grand Canyon* where distinct narrative strands interweave and ultimately converge to form a coherent whole, *Gomorra*'s stories remain relentlessly separate, providing no holistic narrative structure to contain them and to offer at least the aesthetic solace of formal cohesion.[25]

One of the stories that powerfully exemplifies the thesis of Saviano's text, and that could have easily lent itself to didacticism in a more conventional film, is that of Pasquale the tailor. Saviano's opening chapters are organized around a central economic insight – that the Camorra has accrued inordinate power by establishing a parallel capitalist economy based on an entrepreneurship unfettered by legal restraints.[26] While Saviano dedicates a good deal of his book to the analysis of this mechanism, marshalling many concrete examples as proof of its workings, Garrone refuses to subordinate Pasquale's story to this *a priori* thesis. In other words, he lets the story speak for itself. In its very mode of speaking, Pasquale's story contains *in nuce* the narrative strategy of Garrone's film as a whole. Just as *Gomorra* shuttles back and forth among its five plots, Pasquale's story shuttles between his two jobs: his "official" one under the supervision of his oppressive Camorra boss, Iavarone, and his nocturnal one in an illicit Chinese dressmaking firm. In keeping with the film's refusal of didacticism, Garrone's protagonist Pasquale does not verbalize his understanding of Camorra economics. Instead, it is the *dress* that bespeaks the truth of the system. The garment begins as an idea in the mind of Iavarone, who out-bids other dressmakers vying for a commission with a fashion house in the North by obliging his master tailor Pasquale to work at break-neck speed and for a pittance. When the film returns fitfully to the Pasquale plot, we get brief shots of the dress in various stages of completeness. A more conventional director would have kept a constant focus on the garment, providing close-ups of each step in its making, from pattern, to cutting, to stitching, to fitting, and even perhaps to a final triumphant display. Instead, glimpses of the dress seem almost incidental to the story's primary focus on Pasquale, his exhaustion under the regime of his oppressive boss, his elation at the gratitude and reverence of the Chinese. But like Garrone's film, itself the result of planning, cutting, and stitching, the final product is understated. The penultimate scene of Pasquale's story shows his handiwork under the admiring gaze of the television cameras, but the shot goes by in a flash, thus minimizing its melodramatic potential. It is the dress that has given voice to Saviano's lesson on Camorra economics, and it has done so wordlessly, imagistically, and understatedly, asking us to do the work of stitching together its journey from Campanian sweatshop to Milanese retail outlet, to the body of Scarlett Johansson at the premier of the Venice film festival, to the airwaves of an approving world.

Central to the film's inductive procedure is the presence of a mega-image that gives rise to Garrone's moralizing commentary through strictly cinematic means: Le Vele di Scampia, the housing project whose spaces determine the movements of characters, dictate the camerawork, and serve as the objective correlative for the Camorra's sovereign power over its subjects in a number of pivotal scenes.[27] Built between 1962 and 1975 in suburban Naples as the utopian fantasy of a planned community, Le Vele went horribly awry, becoming the place where "bad-living, bad architecture, and bad politics were welded together."[28] The name of the structures alone suggests how good intentions poorly implemented can turn into cruel self-satire. The maritime imagery so poetically invoked by the term *vele* (sails) comes to characterize the apartment buildings as seafaring vessels languishing in dry dock, going nowhere. The internal network of criss-crossing gangways, idealistically designed to promote the interconnectedness of so many separate lives, becomes instead an analogy for Camorra rule over its occupants. The totality of Mob control is reflected in the self-enclosure of this *mala-architettura* whose inhabitants seem to live out their entire existences within its walls. In a particularly chilling shot, Garrone shows a wedding procession advancing along one of the gangways, its squalor barely covered by a blue running carpet, while the usual comings and goings of the *malavita* take their course on the gangway located above it.[29]

In a curious twist, the external world that this *mala-architettura* shuts out through self-enclosure is re-imported by means of clothing. Totò wears a jersey with "England 7" emblazoned on its back. Whether or not he understands the reference to the soccer star Beckham, the camera that trails him through many shots cannot help but call our attention to the incongruity between the world conjured up by the British sports icon and the one inhabited by this fledgling *camorrista*. The young men of the drug distribution system don the pristine new warm-up suits and impeccable tennis shoes of American hip-hop aficionados. One of the thugs who kills Marco and Ciro in the film's last sequence wears a tank-top with "Cincinati" (*sic*) on the back, and the misspelling, along with the huge girth of the man, reveals the grotesque inappropriateness of such an allusion to this quintessentially American sport of lean, tall players who shoot baskets rather than human beings. In a reversal of the outbound geography of these sports jerseys, one of the African drug pushers who plies his trade in the area wears a shirt with the inscription "Italia."

The two figures who are filmed frequently circulating within Le Vele, Don Ciro and Totò, are characters whose roles most intimately exemplify the workings of the System. Don Ciro is the "sottomarino" (submarine), the functionary who delivers money to the families of imprisoned gangsters, and it is by the camera's *pedinamento* of this character that we gain access to the domestic spaces of the lives that depend on Camorra support. With each "delivery" we gain a foothold into a given family's story, as the recipient greets Don Ciro with coffee and a tale of woe that can only be alleviated, in the teller's mind, through an increase in Camorra compensation. In each case, Don Ciro pronounces his mantra "farò presente" (loosely translated: I'll let them know) – a verb phrase whose constant repetition and whose lack of a direct or indirect object reveals the hollowness of his promise to communicate this latest grievance to the higher-ups. The most painful of his repeated encounters within the architecture of Le Vele are those with Maria, whose husband is in jail and whose son has joined the faction that has broken away from the dominant "clan" of their locality.[30] In their final meeting, which takes place on the gangway leading to her house, Maria's doom is foretold in Don Ciro's refusal to even enter her residence. The camerawork in this scene is especially jarring – it maintains a suffocating closeness to Don Ciro and moves unsteadily according to the man's gait, first following him with a shoulder-level shot that reveals the bulges of his newly donned bulletproof vest.

Upon hearing Maria call out his name, Don Ciro turns in her direction and warns her not to leave the house. As he continues walking away from her, the camera executes a 180-degree turn and films him

Garrone's camera trails close behind Don Ciro's back, puffed up by the padding of his bulletproof vest.

frontally, with Maria in the distant background at the end of the gangway near the threshold of her apartment. When she informs him that she is being driven from her home by their clan, Don Ciro responds that he can't help her, his expression downcast as he hastens away. But Maria stands her ground. The gangway now opens into a platform leading to the stairwell, thus offering Don Ciro escape from the woman's importunings.

The cinematography in this scene warrants further scrutiny, for it marks an important next step in the elaboration of Garrone's phenomenology. Not only does the shoulder-mounted camera express the filmmaker's own openness and astonishment in the face of what he finds, but it also "tries on" the subjectivities of *Gomorra*'s main characters, appropriating their points of view through the use of what Pasolini labelled "free indirect subjective" cinematography. Located midway between the extremes of objective and subjective points of view, the free indirect subjective allows us to see through the eyes of a character – to adopt his or her cognitive style – even as the character remains visible to us on screen. In a related development, Jean Mitry and Gilles Deleuze posit a continuum of positions between the objective and subjective poles that allows for the camera's varying degrees of proximity to a character's point of view.[31] This endows the camera with considerable elasticity, enabling it to slip in and out of a character's consciousness much as the skilled writer moves seamlessly across direct, indirect, and free indirect modes of discourse.

In the scene of Don Ciro's last encounter with Maria, the camera comes to fully adopt his perspective, sharing his paranoid sense of being watched. There is no shot/counter-shot editing in this scene – Garrone never gives us Maria's "take" on Don Ciro's withdrawal from her. We remain confined to the frightened man's focalization as he moves through the regimented itinerary of gangways and stairwells that give spatial expression to Camorra control. Like Jeremy Bentham's panopticon,[32] this architecture performs the function of surveillance, monitoring Don Ciro's movements and dictating which apartments he can enter and which he must shun. The list of families on the Camorra payroll, newly revised to exclude Maria's name, serves as the written form of panoptical control that Don Ciro must obey as he makes his rounds. The wariness of his movements within this space, as captured by Garrone's free indirect subjective camerawork, become the equivalent of putting on the bulletproof vest – protective manoeuvring in a hostile and potentially lethal environment.

The other protagonist whose point of view is borrowed through free indirect subjective camerawork and who transits continually along the gangways of Le Vele is Totò. Just as Don Ciro circulates through the housing project as a deliveryman, so too does the boy, but in the latter case as the bearer of groceries provided by his mother's store. In the war-torn environment of Le Vele, where housewives exit at their own peril, the home delivery of groceries is less a luxury than a means of self-preservation. In his hyper-mobile capacity, Totò becomes an acute observer of his Carmorra-charged surroundings, and as such serves as the ideal vehicle for Garrone's own naive exposure to the world of crime. Of particular note in this regard is the scene in which Totò waits at the doorway as Camorra operatives "process" the latest shipment of cocaine. The scene begins with a close-up of a blender, wielded by an exceedingly scruffy, scar-faced man, and then pans down to another set of hands busily and expertly filling capsules with powder before Garrone cuts to Totò standing expectantly at the doorsill of the room. That he remains on the other side of the threshold is important, suggesting his unreadiness to enter this intimate space, the beating heart of the Camorra drug trade. The camera returns to the worktable but cuts back to Totò once more before finally alighting on him as the scene reaches its conclusion. Throughout the episode, we are led to believe that the camera's curious, detail-oriented gaze – one that turns this assembly-line procedure into a fascinating and elaborate exercise in group craftsmanship – coincides with Totò's own admiring perspective.

It is through Totò's story that the film is able to chronicle the insidious process by which young men become Camorra recruits, a process that ingeniously equates entering into criminality with coming into manhood. In one of the earliest scenes of the Totò plot, the protagonist's childishness is brought to the fore. We see Totò splashing about in a plastic wading pool, playing with inflatable water toys as other children his age and younger frolic around him. But we are not allowed to linger on this scene of childhood wholesomeness and normality because Garrone's camera soon cuts to shots of young men doing sentinel duty on adjacent rooftops, as they relay the news of an impending police raid.[33] When the camera returns to the wading pool, it does so in an extreme long shot that shows the mammoth architecture of Le Vele surrounding this idyllic scene of childhood recreation. To make this shot even more disturbing, it is taken from an angle that fully exposes the grim geometry of the interior gangways and the weird ziggurat structure of the building's many levels. It is as if the wading pool, as the pristine space of innocence, were swallowed up by the vast and malignant reach of the architecture that has come to embody Camorra rule. Such moments of childish abandon are the exception, this mise-en-scène tells us, in the Camorra-sponsored rush to manhood.

In a later scene, Totò is told "Now you're a man," after having passed the test of courage under gunfire cited above. Bracketing this rite of passage are two symmetrical scenes that provide before and after snapshots of Totò's leap into manhood. The first shot shows him peering at his mirror reflection as he plucks his eyebrows in a cosmetic effort of dubious virility. In the second shot, the mirror reflects back to him the sign of his newly won battle scar – a bruise on his chest inflicted by the impact of the bullet not completely cushioned by the bulletproof vest.

Given the non-directive nature of Garrone's narrative technique – his refusal to extend a strong guiding hand through the thicket of his five plots – it comes as some surprise that an author surrogate does indeed emerge from the multitude. That figure is Roberto, the one principal character to hail from the extra-Camorra world. A university graduate eager for gainful employment, Roberto has apprenticed himself to the slick and unscrupulous Franco, a contractor for the disposal of toxic waste. Of the very few extreme long shots that punctuate *Gomorra*, most of them belong to the Franco-Roberto plot. Though we could attribute this calculation to the fact that their story involves the large-scale relationships between humans and their natural surroundings, I believe that the camera's impulse to step back and assume a critical distance

The playful scene in the wading pool that had filled the frame in preceding shots is now dwarfed by the massive architecture of this Camorra stronghold, with its ominous hints of Totò's future entrapment by the System.

from the narrative at key moments reflects Roberto's own attempt to come to terms with the unscrupulous dealings in which he is engaged.[34] In making Roberto the internalized figure of the filmmaker, Garrone is, of course, taking his cues from Saviano, who inscribed himself in his written text as Franco's would-be assistant.[35] By retaining the textual character's (and of course, the writer's) first name, the film reaffirms Roberto's role as authorial stand-in, and it does so cinematically in the form of a gaze that can detach itself from the world it surveys. It is such cognitive distancing that gives Roberto the eventual power to walk away from his unsavoury employment.

Garrone announces the critical function of long shots in the very opening frames of the Franco-Roberto story when the two men emerge as tiny specks from some mysterious underground source in the desolate wasteland of an abandoned gas station. Later they will be shown amidst the vast and majestic backdrop of the sun-baked quarry soon to be filled with barrels of toxic waste. Another shot, this time filmed along the axis of a hallway, leads into a room where Roberto sits alone in a corner of the far end. This chamber is the sickroom of a landowner, whose illness could well be a result of exposure to toxic landfill,[36] and whose ponderous daughter sits protectively by his pillow while his son paces nervously as Franco, sitting to one side, negotiates a price for dumping wastes on the family's property. At first, it seems that the family will take a principled stand: "It's not trash, it's poison," the sick man asserts, but we soon learn that the issue of toxicity has been brought up not as a moral reproach, but as a reason for price gouging. Cutting back to Roberto in an attitude of listening, Garrone makes him the focalizer of this venal and squalid scenario. Once the young man takes his leave of the fetid space, the camera chooses to follow him outdoors, where the results of Franco's toxic dumping are to emerge full blown: an old woman suffering from dementia (a second victim of the poisoned environment?) mistakes Roberto for another man and presents him with a basket of preternaturally large and richly coloured peaches. Later in the car, Franco orders Roberto to discard the produce. "Don't you smell the stench?" he sneers. Roberto, having been taken in by the beauty of the fruit, just as he had been duped all along by Franco's own charming facade, announces his resignation. "We end up resolving the problems that others have created," Franco rationalizes, "funziona così" (this is how it works). In walking away from any complicity with the System, Roberto becomes the only character to free himself from its stranglehold. Of the other two characters who renounce their Camorra roles – Pasquale and Don Ciro – uncertainty remains about the degree to which they can definitively extricate themselves from the System. The last we see of Pasquale, he is taking his place behind the steering wheel of a huge tractor-trailer, and though the scenario of the open road may signal emancipation, Pasquale's counterpart in Saviano's novel ends up as a truck driver for the Camorra.[37] Don Ciro is miraculously spared in a raid on his clan by the break-away faction, and as he steps over the dead bodies that blanket the approach to the apartment where he had nearly met the same fate, Garrone's camera assumes an unusual overhead view, as if to survey the battlefield after a military rout. Once clear of the corpses, Don Ciro picks up his pace and hurries down the road leading away from Le Vele. This is the last we see of him, but Don Ciro's degree of entrenchment in the System leaves little hope for the success of so simple an exit strategy.

In narrative terms the film delivers its most tragic commentary on the Camorra world through the fates of its youngest characters, Totò, Marco, and Ciro. Totò's destiny had been sealed in the final step of his escalating role as delivery boy. From bearer of groceries for housewives of Le Vele to bearer of cocaine allotments for pushers on the street, Totò had graduated to bearer of death for Maria.[38] This irreversible step into criminality is taken with great reluctance by the boy, who is truly fond of Maria, but the *camorristi* have been especially adept at manipulating his desire for acceptance, and they make him a pawn in the plot to gun her down. As Totò flees the scene of the murder that he helped facilitate, the camera pulls back to film the action in an extreme long shot that takes in the massive architecture of Le Vele, with all the sinister geometry of its gangways and the jagged climb of its outer walls. Such camerawork leads us back to the scene of Totò in the wading pool at the moment in which he seemed most childlike, when the camera had pulled back to remind us of the precarious nature of a boyhood spent in Le Vele, the architectural manifestation of Camorra rule. Now the inherent pessimism of that earlier scene is fulfilled by the tragic outcome of this second one, setting up a photographic symmetry that brands the story of Totò with the mark of predestination.

If the full-blown experience of childhood is effectively precluded by life under the Camorra, so is that of adolescence, whose rebellious excesses take a predictably malignant turn in a world where violence and criminality are the rule. As previously noted, the normal teenage tendency to fandom leads Marco and Ciro not only to venerate but to emulate Al Pacino's performance of Scarface. Adolescent longing for freedom from parental control in their case translates into rejection of Camorra authority, and the consequent flaunting of their alleged status as free agents of crime. Significantly, their story unfolds entirely outside the confines of Le Vele, and their exuberant freedom is expressed in constant forays on Ciro's motorcycle through varied landscapes and suburban spaces. The last such expedition will take them to the beach (or one very similar to it) where they had earlier celebrated their first success as petty thieves after filching a stash of cocaine and a wad of money from a group of African drug pushers. Thus the final act of their story brings their brief criminal careers full circle in an ending that could not be more different from that of their beloved Scarface, who went out in a paroxysm of violence and gore as he heroically attempted to fend off his enemies' onslaught. Marco and Ciro instead are executed by a pack of grizzled and overweight thugs for whom this is clearly a routine exercise. But rather than end their story (and the film itself) on a sensationalizing note, such as the spectacle of their blood-stained bodies, Garrone has chosen to linger on the utterly pragmatic matter of their disposal.[39] As the killers nonchalantly load the corpses onto the bucket of a bulldozer, their gestures recall those of veteran sanitation workers going about the day-to-day business of garbage removal. Garrone's anti-spectacular treatment of this horrific scene marks the triumph of the mundane, the end of the workday for camorra thugs who must dispose of the waste products of the System in yet one more example of the wrenching and "unsustainable normality of devastation."[40]

PART TWO

Neo-regionalism

Chapter Five

"Per vacanza?" "No, per viverci!" (To vacation? No, to live here!): Giorgio Diritti's *Il vento fa il suo giro* (The Wind Blows Round), 2005

Direction: Giorgio Diritti. *Screenplay*: Giorgio Diritti, Fredo Valla. *Cinematography*: Roberto Cimatti. *Editing*: Edu Crespo, Giorgio Diritti. *Music*: Marco Biscarini, Daniele Furlati. *Sets*: Emanuele Perrone. *Costumes*: Raffaella Ciavarelli, Manuela Marzano. *Cast*: Thierry Toscan (Philippe Héraud), Alessandra Agosti (Chris Héraud), Dario Anghilante (Costanzo), Giovanni Foresti (Fausto), Giacomino Allais (Roberto), Caterina Damiano (Emma).

Synopsis: A Frenchman, Philippe Héraud, conceives a plan to relocate his young family from the Pyrenees to Chersogno, a remote village in the Val Maira area of the Alps southwest of Turin, in order to raise goats and produce cheeses for the gourmet market. The mayor of Chersogno, Costanzo, and an ally on the town council, Fausto, convince their wary neighbours that the Hérauds will help energize and repopulate this languishing locality. The warm collective welcome they orchestrate to greet the Hérauds soon gives way to suspicion and growing hostility as the family's countercultural ways run up against the norms of this rigid and self-protective population. Among the subplots to emerge is that of a brief amorous tryst between Fausto and Philippe's wife, Chris. Another secondary narrative thread traces the story of Massimo, who is eager to enter the shepherd's vocation alongside of Philippe but is prohibited from so doing by his oppressive father. Yet another minor character worthy of interest is Monica, a studious young woman whose suffering on behalf of those cast out by the community fuels her decision to leave Chersogno. The dire sequence of events leading to the film's unhappy ending is triggered by Emma, whose property borders on the Hérauds' and whose resentment of the family's imagined encroachment on her land culminates in violence. The meaning of the film's title, based on a proverb about the cyclical course of natural time and human affairs, is tragically fulfilled when the Hérauds' departure closes the circle so auspiciously opened by Philippe's arrival in Chersogno at the film's start.

In keeping with the free spirit of its protagonist, the makers of *Il vento fa il suo giro* set out to buck the conventions of the Italian film industry, soliciting no state or televisual funding and sidestepping established patterns of distribution, opting instead for a cooperative formula in which the troupe and actors served as co-producers, pooling their resources and accepting the financial liabilities that went along with freedom from outside constraints.[1] The intensely participatory nature of the production extended to the residents of the Alpine location, who volunteered their houses, animals, props, and food in an ironic reversal of the inhospitality that the film's fictional townspeople showed toward the Hérauds.[2] All of the actors were non-professionals, and the only requirement for those playing the roles of townspeople was that they be proficient in Occitan, the ancient Gallic-romance dialect still spoken in the region.[3] Troupe members lived with the villagers for the nine months' duration of the shoot, becoming closely integrated into their community and actively collaborating in caring for the film's animal actors.[4] This profound communitarian investment in the film's production carried over into the actors' performances and technical practices, which endowed *Il vento fa il suo giro* with its air of authenticity, moral urgency, and emotive power. "If the film made itself, and has a certain flavour," Diritti remarked, "it is surely because the people who worked with us in the cast, but also those who helped us in the valleys, shared this project – they lived it with us, they ate, worked, and celebrated with us and hence this sense of sharing, of participation in my view, transmitted itself to the film."[5] And just as troupe members and on-location volunteers were drawn into Diritti's project, so do they in turn engage viewing audiences in the experience of passionate conviction that led the people of Val Maira to share in this unusual, ethically charged experiment.

In formal terms, then, the filmmaking process enacted the ideal that resides at the heart of the story and is encapsulated in the Occitan word *rueido*, signifying the voluntary and selfless coming together of an entire community to undertake strenuous physical labour in times of need, epitomized historically by collective efforts to hide stashes of hay in the nave of the town church to thwart Nazi confiscations during the final years of the Second World War.[6] The term comes up in the first exchange of dialogue featured at the film's opening, as two men in a car make their way up a winding mountain road. "How should I start?" asks a voice in Occitan, a question that serves as a meta-commentary on the very film whose start we are watching. This question is voiced against a dark screen surrounding a small aperture that gives onto the side of a rocky cliff. "Say something about the *rueido*," answers the second speaker, "what it meant for us, for our community, getting together to do all the heaviest work, being united. Then you could talk about the *rueido* at the end of the war, the one you were involved in." As the car enters the darkness of a second and then a third mountain tunnel, a smooth pan leads to a brief flashback, embedded in the mind of the first speaker, who remembers himself as a boy in a church, loading hay from a huge pile onto his back for transport. The flashback ends with a return to the film's present tense, and the voice-over recitation, in dialect: "e l'aur fai san vir" (and the wind blows round), the Occitan proverb that gives the film its title.[7] This fleeting scene contains, in germinal form, the nexus between language, landscape, and temporal return that will play itself out over the course of the film and will constitute its thematic core.

By placing the sonorities of Occitan dialogue against the forbidding backdrop of Alpine cliffs, the film's incipit marries the natural setting with dialect, attributing, in strictly cinematic terms, the longevity of this arcane tongue to the self-enclosure, isolation, and cultural stasis of a world cut off from the historical mainstream. Dating back to its medieval roots in southern France, when the *lang d'oc* separated itself off from the *lang d'oil*, which would become the official language of culture, this minority idiom would remain the language of the periphery – a linguistic throwback that has seemed to withstand the incursions of time and change. As such, it signifies a resistance posture, militantly opposed to the hybridizing and modernizing effects of outside influences. It is significant that the townspeople insist on calling the Hérauds "*i francesi*" as if in lingering resentment over being relegated to the cultural outskirts by the inheritors of *lang d'oil*. In reaction, the Occitan speakers have clung to their linguistic purity – a position articulated by Fausto, who invokes a distant past when the region hosted a diversified populace at the expense of the local cultural identity. "Here lived Jews, Moslems, heretics, and Catholics," Fausto explains. "At one point they almost killed off *lang d'oc* culture because people were tolerant." Once the villagers of *Il vento fa il suo giro* begrudgingly agree to accept the Hérauds in their midst, the limited nature of their welcome – their atavistic tendency toward intolerance – becomes clear. Commenting on the arrival of a big family to their shrinking community, one man expresses relief

One of the shots of the Val Maira landscape whose ruggedness will not deter Philippe from deciding to put down roots among its peaks and folds.

that at least they're "not from the South." Others fear that now "they'll be swamped by Albanians." Midway into the film, when the tide turns against the Hérauds, they are deemed "worse than gypsies." The ease with which thoughts about the newcomers lead to associations with socially stigmatized groups lays bare the exceptional and dangerously fragile nature of the villagers' tolerance for "the other."

In keeping with the exclusivity of Occitan as language and cultural identity, Diritti has forged a cinematic language that echoes such inhospitality at the level of style. Diverging starkly from the usual picture-postcard treatment of Alpine settings, the director of photography, Roberto Cimatti, opted for an austere approach "as is rarely seen on the screen, often filtering the landscapes through the clouds or rain and holding the colour palette to solemn tones: understated green and metallic gray."[8] The sequence of Philippe's initial foray into the Alta Valle Maira is a case in point. In search of a possible area to relocate his family from their home in the Pyrenees, he is greeted by a series of rugged landscapes and episodes of interpersonal indifference that would discourage any but the most intrepid pioneer from seeking a foothold in this zone. Serving as our own entrée into the film's natural setting, a montage of forbidding wintry landscapes takes us past snowy embankments, cragged rock formations, vertiginous cliffs, and abandoned dwellings, all accompanied by an ominous musical score.

Compounding our unease is the camerawork, which fails to align spectators with Philippe's perspective by denying us a stable vantage point, filming first from the road behind the car, then from an elevated position on the site of an abandoned building – almost as if from the viewpoint of a local character spying on the protagonist's movements – and later from a position in front of the vehicle. This technique makes it impossible for us to entertain Philippe's subjective view of his surroundings, and to anticipate his enthusiasm for making this terrain his family's home.

The uninviting nature of the landscape is matched by the coldness of Philippe's first reception by its human fauna. The setting is the local bar, ritual meeting place for men with the leisure to loaf in company.[9] Emblazoned on the front page of a regional newspaper found on the premises is the headline "Thefts Continue in the Upper Valley." Philippe's entrance therefore occasions an understandable stiffening of postures. Without introducing himself, buying a coffee, or engaging in any other pleasantries, Philippe gets immediately down to business: "Are there houses to buy or rent?" One of the listeners asks for a clarification – "Per vacanza?" (For a vacation?) – to whom the Frenchman energetically replies, "No, per viverci!" (No, to live here!). "Per viverci" becomes a kind of mantra for Philippe, who repeats it every time he poses the housing question. In one such instance, he elaborates on his usual retort: "Non faccio vacanza, faccio formaggio!" (literally, I don't make vacation, I make cheese!). The playfulness of Philippe's verbal antics – the substitution of *formaggio* for *vacanza* as the object of *fare* – masks the underlying seriousness and radicalism of his reasons for migrating to this remote mountain enclave. His insistence that he comes not to make a temporary foray into nature, but to *viverci* – to establish a permanent, rooted existence, steeped in the soil, the cycle of seasons, and the biorhythms of animal life, sets up the sharp contrast between his attraction to this rugged terrain and that of the seasonal tourists who rent cozy chalets for two weeks in August. Ensconced in their comfortable lodgings, they can grill on their verandas amidst the grandeur of the Alpine backdrop, visit the village shops in search of local food stuffs, and generally revel in their experience of "roughing it." These temporary sojourners bring with them all the baggage of their urban condition, not only in their suitcases and minivans but in the more abstract sense of economic strength and cultural superiority that they can lord over their provincial hosts. In literary terms, they are bearers of the pastoral dream: the fantasy of escape into a simpler, rustic existence amidst farmers who furrow their fields with ox-drawn plows and shepherds who pipe their songs on oaten flutes.

The clash between those who are in Chersogno *per vacanza* and those who are there *per viverci* takes place in the Hérauds' kitchen, where a small group of seasonal tourists have stopped by to taste cheeses. While they have come as eager consumers of this genuine local product, they harbour an ulterior motive: to donate supplies to a household that they deem substandard for the raising of children. Laden with pastries so the little ones will have something "good to eat" and with used clothes otherwise destined for the equivalent of Goodwill, these visitors become the protagonists of one of the film's more excruciating moments. The scene ends with a close-up of Chris, who scrupulously avoids thanking the well-wishers. Her expression, instead, reflects a proud disregard for this most unwelcome charity, based as it is on the visitors' blindness to the radical social critique built into the family's lifestyle.

This seasonal influx of vacationers has bolstered the regional economy, fattening the wallets of landlords who live in the valley below Chersogno and who are therefore resistant to welcoming the Héraud family on a year-round basis. At the meeting of the town council where Philippe's request to settle in this locale is being considered, two men vigorously defend his motion – the mayor, Costanzo, and Fausto – and they do so on the grounds that this young family will reinvigorate the town, bringing new life and purpose to its aging and dwindling population. This rationale finds its most powerful fulfilment in an outdoor scene of hide-and-seek through the narrow streets and byways of Chersogno. A mere minute and four seconds in length, the montage follows Philippe's wife Chris and all three of her young children as they scamper through the narrow streets, around corners, and past a few scattered villagers, introducing youth and movement into an ancient environment literally set in stone. The cinematography of this sequence is itself liberated – the highly mobile camerawork, staccato editing, and variety of angles and heights from which the footage is shot all serve to involve us in the game as seekers who join the other players in search of their human prey. It is in this scene that Fausto, lured into the game by the child Virginie, enacts his own burgeoning desire to "capture" Chris, in what would be labelled "the soft chase" by scholars of Renaissance romance. The Hérauds transformative effect on the town, in giving new life and movement to its topography, thus finds a personal equivalent in the transformation undergone by Fausto in the presence of Chris. As a result, he telephones his agent (who happens to also be his mistress) to cancel an upcoming tour. This means that he will suspend his career as an itinerant clarinetist, scheduled to perform with a small orchestra for the entertainment of revellers in night clubs and on cruise ships. And it means he will suspend the loveless relationship with his agent. The advent of the Hérauds has obviously triggered an identity crisis,[10] offering him the prospect of a dynamic alternative to the static and sterile condition in which he is mired.

For the mayor, Costanzo, the Hérauds' arrival heralded a way of reactivating the region's link to its archaic past, based on the herding of livestock and the artisanal production of goods. Costanzo voices this hope during a speech delivered at the welcoming ceremony for the Hérauds in which he exalts "the fruits of a labor that is a natural continuation of the activities our ancestors performed here." In private, however, Costanzo worries that the Hérauds' example will incite envy and feelings of inadequacy in this regard. "They're afraid," he says of the Chersognesi, "that someone will succeed where they failed." And later, once communal sentiments turn against the family, Costanzo defends them in the face of complaints about the stench of their livestock, the mess caused by their compost heaps, and the health hazards posed by carrion discarded on public property. "No one," he fulminates, "remembers the work their fathers used to do!"

Diritti's filmmaking does not flinch from the material hardships of the Hérauds' back-to-nature lifestyle. In other words, he cannot be suspected of "pastoral" leanings in the literary sense, given the film's forthright attention to the drudgery, stench, and filth that the family endures. For every scene of Chris ladling out soup in the coziness of the kitchen, there is a glimpse of Virginie bailing out flood waters from the goat stalls, or a shot of the two young sisters enjoying a bubble bath at the invitation of a next-door neighbour, given the lack of adequate plumbing facilities at home. Perhaps the most poignant enactment of these hardships is the sequence in which Chris enters Fausto's upscale house to water his plants while the latter is travelling on tour. This errand offers the pretext for a solitary tour of the premises, and the momentary indulgence in her secret longing for luxury. After watching Chris move about the spotless kitchen, equipped with state-of-the-art appliances, the camera takes on her subjectivity with a slow pan across the adjacent room, lit by windows offering breath-taking views of Alpine slopes (the kind used to lure seasonal vacationers) before alighting on an elegant abstract painting hanging above an orderly desk. From there, we see her settling onto a couch, assuming a fetal position, and then proceeding to the bedroom, where she examines an opened book on the bedside table. But the culmination of this voyeuristic tour comes in the bathroom, where Chris confronts her face in the looking glass and literally tries on an alternative identity, daubing herself with Fausto's cologne and contemplating its sensuous effect on the self that is reflected back to her in the mirror. This long, wordless sequence tells us everything we need to know about Chris's suffering in her marriage to Philippe.[11] Needless to say, her foray into Fausto's domestic space is redolent of their tryst, which had opened up the possibility, however fleeting, of escape from her husband's regime. While she clearly shares Philippe's rejection of modernity (e.g., her fear of living in the shadow of the nuclear plant planned for construction near their previous home), there remains a part of her that cannot help but be attracted to a less materially and emotionally straitened way of life.

While the modern comforts and aesthetic pleasures of Fausto's home occupy a prominent place in Chris's secret yearnings, it is her family's dwelling that occupies the centre of the film's "built environment" as the material manifestation of Philippe's value system and the mayor's hopes for reversing his village's decay. Because none of the locals is willing to offer ready-made lodgings on a year-round basis, preferring to keep them available for summer vacationers, an enormous collective effort is required to create one for this family. That effort takes the form of renovating an aged and abandoned homestead, with symbolic implications for the life of the town itself, and a historic link to the *rueido* – the above-mentioned custom of volunteering to perform strenuous collective work for the sake of individuals in need, or for the good of the community as a whole. (The mail carrier Pina will make this explicit in telling Monica's mother, "They're all working doing a *rueido*," and Fausto will comment on the villagers' return to this traditional rite: "l'aura fai son vir ... ogni cosa ven appress" (the wind blows round, and everything returns). Of considerable import is the fact that the house has been renovated but not modernized – the old wood-burning stove is not replaced, indoor bathing facilities are not installed, the bedrooms and the kitchen/stables will remain in separate buildings. In other words, the Hérauds will be replicating the lifestyle of Chersogno's ancestral inhabitants.

It is here that the language of cinema comes to the fore in a dual and contradictory capacity. Through montage, the film documents the arduous and multifaceted effort of renovation, involving a massive clean-up of all the mouldering debris left by the previous owners, followed by repairing, painting, and fumigating the premises. Thanks to the medium-specific power of cinema to elicit all of the senses, we can feel the chill of the rooms unheated for so long and the dankness of the air, smell its stale odour and hence intuit the prodigious amount of labour that will be required to make this squalid space not only livable but welcoming. For all of the footage dedicated to the dreary business of the clean-up, however, it is the very process of montage that undercuts the strenuousness and duration of these efforts by compressing time into discreet slices of activity, thereby erasing the tedium of the interim moments, giving the illusion of exhilarating speed, linear progress, and ease. Thanks to montage, pleasure comes to override the tiresomeness and weight of the clean-up process, leaving the impression that communal generosity and fellow-feeling will be the lasting legacy of this welcoming act.

All of the goodwill generated by this modern enactment of the *rueido* will be squandered by subsequent failures of hospitality on both the giving and receiving end of relationship. The Italian term for "hospitality," *ospitalità*, has a curious duality; its root *ospite*, meaning both guest and host, suggests the reciprocity that lies at the heart of the concept. As a sacred obligation with deep anthropological origins, it makes stringent demands on the receiver as well as the giver of shelter and sustenance. Where Philippe falls woefully short in this regard is his refusal to admit the local pastor, Don Franco, into his house to bestow the annual priestly benediction. The Frenchman's atheism is no excuse for rejecting what his host culture considers the ultimate form of hospitality – the community's bestowal of its spiritual blessing upon its guests – over and above the strictly material provision of walls and roof. Philippe's gesture, dictated by his own obsession with ideological purity, is but the first in a series of rigid postures that will slowly deprive him of the community's embrace. Other missteps include the disposal of a dead pig on communal grounds, and the free-range pasturage of his herd – behaviours that run up against the villagers' belief in standards of hygiene and individual property rights, respectively. But these irritants hardly warrant the disproportionate punishment meted out by Emma, Philippe's nemesis, who slaughters two of his goats and hangs them upside down from a ruined entrance to the grounds of the local church.

The message is clear, and Philippe is quick to decipher it. By striking at the bodies of these creatures, Emma has struck at the corporate body of the family as a whole – for they are co-extensive, in terms of both the Hérauds' material livelihood and the existential continuity between humans and their charges in the animal world. With the slaughter of these two goats, it is as if the family body had suffered a physical mutilation – as if a limb had been amputated or a vital organ excised. Adding to the shock of this despicable deed is the fact that its perpetrator is a cowherd, and therefore deeply bound to a life of inter-species reciprocity. By dint of her vocation, Emma knew how to inflict maximum damage (short of murder) on her human victim, and her sadistic imagination reached genius levels in staging Philippe's discovery of

Philippe is framed by the spectacle of the slaughtered goats hanging upside down from the lintel of the ruined entryway to the local church.

her grisly act. Not surprisingly, Philippe's first impulse upon seeing the slain animals is to cut them down and end their pornographic display. Of particular note is the location of this spectacle on the grounds of the village church – a setting rife with associations of a Judeo-Christian nature, from episodes of animal sacrifice in the Hebrew bible to New Testament imagery of Jesus as both the Good Shepherd and the sacrificial victim – *Christus Pastor* and Lamb of God. But the most obvious scriptural allusion is to the scapegoat (Leviticus 16), bearer of the Israelites' sins, sent into the wilderness to expel the taint of communal impurity. The Hérauds as a unit, and Philippe in particular, become the ideal vehicles for this exculpatory rite. It is the family's identification with their animals – both positively, in their intimate bond with the natural world, and negatively, in the community's relegation of the Hérauds to subhuman status[12] – that makes possible the literalization of the scapegoat metaphor, the crossing of the boundary between the literal and the figurative meaning of this ancient trope.

But the seeming ease with which the community rids itself of the "impure" element gives way to a far more complex ethical calculus in light of the "collateral damage" caused by the Hérauds' departure: a minor character, Roberto, commits suicide.[13] From the perspective of this death, a subplot retroactively takes shape around this emotionally troubled and cognitively impaired young man, who had become gradually and unobtrusively absorbed into the family's orbit. His tragic end prompts us to replay, in memory, a series of episodes in which he had fleetingly appeared. The film's early moments had included discrete glimpses of him as a vagrant – sleeping on a bench with a wine bottle at his feet, falling drunk by the wayside, sitting on a rooftop during the welcome ceremony for the Hérauds, assaulting Monica and requiring neighbourly intervention to head off disaster. Once the family settles in, these flashes move toward social integration. We see Roberto making himself presentable by shaving, then riding alongside Philippe in a tractor, lying companionably with Monica in a grassy field, joining in the family meal, and helping pitch hay. Most striking are the several scenes of the young man sailing through the countryside, arms outstretched, as if he were some kind of tutelary god or *spiritus loci*. While these moments of quiet happiness barely registered with us at the time, in hindsight they take on inordinate importance as a measure of one character's paradise lost in the aftermath of the family's departure.

Diritti's camera "discovers" the suicide through the eyes of Fausto, who comes upon the ominous spectacle of an ambulance, viewed from the height of a spectacular helicopter ride through the skies above Chersogno, whose very name, *caro sogno* (dear dream), is about to reveal its bitterest irony. Along with Fausto and other passengers, Costanzo has joined this aerial excursion for the filming of a television broadcast about the beauty of the region and the charm of its mores. The starkly promotional purpose of this broadcast emerges in the host's voice-over description of Chesogno as a place that "offers the possibility of a marvellous vacation." The presence of Costanzo and Fausto on this ride shows their surrender to the logic of tourism, so vehemently opposed by Philippe's intention to "viverci," to put down roots in year-round residence, to live in "folkloric time" in concert with the biorhythms of the natural world. This sky-borne tour of the area features an interview with a certain Mr. Ponte, the oldest of its native sons, and it is he who explains the meaning of the *ruiedo*, the ideal of solidarity and fellow feeling that the film's conclusion so violently upends. From the height of the helicopter ride that opens on to a panorama of Alpine splendour, the words of the TV announcer harmonize perfectly with our visual experience of Chersogno from above "una ridente località delle valli di Monviso" (a laughing locality of the Monviso valley). But it was enough to descend to ground level to understand that not everyone laughed in Chersogno, especially now, in the void left by the Hérauds, who had naturally and seamlessly included Roberto in their daily life without fanfare or any self-congratulatory exhibitions of charity. Diritti's camerawork and editing had complied with these quiet and natural gestures of inclusiveness – so much so that we barely noticed these instances, in contrast to other characters' acts of generosity toward Roberto, which had been foregrounded in the film's earlier scenes. As an active participant in the Hérauds' family life, Roberto was no longer marked by his difference – the status attributed to recipients of charitable giving – for the Hérauds had accorded him a full share in their humanity, as deserving of a seat at the table as the rest of the family members whose toil had made their meals possible.

It is through ellipsis, then, that we are invited to imaginatively reconstruct the solitude and desolation that would lead Roberto to take his life in the wake of the Hérauds' departure. A less stringent director would show us scenes of his wandering in despair, or relapsing into the previously glimpsed habits of passivity, abjection, and drink. Instead we learn of the tragedy through Fausto's anguished eyes as the helicopter descends to ground level and Roberto's body, with the noose still around his neck and rope burns plainly visible, is transported on a gurney to a waiting Red Cross vehicle. The setting of this suicide makes no secret of its symbolic meaning – Roberto had chosen to die where Philippe had beheld the sight of his slain goats, hanging from the lintel of the churchyard gate. Because it was this spectacle that triggered the Hérauds' departure and sealed their own identity as scapegoats bearing the sins of the community into the wilderness, Roberto visits their fate on himself, in its most extreme and irreversible form.[14] But unlike the scapegoat, whose expulsion is experienced by the community as a liberation from sin, Roberto's act prompts an intense process of collective soul-searching, of delving into its failure of hospitality in the broadest ethical understanding of the term. "What have we become?" asks Costanzo as the congregation stands before Robert's coffin in the village church. "We've become unrecognizable," he continues – unrecognizable in terms of the community's cherished self-image, built around the ideal of solidarity and fellow feeling enshrined in the ritual of *rueido*. It was during the helicopter ride, in which Mr. Ponte had explained the *rueido* in the television broadcast to promote vacation opportunities in the region, that this "recognizable" image of life in the "ridente località delle valli di Monviso" was most prominently displayed. But only from this aerial height – only from this distance – could Chersogno maintain its image of dreamy perfection. Once back on the ground, the gaze of Diritti (as focalized by Fausto) had to confront an inverse human realty, given that the *rueido*, its much-touted sense of community, emerged as utterly closed to the so-called "altro," the one who needed it most.[15]

But the film does not close on this funereal note. Instead, it delicately broaches the possibility of resurrection, beginning with the eulogy for Roberto, delivered by Costanzo at the behest of Monica, which takes the form of the following poem by César Vallejo, published in 1939 and entitled "Mass":

> At the end of the battle the fighter lay dead. A man came to him
> and said: "Don't die! I love you too much!"
> But the corpse, alas, went on dying.
> Two came to him and again said:
> "Don't leave us! Take heart!
> Come back to life!"
> But the corpse, alas, went on dying.
> Then twenty, a hundred, a thousand,
> Five hundred thousand, came, crying:
> "So much love and yet so powerless against death!"
> But the corpse, alas, went on dying.
> Millions surrounded him,
> pleading together:
> "Brother, don't leave us!"
> But the corpse, alas, went on dying.
> Then, all the men on earth
> stood round him. The corpse eyed them sadly,
> overwhelmed. He got up slowly,
> embraced the first man, started to walk ...[16]

These haunting verses, with their numerical progression, suggest that nothing short of universal love – the conversion to *caritas* on the part of "all the men on earth" – can bring about the resurrection of a single individual. The poem's Christological associations – the echoes of the Lazurus episode, and the identification of "the first man" with Jesus – suggest that the theology of resurrection will need a social component if it is to reach the worldwide scale required to bring the lone warrior back to life. Poised between the impossibility of achieving this universal goal and the hope instilled by the belated success of the first man's gesture, Diritti's film signals a movement in the latter direction. Toward the end of Costanzo's recitation, the camera pans over the small crowd in attendance at Roberto's burial, singling out Massimo, before proceeding out of the cemetery gate.[17]

The resurrection theme recurs in the film's finale, which centres on Massimo, the new Philippe, who will bring back to life the Hérauds' utopian dream. Like Roberto, Massimo had surfaced periodically throughout the film, attracted to Philippe's ménage as an alternative to toiling under his repressive father's control at his family's cattle ranch in the valley below Chersogno. But the story's tragic turn of events has freed Massimo from paternal constraints, enabling him to take up where Philippe left off. The final scene is set in the Hérauds' abandoned kitchen, cluttered with debris, recalling its dark, dank, squalid appearance before the communal clean-up that transformed it into the hearth of a warm and lively household. Undaunted by the task of resurrecting Philippe's dream, and unbuoyed by the promise of a *rueido*, Massimo takes a small but symbolically charged step to start the process anew: he lights a fire in the wood-burning stove.

"Il vento fa il suo giro," the closing captions read, "ed ogni cosa prima o poi ritorna" (and everything sooner or later returns). And so the film circles back to its own beginning, with words that echo the title, translating into standard Italian the proverb that Mr. Ponte had uttered in Occitan in the work's opening moments. This is the first of the multiple levels on which the film performs its rite of return, and it does so by enfolding the work within the wisdom of a proverb harking back to the community's agrarian past. From the very start, then, *Il vento fa il suo giro* announces the cyclical, folkloric time that will govern the narrative.[18] In technical terms, Diritti's work literally reuses some of its own footage, creating a ring structure by splicing its opening frames into the sequence that leads up to the helicopter ride toward the end, and in so doing triggers a sense of déjà vu on the part of the spectator. But within the space contained by this formal circumference, various inner narrative circles are formed, where ends seem to return us to beginnings, only to be broken off by the interference of competing circular developments. The *rueido* offers the most obvious example of this pattern when the collective home renovation efforts on behalf of the Hérauds are greeted as a return to the tradition's roots in the communal activity to prevent Nazi confiscation of the hay. But the historical circle is broken and the solidarity of the homesteading *rueido* proves to have been only a temporary gift once the community's welcome is withdrawn. Rather than complete and reinforce the positive meaning of the *rueido*, the circular structure of the Hérauds' sojourn exposes the limits of this communitarian ideal: to wit, solidarity is a birthright, reserved exclusively for those of the *lang d'oc*.

Strikingly, the film continues, as previously noted, beyond the exit of the Hérauds from the scene. Up to this point, Philippe had carried the film – he and his family had served as the objects of our most intense identification and empathy, even in the instances when his harsh purity may have momentarily alienated us from him. But *Il vento fa il suo giro* leaves the Hérauds' story behind – their future does not interest Diritti, who picks up instead where the opening fragment of the film had left off before flashing back to Philippe's arrival in Chersogno nine months earlier. Only now does the car ride in which Mr. Ponte asks Costanzo, "How do I start?" come to make sense. The question refers to the interview to be held in the sky above the Valle di Monviso, and with the reinsertion of this footage toward the end of the film, another circle of return is completed. But here too the sense of closure is undercut – this time by the film's "coda," which takes the story beyond the end of the helicopter ride, with its tragic revelation, by presenting the community's reckoning with its own responsibility for Roberto's death. And it is here that the final circle is closed as the film returns to the scene of the abandoned kitchen, glimpsed previously during the *rueido* of the home renovation project, and shown now in its current state of abandonment by the Hérauds. But a new circle is about to begin, as Massimo lights the fire in the wood stove, reigniting Philippe's vision and sparking the hope that this determined young man can bring the wind around to a new/old starting point, with the resurrection of the *rueido* in its most inclusive sense – in the community's true openness to the outsider, and to the "other" in its own midst.

Chapter Six

"What History Is This?": Giorgio Diritti's *L'uomo che verrà* (The Man Who Will Come), 2009

Direction: Giorgio Diritti. *Screenplay*: Giorgio Diritti, Giovanni Galavotti, Tania Pedroni. *Cinematography*: Roberto Cimatti. *Music*: Marco Biscarini, Daniele Furlati. *Sound*: Carlo Missidenti. *Editing*: Giorgio Diritti, Paolo Marzoni. *Sets*: Giancarlo Basili. *Costumes*: Lia Francesca Morandini. *Cast*: Greta Zuccheri Montanari (Martina), Maya Sansa (Lena), Alba Rohrwacher (Beniamina), Claudio Casadio (Armando), Laura Pizzirani (Maria), Maria Grazia Naldi (Vittoria), Luigi Palmieri (Grandfather Gisto), Stefano Croci (Uncle Dino), Pietro Tomasini (Uncle Domenico), Francesco Modugno (Antonio), Stefano "Vito" Bicocchi (Signor Bugamelli), Eleonora Mazzoni (Signora Bugamelli), Giovanni Macchiavelli (Guglielmo Bugamelli), Orfeo Orlando (Merchant), Diego Pagotto (Pepe), Bernardo Bolognesi (Gianni, partisan), Zoello Gilli (Dante), Raffaele Zabban (Father Giovanni Fornasini), Timo Jacobs (SS medical officer), Frank Schmalz (Wehrmarcht Officer), Thaddeus Meilinger (SS Captain).

Synopsis: The film is set in the Monte Sole area of Emilia-Romagna between December 1943 and October 1944 during the Nazi occupation of Italy. It tells the story of a large peasant family, consisting of the aged matriarch, Vittoria Palmieri, her bed-ridden husband Gisto, her brothers (or brothers-in-law) Domenico and Dino, her daughters Beniamina and Maria, her son Armando, Armando's wife, Lena, and

---

This chapter is an amalgamation of two essays, each of which has be extensively revised from the originally published version: "The Child as 'custode della memoria futura': *The Man Who Will Come* and the Massacre of Marzabotto," *Quaderni d'italianistica* 34, no. 2 (2013): 133–48; and "Resistance on Screen: Varieties of Witnessing, Modes of Remembrance," in *The Concept of Resistance in Italy: Multidisciplinary Perspectives*, ed. Maria Laura Mosco and Pietro Pirani (Lanham: Rowman & Littlefield International, 2017).

their eight-year-old daughter, Martina, who serves as the film's main character. This child's role as focalizer is marked by a significant form of alterity – she is mute, and our spectatorship is therefore limited to observations of her facial expressions, exchanges of gazes, and rare access to her written thoughts. The film is framed by Martina's return to the now-empty home from which the family had fled during a Nazi raid, and its plot unfolds as a flashback, triggered by the girl's memory of a "primal scene": her witnessing of Armando and Lena's discreet act of lovemaking in the bedroom all three share. The gestation of the child conceived in this episode will dictate the film's temporality, along with the events of the yearly agrarian calendar. But the natural rhythms of the land and of the human life cycle are brutally disrupted by the incursions of the Second World War, and in particular the clashes between Nazi occupying forces and local partisans, which end in the retaliatory slaughter of the territory's entire civilian populace at the hands of the SS. Martina miraculously survives, and she manages to save her newborn brother, to whom she sings a lullaby, thus breaking her silence and foretelling her role as one who will transmit the memory of this searing historical past to future generations.

"Stamattina a San Martino, ne hanno trovati altri quaranta" (this morning, at San Martino, they found another forty [massacre victims]), the anti-fascist priest Don Fornasini tells his mother in the aftermath of the *strage di Marzabotto* – the Nazi extermination of 770 civilians living on the slopes of Monte Sole to the southwest of Bologna in the region of Emilia Romagna.[1] "Li abbiamo seppelliti tutti insieme, mamma, non si poteva rischiare" (we buried them all together, Mama, we couldn't take any risks). In making *L'uomo che verrà*, a fiction film that scrupulously follows the historical record, Giorgio Diritti attempts to give symbolic burial to the mass victims of one of the largest civilian slaughters to take place on the battlefronts of Western Europe during the Second World War. Significantly, in his review of *L'uomo che verrà*, Roberto Chiesi labelled the film an "epicedium"[2] – an ancient Greek funeral lament, chanted by a chorus – in a characterization that accounts for the central importance of the soundtrack, as well as for the film's overall identity as a rite of mourning.

In order to scale down the mind-numbing enormity of the slaughter, Diritti presents an imaginary family living in the area of Monte Sole, and raises their plight to the level of tragic exemplarity. Despite the fictional origin of its characters, the film achieves documentary force as a result of Diritti's extensive research and his painstaking efforts to recreate, with an "attention bordering on the maniacal," the historical events of the atrocity within the material context of rural life in Emilia Romagna during the mid-1940s.[3] Underlying Diritti's documentary zeal in making *L'uomo che verrà* is an ethically charged impulse to bear witness to this history, to rescue it from the dustbins of the archival past in the name of staving off recurrence. Such terms as "urgency," "responsibility," "moral commitment," and "need" abound in Diritti's public statements about what drove him to undertake this daunting project.[4] As a reader of historical texts concerning the massacre, he was left with the powerful impression "that it was necessary to do something: such drama could not be consigned to numbers, or to history books, it had to be told as a story."[5] During his personal encounters with contemporary residents of Monte Sole, this testimonial impulse gained momentum, "as if the family members of the victims and the survivors had given me their memory, asking me to transfer it to others."[6] As direct or second-generation witnesses to the events of Monte Sole, his interlocutors were issuing a plea that Diritti testify in turn to this history, that he use the cinema's medium-specific powers to "transfer it to others" in a way that would instil identification with the victims, a sense of grief for their loss, an assumption of moral accountability for the historical currents that led to this horrific past, and a commitment to actively intervene in the course of public events to preclude future occurrences. In his very choice of the film's title, Diritti envisions "the one who is to come" as the receiver of this testimony, the repository of historical awareness and of its built-in imperative to act.

Among the pitfalls of representing highly fraught historical episodes is the temptation to adopt an a posteriori approach "with all of the risks of manipulations and pseudo-historical kitsch" that such subject matter invites.[7] Diritti's original plan had been to focus on the Stella Rossa Brigade of partisans active in the area, or to highlight the experiences of the local clergy who harboured anti-fascist sympathies. But either of these choices would have privileged a group with its own *a priori* framework for confronting the struggles at hand. In pursuit of a zero-degree approach to the events unfolding in Nazi-occupied Emilia-Romagna, Diritti chose as his film's focalizers members of a family (the Palmieris) within the farming community of the area in the belief that such a strategy would be best served by the peasants' perspective, with its emphasis on survival and natural justice at the expense of theologically or politically charged beliefs.[8] "Perchè non restano a casa loro?" (Why don't they just stay home?), Martina's father Armando asks his landlord, who feels compelled to remain in the Nazis' good graces. "La storia è piena di guerra" (History is full of war), the landlord responds. "La storia? Chi se ne frega della storia e di chi la fa?"(History? Who gives a damn about history and those who make it?), counters Armando. "Diventano tutti importanti chi ammazza e chi ruba ai poveretti. Che storia è questa?" (All those who kill and rob the poor are the ones who become important. What kind of history is that?)

Che storia è questa? This highly fraught rhetorical question reaches far beyond the limits of Armando's dialogue with his landlord to encompass the entire historiographical project of Diritti's film. Above all, it activates the profound ambiguity at the root of the Italian term *storia*, which translates into English as both "history" and "story," blurring the line between canonical, fact-based accounts of past events and narrative constructs of a fictional sort. With the anguished question "che storia è questa?" Armando issues a plea to replace the annals of the "importanti" with the undocumented and therefore imaginatively construed experiences of those who suffer the workings of history from below. For Diritti, Armando's challenge to top-down historical accounts dictated not only the filmmaker's choice of a peasant family's perspective through which to channel the Marzabotto event, but more importantly, his decision to make the family's eight-year-old daughter Martina the film's focalizing agent. In so doing, Diritti joins the ranks of filmmakers who have chosen to filter Second World War history through the eyes of protagonists yet to come of age: Benigni's Giosuè (*Life Is Beautiful*), the Tavianis' Cecilia (*Night of the Shooting Stars*), and the Frazzi's Penny (*The Sky Is Falling*) immediately come to mind. Like Giosuè, Cecilia, and Penny, Martina brings a childhood vulnerability to her perspective that invites us to set aside any protective cynicism or historical knowledge that might cloud our direct and appalled view of her story's contents. As spectators whose gaze is modelled on Martina's, we share the child's innate sense of the rightness and wrongness of things, and are brought to an innocent, and therefore ethically pure, position of judgment with respect to the war-time horrors of Marzobotto.

Of paramount importance is the fact that Martina, unlike Giosuè, Cecilia, and Penny, suffers from a grave impairment – one that shapes our entire relationship to her role as witness. She is mute. Prior to the onset of the film's narration, her infant brother had died in her arms, and the trauma had left her devoid of speech. Unable to testify in words, Martina becomes a singular "spokeswoman"; we must fixate on her visage in order to fathom this child's unique powers of communication. "Martina's muteness is a symptom of a great sensitivity of the gaze," Diritti explains. "It is a dimension, in a state of lack, of superior perceptiveness and attention. In the film, her silence becomes story."[9] Without

In this shot, Martina's face displays the "superior perceptiveness and attention" that Diritti attributes to her, but which find no outlet in the spoken word.

verbal access to her encounters with the world, we must depend upon outward physical manifestations of it, but these lack all eloquence. Diritti's camera dwells extensively on her face, whose expression remains largely opaque, a blank screen-within-the-screen inviting us to project our own imagined reactions to her plight.

Her facial expressionlessness has its bodily counterpart in the stillness and withdrawal that accompany her moments of greatest distress. At these times, she either retreats into the barn, where she assumes a posture that seems to fold in on itself, or she perches on a bench outside the school or farmhouse in absolute immobility. It is as if her muteness extended beyond the organs of speech to envelope her entire being in a cloak of impassivity.

The only direct access we have to Martina's thoughts is her writings – her Christmas poem recited by one of the parish women and, most importantly, a school essay in which she gives voice to her bemusement over the German occupation ("they don't speak Italian and I don't know why they come here when they could be at home with their children)," the nature of their adversaries ("I heard that they're at war against the Allies but I've never seen them"), and her understanding of the partisan cause ("then there are the rebels who fight because they say the Germans must leave. The rebels have arms too. Many of them speak our language and dress like us"). Her experience of this history in real time, unmediated by any rational understanding of warfare that would explain why Germans would leave their children for a land where they can't even speak the language, or why the "rebels" want them to leave, amounts to this child's version of her father's anguished question: "che storia è questa?"

Among the answers to Armando's question is the film's very title, which projects this history into the future when the "man will come" to recount the tragedy of Marzobotto to subsequent generations, as a memorial and a warning, an elegy for a lost world, and a plea for vigilance in the here and now. The messianic thrust of this title, with its religious overtones, is hard to overlook, as Diritti makes clear in the scene preceding the appearance of the title on-screen, when Martina's mother Lena visits a shrine of the pregnant Madonna and touches the icon's swollen belly in the hope that her own child-bearing hopes will find fulfilment. Within the fiction of the film, the man who will come is indeed a saviour figure, the longed-for male child who promises resurrection of the family's future after the death of the Palmieris' first-born son. But the semantic insistence on the *adulthood* of this much-desired offspring projects the hope into a future understood in generational terms. This child will grow into the proverbial New Man, the post-war generation bearing the daunting responsibility for national rebirth in the wake of the fascist *ventennio* (twenty years), the catastrophic alliance with Germany, Italy's fiascos on the Second World War battlefront, the nightmare of Nazi occupation, and the Allied campaign of liberation. At the end of the film, Martina recovers her powers of speech, and this "miracle" must be understood in relation to her sibling's generational significance, as well as to her own personal logic of atonement for the pre-narrative death of her infant brother – a tragedy for which she feels irrational and unrelieved guilt. Though such logic would lead us to expect her withdrawal into a state of permanent silence, if not outright catatonia, given the events of Marzobotto, Martina's re-emergence from muteness at the end of the film makes sense as her reward for keeping this second brother alive. Paradoxically, this return to verbal utterance means that she must bear witness to the *storia nefanda* – literally, unspeakable history – of the genocide that has befallen her people. It is this story that she must transmit to the baby, if the Italian New Man is to symbolically "work through" historical trauma in order to stave off its recurrence.[10]

One of the most charged issues Diritti's film faces in asking "che storia e questa?" is the nature and the role of the resistance in the history of

Marzabotto. Diritti's first move is to insist on the distinctly local identity of the partisans – their emergence from the same soil that produced the farming community of Monte Sole. "We are the same as you," argues Gianni, one of the leaders of the Brigata Stella Rossa, as he visits peasant homes in search of new recruits. The partisans speak the same dialect as do the members of the Palmieri family, and the leaders of the brigade, Gianni and Lupo, exhort their comrades to action in the most rustic language, shorn of any of the patriotic rhetoric associated with the cause. Especially striking is the leaders' insistence on purging their activism of any ideological rationale that would link it to a broad-based, national or international movement and thus weaken its fiercely indigenous nature. "Don't get any political ideas in your head," Gianni admonishes the group in his inaugural speech to the newly expanded brigade. "You know why you're here? I'll tell you why. You're here because back there, there are fascists and Germans. But this is your home, and that of your grandfathers and grandmothers, and it's where your family lives." To remind us of the apolitical nature of this emphatically local movement, driven by an archaic belief in the peasants' claim to a land they have tilled for generations, a later snippet of dialogue announces a partisan's defection precisely due to Lupo's distaste for ideology. This leader's apolitical stance introduces a note of irony in his brigade's title – the adjective *rossa* is emptied of all historical and ideological content and comes to be a purely ornamental signifier, linked to the dashing red scarf that Lupo sports in his every on-screen appearance. By removing the Marxist implications of their cadre's name, Lupo precludes any intermural associations, thus reaffirming the group's anthropological roots in the soil of Monte Sole. But the most striking and devastating proof of this movement's localism is the identity of the spy who infiltrates and betrays the group. He is "Pepe," the so-called nephew of a travelling merchant from Bologna. Hailing from the big city, led to the Palmieri family by his ostensible "uncle," Pepe announces his desire to join the "rebels." This nefarious twosome represents not only an urban elsewhere but a merchant economy in which goods, and false allegiances, are peddled by men with no primal connection to the land and to the community it has sustained over time.

Throughout *L'uomo che verrà*, Diritti strikes a delicate balance between sympathy for the resistance and a detached view of the hardships it inflicts on the local populace. Though the Nazis are far more brutal and damaging in their confiscation of foodstuffs, emptying the Palmieri barn of all its livestock, the partisans are also guilty of depleting the peasants' scarce inventory of resources. To temper the harshness of the latter's actions, Diritti documents the partisans' goodwill in listing the items they extorted from the family – two loaves of bread, four eggs, zero hens, zero rabbits – with the idea of compensating them at some later date. Throughout the scenes dedicated to recruitment, initiation, travel through snowy landscapes, and encampment in primitive redoubts, Diritti reveals the courage and material difficulty of the partisan choice. But the hagiographic view meets with powerful countervailing concerns: the partisans' responsibility for unleashing the Nazi genocide and their failure to intervene in its course. It is the assault on a Nazi jeep, killing all three occupants, that leads to a full-scale battle in which the Stella Rossa Brigade beats back its German attackers, which in turn leads to the extermination of the 770 civilians living on the slopes of Monte Sole. (The Nazi calculus of ten Italian lives for every German fatality had obviously given way to a far more haphazard and inflated form of retaliatory bookkeeping.) The scene in which several battle-weary partisans view the round-up of their civilian compatriots from a safe distance prompts a set of warring impulses in us viewers: rational understanding of the fighters' impotence along with emotional incomprehension of it. We partake of the partisans' vantage point as the badly wounded, nearly unconscious Dante is accompanied by a comrade to an outpost where they join a pair of fellow militants who are standing guard above the village. "We were routed at Cadotto," the new arrival announces, and with this allusion Diritti strategically brings to mind the Nazi surprise attack on the partisans that killed Lupo and permanently disabled his brigade. One of the guards, who holds a set of binoculars, passes them along to the newcomer and reports, "They're taking them away." On the sound track we hear Nazi orders being shouted amidst the growing strains of dirge-like chanting. The camera now cuts to what the partisan sees through the telescopic lenses – German soldiers forcing a line of villagers along a road through the mist. This harrowing vision is followed by a cut to the profile of the partisan with the binoculars – accentuating his role as observer/bystander – before panning to Dante, who collapses from fatigue, pain, or worse. By strategically alternating between the plight of the battle-torn partisans and their passive witness of the round-up, Diritti displays an uneasy ambivalence toward their place in this searing history. In rational terms, we know that this tiny cadre could do nothing to change the course of events, and that any action on their part would be a kamikaze adventure of the most foolhardy sort, and yet emotionally we cannot help but wish for some heroic move in that direction.

But it is Martina who most starkly and consequentially channels the film's bifurcated view of the partisans' relationship to the massacre of

Monte Sole, and we must therefore pause to consider the shift that her attitude undergoes toward the group throughout the course of events. In the film's first rendering of her interaction with the Stella Rossa Brigade, the camera presents imagery of the most idealized sort: Martina, making her way through an idyllic landscape, encounters the dashing and romantic Lupo, wearing his trademark red scarf, leading his men against a spectacular Apennine backdrop. In a gallant touch, one of Lupo's followers gently lifts Martina up onto his comrade's horse to give her a ride home. This storybook image of the local resistance brigade suggests that she has internalized the mystique attributed to Lupo and his men by the community at large. The scenery, depicting the dramatic contours of the Emilian countryside in a view whose horizon coincides with the upper boundary of the film frame itself, embeds the horsemen so thoroughly in its expanse as to confer upon them a heroic stature commensurate with the grandeur of their natural setting.

The community is not alone in its romanticized view of the resistance – the partisans themselves engage in a moment of self-glorification affectionately satirized by Diritti in the aftermath of their military victory against a full-fledged Nazi assault. To celebrate their triumph on the battlefield, the warriors stage a display that makes up in pride what it lacks in material splendour: two partisans, sitting atop a single horse, parade across the screen to the music of act 1, scene 1 of Aida ("Sul Nilo al sacro lido"), which issues from a gramophone carried by the second of the two exultant riders. Another subscriber to the myth of partisan prowess is Signor Bugamelli, an affluent Bolognese refugee who has chosen to bring his family to the Monte Sole region in the naive belief that the countryside will shield them from the ravages of war. When a Nazi scare sends the men fleeing into a forest hideout, Bugamelli's hopeful question – "The partisans will defend us, right?" – meets with eloquent silence as the camera pans the impassive faces of his peasant interlocutors.

Most striking in Diritti's evolving representation of the Stella Rossa Brigade is the scene in which Martina's own reverence for the group gives way to horror. Indeed, the moment in which she is forced to replace one with the other marks the first of the crises that will beset her for the remainder of the film. Martina's fall from ideological innocence to tainted knowledge begins on a deceptively idyllic note as she comes upon a large toad in the woods and follows it to the side of a pond. Across the water is a German soldier, vigorously digging a hole. She recognizes him as the "softest" of the Nazis – the one who had diffused a tense scene by juggling the eggs extorted from the Palmieri family in an earlier episode, and who in a later encounter was visibly moved by the sharing of bread with the peasant community. Watching his exertions now, Martina's happy recognition turns into anxiety and confusion as a partisan wielding a rifle approaches the German from behind. A second partisan appears, surveying the surroundings to make sure there are no witnesses to the proceedings. This is Dante, the recruit who had told Lupo, upon entering the partisan ranks, that he would perform any duty short of killing another man. The camera now cuts to a close-up of Martina, her face intensely focused on the unfolding tragedy of the young German's execution at the hands of Dante. This is followed by a frantic sequence of hand-held shots, sometimes preceding Martina, sometimes tracking her movements from behind or in profile until she finally arrives home where, unable to communicate her crisis to her mother, she withdraws into the barn, her sanctuary in time of emotional upheaval. Cross-cutting to the partisan outpost, back to the traumatized girl, and again to the partisans, now with a focus on Dante's expressionless face, the editing process renders a judgment on the dehumanizing effects of violence even when it is put to the service of a cause that is necessary and just.

But despite his unvarnished portrayal of the resistance, confronting its weaknesses as well as its strengths, Diritti never loses sight of the massive scale and horrific atrocity unleashed by the occupying forces on an innocent and helpless civilian population, rendering unthinkable any false analogy between partisan provocation and Nazi retaliation. Thanks to Martina's witness, which in its silence has required us as viewers to intuit her reactions to events, we have been made second-order witnesses through a particularly intense form of imaginative identification. To reinforce Martina's powers of silent communication, the film's musical soundtrack assumes a place of special prominence, indicating her state of mind during moments of acute anxiety as the tragedy unfolds.[11] One acoustic manifestation of extreme anxiety and inner turmoil is characterized by the high-pitched chanting of what seem to be children's voices perceived in a delirium as Martina and another girl watch the above-mentioned partisan ambush that kills three occupants of a Nazi jeep. This hallucinatory motif, which had originally been confined to Martina's subjectivity, is generalized to all the children as they flee their temporary lodging in the schoolhouse. It will ultimately merge with the story's "theme song," chanted by adult voices, when the victims are led to the site of impending slaughter in the cemetery of Casaglia.

The film's most telling musical sound effect, because most indicative of Martina's power to shape the narrative and to speak for Diritti's intent in making *L'uomo che verrà*, is a simple *ninna nanna* or lullaby,

Martina, cradling her newborn baby brother in her arms, sings the *ninna nanna* learned from her mother, while facing the backdrop of her homestead, now devoid of the abundant life it once harboured within its walls.

sung in Emilian dialect, at the beginning, middle, and end of the film. We hear strains of it early on, but it assumes its full-fledged identity as music to lull a child to sleep only later, when Lena sings it to Martina as they cuddle in bed. Most momentously, the song recurs during the film's finale as Martina softly produces it – her first vocalization since the death of her baby brother – to soothe the new infant whose life she has been able to save. In so doing, she signals her transformation into a mother figure, and her assumption of a responsibility that goes beyond the film's narrative bounds to include her role as witness dedicated to the transmission of memory to post-war generations.[12] The chorality of much of the film's music, and the source of the lullaby in the folk culture of the Emilian countryside, suggest that this entire community will be speaking through Martina's testimony – that she will be its "custode della memoria futura" (custodian of future memory).[13]

There is another musical motif that transcends any individual character's subjectivity and comes to stand as both the choral expression of a peasant culture lost to history and the film's own formal commentary on that loss. As such it takes on the air of hymnody, of sacred music, in keeping with the burial rites that Diritti's film symbolically performs. During the final frames of *L'uomo che verrà*, as the end credits roll, two seemingly antithetical musical forms alternate – the lullaby and the dirge – suggesting that the only way to commemorate and mourn the dead of Marzabotto is to usher in new lives committed to building a world free of war and its attendant atrocities.[14] It is in this sense that we may see Diritti as updating the example of Ermanno Olmi, whose body of work represented an ongoing alternative to ideologically driven filmmaking since the early 1960s.

Much has been made of the influence of Olmi on Diritti's career, and with good reason.[15] Diritti was a student in "Ipotesi cinema," the film school founded by Olmi, making the younger filmmaker a direct recipient of the master's approach. Of particular relevance to *L'uomo che verrà* is Olmi's epic film of the Bergamask countryside, *L'albero degli zoccoli* (Tree of the Wooden Clogs, 1978), which chronicled the fortunes of a single family within a little peasant community lodged in the same farmhouse complex, throughout a full cycle of seasons toward the end of the nineteenth century. In addition to sharing a documentary focus on the *quotidianità* of peasant life within a set of very specific geo-temporal coordinates (including the insistence on dialect), both Olmi and Diritti make children the focal points of their films' narrations. In *L'albero degli zoccoli*, it is the young son of the Battisti family, Minek, whose academic potential sets the story in motion and whose gaze of sadness and longing brings it to a close. Furthermore, both directors elevate the religiosity of their peasant protagonists into a model for their own relationship to the worlds they represent on film, adopting a reverential stance, much as Lena had in her above-mentioned visit to the shrine of the pregnant Madonna. In accordance with this shared sacralizing impulse, both films enact a scriptural scenario – that of the Fall from a state of primal innocence and wholeness into one of guilty knowledge and exilic despair. For the Battisti family in Olmi's film, that Fall is the result of an internal force – the family's decision to send Minek to school, and thus to literally gain the knowledge that will banish them from the Eden of their archaic world. For the Palmieri family, instead, it is history that expels them from a prior state of grace, condemning them either to immediate and violent death or to a condition of irreparable loss and the necessity of bearing witness to it. By locating the source of the Fall in external historical circumstance rather than in humans' innate desire for knowledge, Diritti grants agency to those who would learn from history and be moved to intervene in its course. In this sense, *L'uomo che verrà* may be seen as updating Olmi's vision, and bringing it into alignment with the progressive yet non-ideological *cinema d'impegno* of our current age.

Diritti builds this committed stance into the film's framing device, which foregrounds and enacts its own testimonial status as defined by the "now" of the storytelling process. *L'uomo che verrà* opens with a subjective camera shot that moves slowly and smoothly through a series of rooms, all containing empty beds whose disarray suggests the hasty departure of their occupants. After focusing on one particular bed, Diritti cuts to a reverse shot of a short-haired, primly dressed little girl before cutting back to the bed, now occupied by the same girl, this time sporting long hair and a night cap. With this second cut, the film has transitioned back into the past, where it will remain until the final sequence, making the entirety of the action an extended flashback. At the film's conclusion, events will have finally "caught up" to the opening scene. *L'uomo che verrà* is thus the story of its own telling, the narrative of how Martina acquired the power to bear witness to the destruction of her world.

Martina is the "custode della memoria futura," wrote Paolo D'Agostini,[16] and as such her wandering through the rooms of the farmhouse during the film's opening frames enacts the metaphor of the chambers-of-the-mind, drawing upon the ancient rhetorical technique that dictates the assignment of items for memorization to specific rooms in an imagined house. The very gap between the fullness of the life lived in those rooms, as conjured up in the film's first half, and their spectral emptiness in the "now" of the frame-story serves as a measure of the loss that historical events will visit upon this family, and by extension upon the peasant community for which it stands. Because the opening spectacle of empty rooms and abandoned beds hovers over our consciousness during the course of the film, the return to this scene at the end of *L'uomo che verrà* sets up an internal system of memory – a déjà vu that brings the frame-story back to its starting point, but with one crucial difference. In the concluding replay of the film's opening fragment, Martina's bed remains empty – there is no earlier self to occupy the bed, and to start the story again. Now it is up to "the man who will come," the newborn receiver of Martina's witness within the fiction of the film, and the audience surrogate at the meta-level of the work's reception, to reactivate the story of Marzobotto.

In the final analysis *L'uomo che verrà* may be read as the extended answer to Armando's anguished question "che storia è questa," providing a powerful counterhistory to challenge the abstract, statistic-laden accounts "that we find in the books and academic studies."[17] Mining the ambiguity of the Italian word "storia," the filmmaker has replaced official history (written by and about the *importanti*) with storytelling, the fictional means for getting at the deep truth of personal suffering under the weight of economic, political, and military abuse, and in this particular case, where such abuse leads to atrocity. Marshalling the signature attribute of the cinematic medium – its status as a technology of seeing – in the pursuit of his ethical aims, Diritti's work instils in its viewers a self-conscious awareness of what it means to watch re-creations of this highly fraught past. In the words of Karl Schoonover, the challenge of such a project is to "transform seeing from a passive state of consumption into a powerful means of moral reckoning"[18] and in so doing to make audience members "moral onlookers,"[19] willing to take on the ethical burdens of historical knowledge, and to scrutinize their own relationship with a past whose impact on the Italian national self has yet to be fully assimilated. With such a viewership in mind, Diritti crafts his film as an impassioned plea to render obsolete Armando's question "che storia è questa?" for a future in which the voices of the historically under-represented will finally be registered and their call for justice finally heard.

PART THREE

Migrants

Chapter Seven

Channelling the Geographic Unconscious: Federico Bondi's *Mar nero* (Black Sea), 2008

Direction: Federico Bondi. *Screenplay*: Ugo Chiti, Federico Bondi. *Cinematography*: Gigi Martinucci. *Music*: Enzo Casucci, Guy Klucevsek. *Sound*: Mirko Guerra. *Editing*: Ilaria Fraioli. *Costumes*: Alessandra Vadalà. *Sets*: Daniele Spisa, Dan Toader. *Cast*: Ilaria Occhini (Gemma Pratesi), Dorotheea Petre (Angela), Corso Salani (Enrico Pratesi), Vlad Ivanov (Adrian), Maia Morgenstern (Madalina), Theodor Danetti (Angela's father), Vincenzo Versari (Lupi), Giuliana Colzi (Milena), Marius Silagiy (Nelu).

Synopsis: The film opens with the arrival of a young Romanian immigrant, Angela, to Florence, where she has been hired as a *badante*, or domestic caregiver, for Gemma Pratesi, newly widowed and physically impaired enough to preclude her living alone. Initially resentful of her need for assistance, and reluctant to acknowledge the humanity and competence of Angela, Gemma gradually comes to accept her reliance on the young woman and her growing affection for her. Mother of an only child, Enrico, who has married and moved to Trieste, Gemma experiences a particularly acute need for aid and companionship after a minor accident. In a measure of her change of heart, she defends her caregiver in the face of vicious comments by a neighbour, Milena, whose husband's attraction to the young woman and whose own hatred of immigrants leads her to question Angela's legal status and to threaten police action against her. Gemma's full-throated defence of Angela includes not only the claim that legalization papers have already been

---

This essay originally appeared in *Destination Italy: Representing Migration in Contemporary Media and Narrative*, ed. Emma Bond, Guido Bonsaver, and Federico Faloppa (Bern: Peter Lang, 2015).

filed for her, but also that Romania is about to enter the European Union and that "they'll be one of us!" In the meantime, Angela has maintained phone contact in Romania with her husband Adrian, and it becomes clear that the couple had hoped to start a family, but a pregnancy test upon her arrival in Florence proved that their efforts had so far been in vain. Over the course of the next few months Angela forms bonds with fellow Romanians in Florence thanks to the presence of her sister-in-law Irina, who has become well integrated into the expatriot community. At a New Year's Eve party, a handsome singer-celebrity shows a romantic interest in Angela, who is instead preoccupied about her husband's failure to answer the phone in her multiple efforts to reach him. Desperate to track Adrian down, Angela vows to return to Romania, triggering a reaction of anger and hurt on the part of Gemma, who decides to undertake the journey with the young woman in a reversal of roles both comic and poignant. As a guest in Angela's apartment while the young woman searches for her husband, Gemma is visited by her hostess's father, and though neither can comprehend the other, his very presence prompts a beautiful and profound self-reflection on the elderly woman's part. Angela's quest to find Adrian takes her to the farmhouse of his mistress, where an intense exchange of gazes between the two women leads to the errant husband's return home. In a final twist, we see Gemma on the boat heading toward the Black Sea, but she is not alone. With her is Madalina, Angela's sister, who has chosen service to Gemma as a release from an abusive marriage.

A film of limited material means and narrative scope, *Mar nero* nonetheless engages some of the most searing issues surrounding today's global migrant crisis. The film's very modesty belies its broader ambitions, pushing against the walls of its tiny apartment setting and its confinement to a single interpersonal relationship to construct a parable of hard-won hospitality with far-reaching psychological and cultural implications. Of singular importance to an understanding of Federico Bondi's achievement in this, his feature film debut, is its rootedness in the director's personal observations of a family member's evolving relationship with her caregiver. "A story intimately bound to my autobiography," Bondi explained, "the elderly protagonist [Gemma] was my grandmother. I was inspired by her. Angela, the *badante*, the young Romanian girl who has been in Italy for a month, was precisely Angela, the *badante* of my grandmother. During the years of frequenting my grandmother, I had the good fortune to witness this transformation. My grandmother was a hard woman, unbearable in certain ways, cynical, but also a person full of affection to give and to receive."[1] It is this autobiographical impulse that endows the film with the authenticity of lived experience and of emotional truth, grounded in minute observations of language, gesture, social behaviour, and the particulars of physical setting.[2]

From this starting point, the protagonists' domestic drama radiates outwards to embrace the broader political realities and humanitarian issues that surround the film's inner story. In a striking example of the correspondence between events occurring on the public and private levels, Angela attends a New Year's celebration organized by the Romanian expatriot community of Florence.[3] "For months we asked ourselves if Romania were ready for Europe," declares the master of ceremonies. To the general hilarity and approval of the crowd, a woman loudly responds, "But is Europe ready for Romania?" In the story of Gemma's relationship with Angela, the filmmaker has devised a narrative vehicle for the enactment of that very process of readiness. Gemma's aging and decrepit condition stands for an Italian (and by extension, European) body politic in obvious need of the revitalizing care that a workforce from the emerging world can provide. "The doctor always said to me that I should be on the move," Gemma explains as a justification for her trip to Romania, and with this, she provides a prescription for the collective health of the larger body politic for which she stands. Significantly, Gemma chooses not to take the doctor's advice at its most literal – to *fare movimento*, that is, engage in simple physical activity – but rather to progress beyond the limits of her current condition in existential terms. Indeed, her geographical movement from Italy to the Romanian hometown of Angela is the material result of a movement that has already taken place within her own psyche – a *movement out* of an exclusive and sclerotic concern with the self and *into* an attitude of vital intercultural curiosity. It is in the film's delicate rendering of Gemma's transformation that *Mar nero* offers itself to us as both testimony and exemplum – testimony to the filmmaker's abovementioned observations of his grandmother's experience with a foreign caregiver, and model of the turn toward genuine hospitality that the film seeks to instil in the viewing public.

The key to Gemma's metamorphosis is her acceptance of Angela *as* subject – a process considerably delayed by the older woman's habit of continually calling her *badante* by the name of her unsavoury predecessor, Luda. This is a telling mistake. Exhibiting the kind of inductive thinking that leads xenophobes and racists to generalize from a single negative experience, Gemma is slow to exempt her new domestic companion from the blanket condemnation to which the entire category of caregivers had been consigned in her own thinking. Equally telling, therefore, is the moment when Gemma first addresses Angela correctly. This scene is set in the cemetery where the older woman has just placed flowers on her husband's grave, and has explained her desire *not* to linger at the site. As they take their leave, Gemma asks Angela when her mother died, and with this sign of curiosity, she reveals her readiness to grant the young woman an identity that exceeds the narrow bounds of serfdom, and opens up the possibility of a maternal role for herself. Gemma's desire not to linger over her husband's grave suggests a willingness to consider mourning as a therapeutic process that ultimately enables the survivor to move on to other healthy and fulfilling relationships in the here and now.

What has brought Gemma to this point regarding Angela has been a slow and delicate education in listening. The first sign that Gemma is ready to take an interlocutory role occurs when the younger woman tells her employer that in Romania she had been a hairdresser and manicurist. In an unprecedented display of actually *hearing* Angela, Gemma wryly asks, "Toenails too?" ("Anche i piedi?"). It should come as no surprise that the discovery of Angela's cosmetic skills would be the first thing to break down Gemma's resistance to her, given the older woman's focus on appearance. A second instance of dialogue that promotes the breakdown of Gemma's defences is more subtle in its workings. Hearing that Angela and her husband use a boat as their only means of transportation, while others have cars and horses, Gemma is moved to share her equine memories from childhood. Strikingly, this throwback to an earlier time in her own life does not lead her to draw the obvious conclusions about Romanian economic backwardness. Instead, it takes Gemma deeper into solipsism, as her reverie comes to alight on the suffering of horses when nails were driven into their hooves during the shoeing process. This train of thought leads back to the self, to the pain of arthritis that becomes her "cross" in the hyperbolic and melodramatically inclined Gemma of the film's early scenes.

But her listening soon comes to mark a growing identification between the two women. When Angela explains that she wants to earn money so that she can give her (at this point, hypothetical) child everything, Gemma remarks on the sacrifices that she and her husband underwent to send their son, Enrico, to school.[4] And later, when they broach the subject of spousal relations, Gemma reveals her earthy side by observing that marital discord during the day can lead to blissful reconciliations at night. By hinting at the erotic element in her own marriage, Gemma establishes a further link between the two women in her acknowledgment of their shared identity as sexual beings, whose past pleasures (in both cases) and future ones (in Angela's) should be reason for bonding and celebration.

As important as these passages of dialogue are to the film's explorations of Italy's encounter with the immigrant "other," it is Bondi's strategic use of medium-specific techniques that recommend *Mar nero* to our closest critical attention. Through the careful coordination of camerawork with the perceptual experiences of its two protagonists, the film is able to scrutinize their subjectivities as each comes to a more profound understanding of the other's world. From the very first frames of *Mar nero*, after the opening credits have ceased to roll, the film locates us within the focalizing consciousness of Angela. We are shown a landscape rushing by just as she would see it from her seat in one of the regional trains so common to Tuscany. Though her arrival at the Stazione di Santa Maria Novella is filmed from an objective position outside the building, showing her tiny figure in long shot as she emerges from it, this camera effect simulates her own self-perception as miniscule and lost amidst the vast spaces of a new and alien environment. Throughout the first part of the film, in fact, Bondi will employ the free indirect subjective technique theorized by Pasolini, whereby the camera assumes a character's point of view even as we see that character objectively on screen.[5] Analogous to free indirect discourse in literature, this device allows the filmmaker to appropriate a character's particular cognitive style – to "try on" the way that character views the world – without the restrictions that the use of a purely subjective camera would entail.

In other scenes Bondi appropriates the neorealist technique of *pedinamento* to record Angela's encounters with her new environment, giving particular attention to the immigrant's daily routine. Striking examples of this include the dazzling array of food choices available in the meat and poultry counters of the supermarket and the plethora of products offered on the cosmetic shelves of the department store. The impact of such scenes for us viewers in the economically advanced world, however, can only be felt in a second moment, once our own familiarity with the spectacle of consumer excess gives way to a realization of the utter astonishment with which a refugee from a developing country would greet such lavish displays.

From a political standpoint, Bondi's most consequential move is to align our perspective with Gemma's as she confronts the Romanian homeland to which Angela will eventually lead her. It is here that the film's title gains resonance in announcing the geographic imaginary that *Mar nero* offers to its viewers, just as Angela does in her relationship

Angela exits the Stazione di Santa Maria Novella in a shot whose framing dwarfs her amidst the heavy scaffolding of the lobby architecture.

with Gemma. Of utmost importance is the film's focus on bodies of water, whose associations with travel, adventure, and romance would be far more apt to stir intercultural curiosity than would the mere naming of countries, especially when those countries have been routinely condemned in the court of public opinion. While the poetic workings of synecdoche, metonymy, and antonomasia are easily and enchantingly set in motion by allusions to the Mar nero or the Danube, the designation "Romania" has only the dreariest of "prose" associations – in particular, those publicized locally by hearsay, and more generally by news outlets, whose coverage of Romanian criminality has been generalized to that entire immigrant population.[6] Within the film, the spokesperson for this particular anti-immigrant bias is Gemma's loathsome neighbour Milena, who spews out a litany of racist stereotypes and threatens to report Angela to the authorities as an illegal alien. With the look of an aging prostitute, and the spitefulness of a cast-off wife, Milena is herself a stereotype, plagued by sexual jealousy (her husband is clearly attracted to Angela, as he had obviously been to her predecessor Luda) and prey to the irresistible lure of social scapegoating.[7]

In the film's first half, it is Angela's mention of her husband's commute to work by boat that piques Gemma's geographic curiosity. "Are you near the sea?" she wonders. "Not sea" ("Non mare"), Angela explains in her beginner's Italian, "sea near, Danube. Big river" ("mare vicino, Danubio. Fluvio grande"). Thus, despite its marine title, *Mar nero* is really about rivers,[8] and not surprisingly, the film's Florentine half features the Arno in a scene that puts Gemma's Tuscan-centrism into high relief. Gazing down on the Arno from a scenic outlook (probably Piazzale Michelangelo), she mentions the flood of November 1966. When Angela shows no sign of recognition, Gemma erupts into expressions of disbelief, signalling her obtuseness with regard to this young women's limited access to knowledge beyond her own location in time and space.

Of pivotal importance to the construction of the film's geographic imaginary is the way in which Florence functions as a topos, both as a literal place and as a place in the mind. Since the city is presented through the focalizing consciousness of Angela, it is divested of all high cultural associations as the seat of Renaissance genius; the showcase of architectural, artistic, philosophic, scientific, and literary achievements; the Brunelleschian, Buonarottian, Medicean monument to itself. In short, for Angela, "Destination Florence" is anything but a tourist mecca – it is "Destination Any City" that can offer her a foothold on prosperity. For this reason, the film skirts the historic downtown, showing us only the Santa Maria Novella train station, scrupulously avoiding the spectacle of the church for which that station was named. Upon Angela's arrival, all we are shown is an avenue leading out of the city to the family's lovely country home. But Angela's experience of this iconic destination for *agriturismo* (rural tourism) is minimal – she is not even invited out of the car to make her initial acquaintance with Gemma. For Angela, the glorious Tuscan countryside is nothing more than the antechamber to this awaited and feared first encounter. For the rest of the Florentine segment, the setting is limited to Gemma's apartment (located in Gavinana, a working-class neighbourhood rarely represented on screen)[9] or to the markets and parks characteristic of any Italian urban setting. The one exception to this anti-tourist perspective is the above-mentioned scene in which Gemma shows Angela the Arno, but this functions more to reveal the older woman's provincialism than to introduce the younger woman to a trademark Florentine feature. In fact, the only ongoing indications of the film's urban setting are Gemma's strongly inflected accent and her occasional use of dialect ("vo' via, bischera, boccalona"). Gemma's speech patterns, weighted with "fiorentinità," set up a powerful counterpoint with Angela's pigeon Italian, constantly underlining the cultural distance between the two women, even as that distance shrinks under the pressure of their strengthening emotional ties.[10]

The words "Come on, eat! You haven't taken anything since yesterday" (in English translation) show further evidence of the role reversal between the frail older woman and her caretaker that has led Gemma to insist on accompanying Angela in the search for the latter's errant husband.

The *emptying out* of the city's cultural mystique in the light of Angela's generic immigrant experience triggers an equal and opposite process of great significance: Gemma's *filling in* of the signifier "Black Sea" with all of the discoveries that her newly acquired geographic curiosity has made possible.[11] The literal expansion of Gemma's horizons is announced by her first words on the boat leading to Angela's hometown in Romania. "Altro che Arno" (so much for the Arno), she exclaims as they make their way along the waters of the Danube. But this de-provincializing step heralds the advent of another, more profound form of openness, as evidenced by the very next words uttered by Gemma in this scene. "Eat," she orders Angela. "You haven't taken anything since yesterday."

Gemma's entrance into this new geographic space coincides with her entrance into a radically changed subjectivity – one that replaces her old imperious self-absorption with an attentiveness to the well-being of another that verges on the maternal.[12] In an important measure of her emergence from narcissism, Gemma stares intently at a horse-drawn cart – a gesture that takes the viewer back to the earlier scene of her monologue about the childhood memory of equine suffering. Whereas that earlier reverie had led only to a solipsistic comparison with her own plight, the image of the horse-drawn cart now forces Gemma out of herself, to acknowledge the objective predicament of life lived under a backward economic regime. Without resorting to didacticism, this scene delicately suggests the parallel between the privations of the immediate post-war Italian condition under which Gemma grew up and the plight of a contemporary developing country whose hardships have been the driver of emigration.[13]

Of signal importance to our understanding of Gemma's function in *Mar nero* is Bondi's choice to cast Ilaria Occhini in this leading role. Given her iconic status in the realms of Italian theatre, television, and film, Occhini's presence in *Mar nero* serves as a self-reflexive commentary on the encounter between the "institution" of mainstream spectacle and the new reality that is "Destination Italy." At this abstract level, *Mar nero* can well be read as an allegory of the cinema's quest for the means to accommodate this new national story – that is, the geriatric Italian body politic's need for caregivers from abroad. Playing the role of the aged grand dame who both requires and resists the presence of a *badante*, Occhini personifies the past and present of the mainstream media as they face this representational challenge. To that end, she delivers a carefully layered performance that ranges from the extremes of melodramatic exaggeration to understated and nuanced expressivity. In the early scenes, Gemma is nothing more than a caricature of herself – she is literally *carica*, loaded or charged with the misery of her condition as a new widow and sufferer of painful, though non-life-threatening, physical complaints. With her evolution toward greater openness and fellow feeling, Gemma's persona literally lightens, and her performance of selfhood becomes "de-caricaturized." This shift is quite pronounced in the Romanian scenes, and particularly in the one involving the monologue delivered to Angela's father Nicolae, who cannot understand a word she says but who listens in an attitude of rapt attention that spurs Gemma on to ever more vivid expressions of her newfound and adventurous sense of self.

> I'll return to Florence. I'm a bit sorry about that. Anyway, after this place here, I won't go back to my house. My son would like me to go to Trieste, with that wind, or to a nursing home to play a dead body on vacation. No, no, I'll grab my stuff and be off. I'll go to Umbria. I've never seen it.

At the conclusion of this monologue, the camera alights on a painting displayed on the opposite wall of Angela's living-room, suggesting that perhaps it had triggered Gemma's fantasy of flight. A sentimentalized, greeting-card picture of a wintry landscape with a cottage nestled in the snow and a cheerful pond in the foreground, this scene consigns Gemma's reverie to the realm of kitsch without in any way judging or disparaging her for it. Despite the patent unreality of her plan, it nonetheless reveals the profoundly liberating effect of Gemma's encounter with "this place here." And though her monologue reveals Gemma to be still bound to a performative and histrionic mode of self-expression, the content of her utterances could not be more different from the guilt-inducing *pesantezza* (heaviness) of her earlier ones.

Her performance reaches its maximum degree of lightness in Gemma's final exchange with Angela. It is the morning after Adrian's return, but the elderly woman is as yet unaware of the man's presence at home. Having awakened to an otherwise slumbering household, Gemma peeks into the bedroom to find Angela in the arms of her sleeping husband. The two women make eye contact, and when Angela indicates her decision to stay in Romania with Adrian, through the language of silence and stillness, Gemma dispenses with words altogether, and signals her understanding of the young woman's choice by simply smiling and nodding her assent. According to the terms that we have established for reading Ilaria Occhini's casting as a signifier for the tradition of mass spectacle as it struggles to meet the challenge of "Destination Italy," it is the discarding of the old histrionics and the crafting of a delicate, understated, and profoundly interpersonal mimetic style that emerges as Bondi's answer to this representational dare.[14]

The nexus between geography and subjectivity is by no means limited to the film's Romanian denouement. Throughout the first part of *Mar nero*, Bondi forged a medium-specific language for establishing Angela's connection to a geographical "elsewhere." This was achieved by the insertion of five discrete landscape sequences, hailing from some alien and unidentifiable place, throughout the course of the Florentine segment. These include (1) a slow pan along a riverbank filmed from a moving vessel; (2) a centred, frontal shot of a man seated at the prow of a rudimentary boat as it glides downstream; (3) a centred close-up of the boat's prow against the background of the river; (4) a repeat of insert 1; and (5) a centred, frontal, medium shot of a man, the same man as in insert 2, now walking up a road. Because these inserts are tethered to no identifiable narrative context, we must depend entirely upon the logic of editing to decipher their meaning. The leisurely, gliding movement along the river in insert 1, which forms the background of the credit sequence, gains contrastive value when juxtaposed with the swift passage of landscape images seen from the window of the train rushing Angela to Florence. With this juxtaposition, the film sets up a dichotomy between the two different *modi vivendi* implicit in these styles of transit: one slow and "naturalized" by the purity of the fluvial environment, the other hurried and mechanized by the workings of railroad technology. The editing of the second insert is key to establishing the unexpected parallelism between the two women's sentimental lives. Suffering from loneliness and the oppressive heat of the Florentine summer, Gemma complains to her recently deceased husband, "It's really hot, Nedo." Bondi now cuts to insert 2 featuring a man in the prow of a boat, and then returns us to the Florentine setting with a shot of Angela awake in her bed. We will learn later that the man of the insert is Adrian, but at this earlier point in the narration it is only the juxtaposition between Gemma's remark to the imagined Nedo and the insert of a vigorous young man in some indeterminate "elsewhere" that hints that both women are longing for their absent mates.

What remains unclear is the "status" of these inserts: are they memories or daydreams within the subjectivity of Angela, or are they objective events that are taking place in synchrony with the actions of the scenes unfolding in Florence? Howsoever we choose to understand these indeterminate shots, they serve to connect Angela to her "elsewhere" in a way far more intriguing and compelling than mere dialogue about cultural differences could possibly convey.

Once the narrative takes us to Romania, these inserts become intelligible – they are the settings for events that take place in the film's second half. The recurrence of these settings, now appearing in their proper narrative context, creates a powerful déjà vu effect. It establishes an internal memory system that endows viewers with an uncanny and inchoate sense of familiarity throughout the film's Romanian segment. In this mysterious and disconcerting assemblage of images, we realize that the inserts have set up a kind of filmic unconscious – an inventory of signs whose meaning could not be contained within the logic of a rational and linear narrative sequence. As such, they assume the function of Pasolinian "im-segni" – image-signs that underlie the "prose language" of cinematic tradition and that constitute a raw and pre-grammatical film idiom of unique poetic force.[15] Hailing from the world of memory, dream, mime, and brute reality, this primal imagery constitutes the "mythic and infantile sub-film"[16] that underlies every film, even the most conventional one, and provides its dynamic thrust. In *Mar nero*, the inserts that punctuate the narrative's Florentine part may be seen to lay bare the workings of that primitive Pasolinian sub-film.

That this unconscious takes *geographic* form is vital to Bondi's didactic intent in *Mar nero*. By exploiting the power of the image-signs to activate unconscious desires toward the exotic "elsewhere," and by engaging viewers in the process by which those image-signs come to be identified with the mother country of an unfortunately maligned immigrant population, Bondi's film seeks to replace fear and resistance with intercultural curiosity and interpersonal desire. Beyond the somewhat "prosaic" nature of the storyline and the predictable pedagogy of Gemma's dialogues with Angela, *Mar nero* offers a striking example of a cinema that mobilizes its medium-specific powers to promote a profoundly hospitable and actively welcoming approach to life in Destination Italy.

Chapter Eight

"Your Position Please": Gianfranco Rosi's *Fuocoammare* (Fire at Sea), 2016

Direction: Gianfranco Rosi. *Assistant Director*: Giuseppe Del Volgo. *Writers*: Gianfranco Rosi, Carla Catani (idea). *Cinematography*: Gianfranco Rosi. *Editing*: Jacopo Quadri. *Graphic designers*: Alberto Baccari, Andrea Castelletti. *Sound*: Stefano Grosso, Vladan Nedeljkov, Giancarlo Rutigliano. Aleksandra Stojanovic. *Cast*: Samuele Pucillo, Mattias Cucina, Samuele Caruana, Dr. Pietro Bartolo, Giuseppe Fragapane, Maria Signorello, Francesco Paterna, Francesco Mannino, Maria Costa.

Synopsis: Set on the tiny island of Lampedusa, located seventy miles from the Libyan coast, this documentary is organized around six interweaving narrative strands. The first traces the story of Samuele, a twelve-year-old native of the island, who spends his spare time hunting small birds with a homemade slingshot, playing war games with his friend Mattias, and ultimately undergoing a coming-of-age initiation into maritime life. The film's second narrative focus is the plight of the migrants rescued from the waters off of Lampedusa and brought to reception centres on the island. The third and fourth strands, closely entwined, oscillate between the radio station, run by the DJ, Pippo, and the home of Zia Maria, who listens to the radio while doing housework and who requests songs dedicated to her son and husband. A fifth strand follows an anonymous diver who sets traps for sea urchins and whose story is recorded by spectacular feats of underwater photography. The sixth and final strand features Dr. Pietro Bartolo, the physician who manages the medical care of the new arrivals and whose lugubrious task it is to oversee the handling of the cadavers, including the gathering of tissue samples for bureaucratic purposes.

In awarding first prize to Gianfranco Rosi's *Fuocoammare* at the 2016 Berlin Film Festival, committee chair Meryl Streep declared it "a daring blend of captured footage and storytelling that allows us to see what a documentary can do. It demands its place in front of our eyes, compels our engagement and action."[1] At the news conference following the ceremony, Rosi described the film as an intervention in the migrant crisis unfolding on the southern-most borders of the continent. In Rosi's words, *Fuocoammare* "bears witness to a tragedy unfolding before our eyes. We're all responsible. After the Holocaust, this is one of the biggest tragedies that we're living through. For the Holocaust, we had images after [the fact]. With [the migrant] tragedy, we're bombarded with images." This means that his film is part of the imagistic "bombardment" taking place *during* the course of the crisis, in the hopes of inspiring an activist response *in medias res*.[2]

But unlike the "bombardment" of imagery transmitted on the evening news or published in various forms of print, Rosi has chosen an approach to the crisis that contradicts the violence of his own word choice. His film's sobriety, its quietness, and its patience are the antithesis of the imagistic assault mounted by the media, which induces shock and dismay but keeps the tragedy at a distance, allowing paralysis to set in. Rosi's technique, while never evasive, shuns the shock effect of mass media treatments by building a slow and multifaceted understanding of the crisis *as lived* on the waters surrounding Lampedusa, and on the island itself. If I were to apply a rhetorical term to Rosi's approach, it would be "litotes" – the tendency to understate his narrative and technical means in chronicling the events besetting the island in the face of this ongoing catastrophe. As a rhetorical device, litotes demands that its audience acknowledge the gap between the understated mode of representation and the gravity of its subject matter, thus drawing spectators into an ethically charged stance in the interpretive space opened up between the subject matter and its formal representation.

Rosi's strategy was the product of a considered decision upon arriving in Lampedusa at the onset of his project. Originally commissioned by the Istituto Luce to make a ten-minute short subject, the filmmaker immediately understood that the "facts on the ground" were far too complex to be rendered within such narrow confines. Instead, Rosi embarked on a year-long experience of full immersion in the life of the island, aided by Peppino Del Volgo – his on-site guide and companion – who introduced him to the cast of characters engaged in the daily routines around which the film would revolve. Rosi's intimacy with the world of the island, his insistence on wielding his own (extremely light and agile) camera, and his refusal of assistants other than Del Volgo himself meant that he could create filming conditions of the utmost spontaneity and lack of self-consciousness on the part of his characters. In Rosi's words, there was "nothing premeditated" about the footage he shot – his directing technique was the result of "autofecondazione" (self-fertilization). There was no master plan in place as he embarked on the filming of *Fuocoammare*, and though its subject matter is inherently political, no ideological message took the lead in determining the filmmaker's encounter with Lampedusa.[3] With very few exceptions, this means that the standard tools of the documentary were dispensed with – interviews with talking heads; the use of maps and captions specifying where, when, and who; inserts of archival materials such as written documents, photographs, video clips, and external didactic devices in general were absent from the repertory of Rosi's film. In essence, the roots of *Fuocoammare* are entirely experiential – the fruit of Rosi's year-long exposure to life on Lampedusa, though entirely purged of the first-person subjectivity that guided the camerawork and forged the relationships integral to the film's process of "autofecondazione."

Among Rosi's few concessions to standard documentary technique are the film's introductory intertitles: "The island of Lampedusa has a surface of 20 square kilometers, it is 70 miles from the coast of Africa, 120 miles from that of Sicily. In the last 20 years, around 400,000 migrants arrived at the shores of Lampedusa. In the attempt to cross the Canale di Sicilia to reach Europe, we estimate that 15,000 people died." This dry, statistics-laden text establishes the doubly paradoxical position of Lampedusa in spatial terms: it is closer to Libya than to Sicily, and its tiny sliver of land serves as the gateway to the entire continent of Europe. With this didactic introduction to a world-historical issue that conjures up well-known images of overcrowded vessels heading for disaster, the film instead plunges us into a solitary, land-bound space inhabited by a single child cutting the branch of a tree and whittling it to make a slingshot. With infinite patience, the camera lingers on this boy, the twelve-year-old Samuele, who will star in one of the film's two major plot lines – a coming-of-age story unfolding without any connection to the migrant crisis taking place on the tiny outpost between Libya and Sicily.[4] In this opening sequence, there is no sign of modernity in the primeval grove where Samuele harvests the wood for his weapon, and were it not for his jeans and windbreaker, his activity could take place in any era of recorded history. How shocking, then, is the editorial leap from Samuele's wood-whittling efforts to the next scene, featuring a shot of a radar tower rotating its high-tech beacon, accompanied by a voice, in heavily accented English, that asks: "How many people?" "Two hundred fifty," another voice responds, adding "I beg you." "Your position please?" the first voice inquires, and when no response ensues, the inquiry is repeated several times to no avail. The film now cuts to a long shot of the radar tower, followed by a glimpse of a search light beamed on the surface of the sea before showing the interior of a control room replete with screens and a window onto the ship's deck where a helicopter is poised to take off. Though never explicitly stated, we have just witnessed the preparations for a rescue mission, whose results will not be directly reported until later. Only after editorial leaps across two more of the film's multiple narrative strands will we learn the statistics of life and death in the wake of this catastrophe. The intervening scenes will take us to the local radio station, run by the DJ Pippo, and then to the kitchen of Zia Maria, who is listening to the broadcast of a traditional Sicilian song while peeling tomatoes. We hear the news on this broadcast, sandwiched in between the song and a report of a power outage scheduled for the following day, that 34 bodies have been recovered and 206 survivors have been pulled from the sea. "Poveri cristiani" sighs the listener. Though the subtitles translate this line of dialogue as "poor souls," the Italian word choice uses *cristiani* as an umbrella term to include all human beings within its redemptive reach.

The film revisits Zia Maria several more times, in scenes that always link her to the local radio station and the traditional sonorities of Sicilian life. While the station is equipped with state-of-the-art technology, as seen in the sophisticated video screen mounted on the DJ's monitor, Zia Maria's tastes run either toward archaic folk tunes, replete with lyrics in dialect and melodies redolent of Sicily's Arabic past, or toward songs of more recent but nonetheless local provenance. In one scene she dedicates the song "Fuocoammare," of post–Second World War vintage, to her son Nello to console him for losing a day of fishing to bad weather, and another song to her husband Giacomino "con tanto tanto amore" (with so very much love). This latter dedication, with its ardent adverbs, builds up expectations for an emotionally satisfying portrait of marital life, but when the camera pans to the object of Maria's adoration, the elderly Giacomino sits immobile, his expression vacant as his wife completes the ritual of preparing and serving his afternoon espresso. This scene provides a fleeting snapshot of a lifetime of orderly domestic routine within a world otherwise ruled by the vagaries of weather and the ravages of advanced human age. The film's engagement with Maria's obsessive housekeeping reaches its zenith in the long-shot sequence of bedmaking that completes her story line. The camera patiently follows her expert movements as she meticulously spreads, folds, and smooths the bedding before turning her attention to an unidentified man's photograph surrounded by votive candles on an adjacent table, and the statues of the Madonna and Padre Pio placed elsewhere in the room. Throughout Maria's final scene, a radio transmission of Rossini's *Mosè*, "Dal tuo stellato soglio" is heard in the background, forming a sound bridge to the film's concluding visit to the broadcast studio, featuring a close-up of the DJ, himself obviously moved by this musical selection.

Radio technology is by no means the only intermedial focus of *Fuocoammare*. Throughout the film, screens-within-the-screen abound, including the two examples in the above-mentioned scenes of the radar control room and the radio station. Needless to say, the mise-en-abyme effects of embedded screens reflects self-consciously on the medium of film itself, and in the case of *Fuocoammare* the inner screens serve as portals of knowledge and springboards to action – ideals to which Rosi has explicitly dedicated his work. A pair of other screens appears prominently in the film, and they each serve to enrich the characterization of Dr. Pietro Bartolo, the physician who oversees the care of the island's new arrivals. During his very first appearance in the film, Dr. Bartolo is administering a prenatal sonogram, and throughout this scene our focus is divided between the instrument's movement over the patient's abdomen and the screen registering indecipherable wave patterns whose meanings the doctor seeks to explain. The action is slow-going, and the camera lingers on Bartolo's attempt to fathom the whereabouts of a twin fetus, afloat in the amniotic fluid, which he pronounces to be scarce due to the hardships experienced by the mother-to-be. The navigation of this inner ocean parallels, in microcosm, the radar efforts to locate a sinking vessel in the waters off the coast of Lampedusa. Dr. Bartolo's exploratory attempts meet with success when he detects the fetal head, whose outlines become visible to the mother on screen, and to us as observers at two removes from this burgeoning new life.

The second embedded screen associated with Dr. Bartolo's character leads to knowledge of a far more tragic sort. This scene is a dramatic monologue, delivered slowly and gravely before a large computer slide of a boat teeming with 840 stranded passengers. The doctor's commentary stands as the film's only example of the "talking head" convention so common to documentary practice, and in fact it was shot after Rosi had completed the footage gleaned from the "autofecondazione" of his experiences with the island's populace and its natural setting. Bartolo's testimony represents the moment of the film's direct appeal for an ethically charged response on the part of the viewers. "It's the duty of every human being who is human to help these people," he exhorts us, before transitioning to the first-person plural and hence the collective

Dr. Bartolo narrates the tragedy of the dangerously overcrowded ship pictured on his computer in one of the many representations of screens-within-screens throughout the film.

work of rescue for which he takes the medical lead. "When we succeed, we're really happy, glad. Unfortunately, it's not always possible. So I have to witness awful things" such as the recovery of bodies, of pregnant women, of children, of newborns with the umbilical cords still attached, and the attendant work of collecting tissue and bone samples for post-mortem identification purposes. His focus on obstetric details recalls the earlier scene of the sonogram, so hopeful as a portal into new life. Instead, the computer screen behind Bartolo's concluding monologue shows slides of a ship whose passenger-overload will lead to disaster, and a further image of a severely injured adolescent, suffering chemical burns from the fuel spilled on the floor of his rubber boat.

While akin to the convention of the "talking head," Bartolo's testimony lacks the slick, highly rehearsed recitations of the experts interviewed in standard documentary practice. Instead, his speech is punctuated by silences, moments in which he appears to turn inwards, struggling to put into words his own anguish in the face of repeated tragedies to which he never becomes inured. This long and laboured testimony delivered from the "receiving end" of the migrant crisis finds its striking counterpart in the narration of a Nigerian survivor earlier in the film. While critics applied the term "rapper" to this singer-speaker, if I were to choose a Western analogy for his role, I'd liken him more to the rhapsode of Homeric tradition. But of course, his performance clearly stems from local folk customs in which a leader's account (in this case, in English) is performed against a background of choral chanting in the native tongue. His story traces the journey from Nigeria through the Sahara to the shores of Libya and the sea crossing of ninety people, of whom only thirty survived. The travelogue includes references to the hardships of the desert, starvation, thirst alleviated only by the drinking of urine, flight from ISIS, rape, murder, and imprisonment, but it finishes on a triumphant note: "we went to sea and did not die." To the Western ear, the simplicity of this account, its power, and its religious tinge ("God saved us") hark back to the archetypal sea crossing of Exodus, the sojourn in the desert, and the arrival in the Canaan. But here the ironic gap becomes an abyss, in the knowledge that Moses has been supplanted by traffickers, that the sea did not open to let them walk on *terra ferma* but swallowed them up, sparing only a fortunate few, and that the Promise Land turned out to be an internment camp, followed by a dubious welcome further north, if not outright deportation back to Africa. The classical precedents for perilous crossings and extended wanderings throughout the Mediterranean world (the *Odyssey* and the *Aeneid* obviously come to mind) also provide stark contrasts to the saga of these exiles, devoid of leaders and lacking any providential guidance to bring them to safety in a better place.

But it is the memory of a more recent Mediterranean crossing to which the title of Rosi's film bears witness. The history of the Allied advance from Northern Africa to Sicily created the *fuocoammare*, the fire at sea, which flared in the night sky when British rockets struck a Sicilian fishing boat, La Maddalena. "The sea turned red," Samuele's grandmother told him. "It was wartime." This event became the subject of a popular song, whose words have since been lost, but whose music was used to furnish both the opening soundtrack of the film and one of the selections requested by Zia Maria for the local radio broadcast on a day when weather prevented her fisherman son from going out to sea. While this catchy, upbeat music gives no indication of the tragic occurrence that inspired it, Rosi interprets this gap as an index of the split realities of life on Lampedusa, "where there is tragedy but also ... the distance [established] by light-heartedness."

That distance – that ability to experience tragedy yet live separately from it – is the guiding principle behind several of the film's narrative strands.[5] One such thread involves the exploits of an underwater fisherman. Nameless, intrepid, and clad in elaborate diving gear, this character attracts Rosi's curiosity both on land and at sea as he treks from his modest home on the rain-drenched streets of the town across a rocky terrain to the forbidding coastline, where he does a series of breathing calisthenics before plunging deep into the wintry currents, leading Rosi to remarkable feats of underwater photography in the process. We spectators, unaware of this diver's purpose in braving the elements, eventually come to understand that he is a trapper of sea urchins – a prey far too humble to warrant the heroic efforts involved in their capture. While Rosi admits to his own perplexity about this subplot – "sometimes I include things I don't quite understand" – his musings in this particular regard are telling. That this individual could plough the depths of the very waters that spelled disaster for the shipwrecked migrants proves that "the sea is not just a tomb ... In the [diver's] apnea, there is a breathing space, a moment of reflection." In a less generous afterthought, Rosi notes that the diver's obliviousness to the tragedy unfolding in these same waters enacts "a desire not to connect." This character's use of an underwater flashlight to light his way provides an imagistic link to the beacon of light trained on the water's surface during night-time rescue operations, making explicit the parallel between these two activities, with all of the ethical implications that such a comparison entails.

But by far the most prominent example of indifference to the migrant crisis emerges in the story of Samuele, told in fourteen vignettes sprinkled throughout the film that chronicle his activities, from crafting slingshots and wandering about the island's harsh landscape to slurping up spaghetti drowned in calamari sauce, flubbing an English vocabulary drill at school, and undergoing doctors' appointments for eye testing and shortness of breath. Because this is also the time for Samuele to begin his education on the water, the sea-faring episodes begin in the cabin of a stationary boat with the boy's extensive questioning of his uncle, who has travelled the world as a sailor and whose reports contain none of the exoticism or romance of such a life, only its boredom and privations. Samuele's maritime education continues in a scene strikingly juxtaposed with that of the Nigerian rhapsode, who ended his harrowing account, as we saw above, with the line "We went to sea and did not die." Now the film cuts to Samuele, sprawled on the deck of his uncle's boat as it cuts through the waves, sending the boy to the railing in the throes of seasickness, while a newly caught cuttlefish breathes its last on the floorboards at his feet. His uncle's advice is that he develop his "sea legs" by spending time on a pontoon, or on a boat docked beside it. The final chapter in Samuele's education involves a rowing lesson that takes an amusing turn when his little craft gets caught in the moorings of boats tied to a nearby pier. The understated humour of the incident emerges in Rosi's choice to cut from the spectacle of Samuele's doomed efforts at self-extrication to a shot of his boat being towed by the expertly navigated craft of an older friend.

In none of these exercises does Samuele directly experience the migrant crisis – proof of the detachment that is possible even on such a tiny slice of land, despite the global implications of the drama playing out on its shores. Samuele's attitude of detachment, excusable for a child at the threshold of adulthood, is not confined to his literal storyline, but rises to the level of allegory thanks to an optical impairment diagnosed at the film's midpoint. During an eye doctor appointment, as Samuele looks straight into the camera through a set of glasses used to measure visual acuity, we learn that he suffers from "lazy eye" syndrome. "Your brain does not register the images from your left eye," the doctor explains. Wearing a patch on the good eye will "force your brain to use the lazy eye and to make it work ... very slowly, we must accustom you to using it." The implications of this diagnosis and treatment for Rosi's consciousness-raising aims in *Fuocoammare* are not far to seek.[6] The innate human reluctance to confront painful truths creates a blind spot in the brain, correctable by external intervention that strengthens the metaphorical lazy eye.[7] Rosi's film is that external intervention. It should be emphasized that Samuele's casting in the film had nothing to do with this optical weakness. The emergence of this poetically charged malady was pure coincidence – an example of the *autofecondazione* arising from Rosi's evolving relationship with Samuele over the course of time. The lazy eye was the "metafora casuale ma perfetta – la nostra politica ha l'occhio pigro" (casual but perfect metaphor – our political system has a lazy eye). Needless to say, it is the "un-lazy eye" of radar technology, highlighted throughout the film in the rotating surveillance towers on shipboard, that transmits the knowledge to counter the malady of public indifference.

While premeditation played no part in much of the film's design, one preordained element did determine the course of Rosi's work on *Fuocoammare* – the decision to anchor his film in the experiences of a young boy. Strikingly, that choice did not fall on a migrant child, and with the exception of the Nigerian rhapsode, no individual refugee was singled out for attention in the scenes devoted to their plight. What we get, instead, are collective images of their ordeal, conveyed through the language of numbers: 250 on board, 150 on board, 90 on board, 840 on board. The footage of rescue operations abounds in medium and long shots of the mechanics involved in transporting the survivors, often draped in iridescent thermal blankets, to rubber boats and then to larger vessels before landing on shore, and finally taking them on buses to reception centres for initial pat-downs and picture-taking purposes. In the most harrowing shots, Rosi filmed a mass of entangled corpses in the airless hull of a ship whose engine fumes transformed this space into a gas chamber.[8] Throughout the episodes of rescue, the camera cuts to facial close-ups of migrants who look straight into the camera, sometimes displaying discomfort though not downright refusal to be filmed. In these shots, it is clear that the subjects have consented to be photographed, and the camera always maintains their dignity, and the sense of a damaged inner life under their expressions of suffering and endurance. Such close-ups dominate the scene in the reception centre, where men are shown lined up against a wall to be frisked, and photographs are taken with placards featuring the number assigned to each individual, along with a label marking Lampedusa/Linosa (the latter an adjacent island in the Pelagians) as his or her place of arrival. One woman in a hijab is urged to show her hair, and a brief moment of tension arises when she resists, but then she relents by showing a thin line of locks above the forehead. In an extremely poignant shot, one migrant attempts to arrange his features into a smile – a vestige of the photographic etiquette of a better time. The sequence ends with a man who gazes into the camera with infinite melancholy, his handsome face fixed in what looks like an ebony mask. As Paolo Mereghetti insightfully put it, "even the reception camps are filmed with modesty and respect. There is never voyeurism in Rosi's images, but rather, the effort to show what eyes that are too lazy, feign not to see."[9]

Amidst the pathos and suffering of the reception centre scenes, comic relief emerges in the soccer game organized by the refugees to pass the time and discharge the pent-up energies of young men too long restrained in cramped vessels and bureaucratic line-ups. The humour begins with a joke on us spectators, when one character proclaims, "After Somalia, Libya; after Libya, Sudan; after Sudan, other countries," in what sounds like the solemn listing of stops on a non-linear journey of migration. Instead, we're witnessing the laying down of rules for a soccer league, complete with arguments about the inclusion and elimination of teams, in what amounts to a satire of international relations, ending in harmony and agreement. There follow clips of soccer games accompanied by chants of "Go Syria," "Go Eritrea!" creating a facsimile of successful international relations over and against the dystopian reality of their current plight.

Significantly, the rescue workers receive no such cinematic treatment. Their faces are obscured by antibacterial masks, their bodies are encased in protective white uniforms, and their operations are carried out in the most matter-of-fact manner, devoid of self-dramatization. The quiet heroism of these rescue efforts, Rosi's avoidance of rhetoric in these scenes, is one of the most powerful undercurrents of the film, reaching its apogee in the focus on body bags, hoisted on board and laid out on deck. With dignity and discretion, Rosi's camera chooses to linger on a shot of three workers in impeccable white uniforms who gaze out to sea in an attitude of waiting, with two of the body bags partially in view in the front foreground. What the workers await is soon revealed in the cut to the aforementioned scene of mass death by asphyxiation in the hull of the boat whose living victims have already been transported to safety.

Among the many imagistic cross-references of this beautifully structured film is that of the face, featured prominently in the footage devoted to the migrant narrative, but prefigured in earlier episodes. Chief among them was Dr. Bartolo's previously mentioned "discovery" of the second facial profile on the sonogram screen, and its promise of new life, over and against the dire images of the slides on the doctor's computer representing the tragic crossing of the 840, threatened with shipwreck and burned, sometimes fatally, by diesel fuel. The fetal image, the only one on the sonogram screen legible for us viewers, suggests a triumph of prenatal technology, and reminds us of the maritime rescue efforts that made it possible for this pregnancy to progress to term. A second explicit focus on faces occurs during the war games played by Samuele and Mattias in a cactus grove. After carving the plants' fleshy leaves into primitive facsimiles of the human face, the boys let loose a barrage of slingshot fire, inflicting grievous wounds on some of these leafy countenances, which then require bandaging up with several layers of masking tape.[10]

This scene of target practice fits into the film's larger thematic focus on weaponry, enshrined in the British rocket fire that produced the *fuocoammare* and exemplified, in a primitive register, in Samuele's slingshot. Later in the film, the boy will graduate to more sophisticated munitions when he brandishes an imaginary machine gun in pursuit of aerial prey. But as his story progresses, this advance in weaponry is interrupted by a foray onto the prairie at dusk, as Samuele makes his way, unarmed, into a thicket of vegetation. This is the most intimate and lyrical scene of the film, illuminated by the boy's flashlight, which reflects off of the twigs to produce a filigree effect. Wearing his eye patch, he penetrates into the heart of the thicket, where he discovers a small bird on a low-lying branch. Rather than target the creature, Samuele communes with it, making a chirping sound that the bird answers in kind, and petting it with the end of a twig broken for peaceful purposes.

Samuele, wearing the patch over his lazy eye, mimics a bird call and receives a response from the tiny creature that patiently accepts the boy's efforts to examine it under the glare of his flashlight, and to pat it with a twig.

In keeping with the film's optical allegory, we can read Samuele's newfound gentleness as proof that the rehabilitated left eye has enabled him to entertain an alternative viewpoint – one that replaces relationships of violence and power with those of equality and communion. But the film's final frames undo the possibility of this happy ending, leaving Samuele perched on the pontoon bridge, without his eyepatch, armed with the imaginary rifle that he compulsively shoots and reloads. This disturbing finale invites larger questions about the degree to which human aggression is innate and ultimately unmodifiable, or culturally conditioned and hence amenable to change. Samuele's primeval hunting instincts seem to point in the former direction, and his machine gun fantasy indicates that contemporary cultural incentives to violence may be abetting those tendencies, bringing them technologically up to date.

"Your position please?" This was the query posed by the helicopter dispatcher in response to the desperate call for help in one of *Fuocoammare*'s early scenes. This question, writ large, hovers over the entirety of Rosi's film. At its most concrete, the query concerns the geographic coordinates of the imperilled vessel, but it could just as easily apply to the position of Lampedusa itself, suspended between Africa and Europe, between the developing and the developed world, between the ethical claims for humanitarian aid and the political limits on it, between ancient cultural archetypes and modern innovation, between primitive and contemporary technologies – in short, between Samuele's slingshot and the sophisticated search-and-rescue equipment of the Italian Guardia Costiera. But the ultimate addressees of the question are the viewers of this film, witnesses to the ongoing migrant crisis through the bombardment of mass media coverage while the events themselves are taking place, while there is still time to intervene. When Rosi asks us, through this understated account of the crisis whose gravity emerges all the more powerfully for its quiescence, "your position please," what will we answer?

PART FOUR

Leadership

Chapter Nine

The Ironist and the Auteur: Paolo Sorrentino's *Il Divo: La vita spettacolare di Giulio Andreotti* (*Il Divo*: The Spectacular Life of Giulio Andreotti), 2008

Direction: Paolo Sorrentino. *Screenplay*: Paolo Sorrentino. *Cinematography*: Luca Bigazzi. *Editing*: Cristiano Travaglioli. *Sets*: Alessandra Mura. *Costumes*: Daniela Ciancio. *Music*: Teho Teardo. *Cast*: Toni Servillo (Giulio Andreotti), Livia (Anna Bonaiuto), Giulio Bosetti (Eugenio Scalfari), Flavio Bucci (Franco Evangelisti), Carlo Buccirossi (Paolo Pomicino), Giorgio Colangeli (Salvo Lima), Alberto Cracco (Don Mario), Piera Degli Esposti (Signora Enea), Lorenzo Gioielli (Mino Pecorelli), Paolo Graziosi (Aldo Moro), Gianfelice Imparato (Vincenzo Scotti), Massimo Popolizio (Vittorio Sbardella), Fanny Ardant (Herself), Renato Zero (Himself).

Synopsis: The film opens with a glossary of names, organizations, and events involved in the dizzying array of scandals, suspected criminal entanglements, and power mechanisms that characterize Giulio Andreotti's tenure at the helm of the Christian Democratic party over the last decades of the twentieth century. Actor Toni Servillo, cosmetically moulded into an astonishing likeness of the historical Andreotti, appears on screen bristling with acupuncture needles in his search for a migraine remedy. In this creepy guise, he delivers a short soliloquy about his success in defying a doctor's prognosis that he had only six months to live, while "the others" have all succumbed. A rapid-fire montage follows, chronicling the assassinations of journalist Mino Pecorelli, bankers Robert Calvi and Michele Sindona, liquidator lawyer Giorgio Ambrosoli, fellow Christian Democrat Aldo Moro, and anti-Mafia activists General Dalla Chiesa and Giovanni Falcone. The

---

This chapter originally formed part of "*Il Divo:* A Discussion," *The Italianist* 30, no. 2 (2010): 245–57. Reprinted by permission of Taylor & Francis.

action proper of the film begins with the onset of the protagonist's seventh term as prime minister in 1992 and ends with his 1995 trial for Mafia ties. During that three-year period, the Andreotti government falls when one of his key allies, Vittorio (The Shark) Sbardella, defects. This spurs a campaign among Andreotti's remaining loyalists for the election of their leader to the rank of Presidente della Repubblica – an honourary post that nonetheless confers on its holder a considerable measure of power and prestige. In a second rapid-fire montage of violent deaths – this time by suicide – Sorrentino catalogues the victims of "Tangentopoli," the judiciary investigations into bribe-friendly government officials that exposed the rampant corruption of the Christian Democrats and their coalition partners, the Socialists. During an interview with the protagonist, Enzo Scalfari, editor of Italy's highly influential left-leaning newspaper *La Repubblica*, confronts Andreotti with his implication in "every scandal that has afflicted [his] country" in what amounts to an inventory of the protagonist's clandestine wrongdoing. With the capture of Totò Riina, notorious mastermind of the Mafia's war against the state, the testimony of the *pentiti* – mobsters who cooperate with the law – leads to accounts of Andreotti's fabled "kiss" with the "boss of bosses." In one of the film's most striking scenes, Sorrentino stages an imagined monologue on the part of his protagonist, who stares into the camera and vehemently defends his history of public malfeasance in the name of a divinely ordained mission to preserve the status quo. In the film's final sequences, Andreotti is subjected to a barrage of charges levelled against him by governmental committees, journalists, and ultimately a panel of judges. Throughout all this, only one of the deaths he caused over the years continues to haunt him – the murder of Aldo Moro, which could have been averted had he agreed to negotiate with the Red Brigades. The film ends as it began, with written captions on screen – this time with texts announcing Andreotti's absolution from charges of Mafia association and of ordering the death of Mino Pecorelli.

"Your irony is atrocious," the priest Mario comments in the confession booth to which Giulio repairs several times throughout *Il Divo*. "Irony is the best cure for death," Giulio counters.[1] "And the cures for death" he adds, "are always atrocious." Though the dramatic setting of the confessional may lead us to believe that Don Mario is referring to irony of a strictly verbal sort – the rhetorical device by which literal utterance and intended meaning are set in opposition to one other – the priest's accusation goes far beyond Giulio's penchant for the witty turn of phrase, to an attitude of detachment that licenses virulent actions within the public sphere. And it is this particular form of irony, understood as a relationship of dissociation and disjunction, that comes to dominate the film's entire strategy for representing a character who himself lives life "ironically." In the case of Giulio, "irony is the best cure for death" for reasons both cognitive and political – it allows him the intellectual distance to step back and think dispassionately about his own existence as it rushes toward its mortal end, while affording him the power to undertake "atrocious cures" by orchestrating the destruction of those who would threaten his own survival: political, literal, or both.

Ironia, construed as "sentimento di pacato, disincantato e divertito distacco nei confronti della vita e dei suoi problemi" (a sentiment of calm, disenchanted, and amused detachment in the face of life and its problems) according to the broadened definition of the term,[2] thus governs the relationship between surface and substance in Sorrentino's portrait of the man behind the longevity and the moral ambiguity of Italy's First Republic. Because Giulio's own attitude of ironic self-distancing makes him an unreadable "signifier," impossible to interpret at the literal level, Sorrentino must follow a double representational strategy, at once adopting his protagonist's detachment at the level of form while nonetheless denouncing the moral abdication that such detachment entails.

Thanks to this two-tiered approach, *Il Divo* comes to mark a new phase in the Italian cinema of civic engagement – one that defines itself in a relationship of "afterness" with respect to the tradition of neorealism and its offshoots in the second half of the twentieth century. Sorrentino's film signals a major step beyond this storied precedent, at once challenging its linguistic orthodoxy – the belief in the referential reliability of filmic signs – while reinforcing the urgency of its imperative to monitor the Italian national condition. The "afterness" of Sorrentino's achievement in *Il Divo*, then, inheres less in the impulse to supersede the earlier moment than to advance it through a process of linguistic remodelling that incorporates contemporary media codes while preserving the moral agenda of this hallowed tradition. In so doing, Sorrentino's work offers a compelling example of what Pierpaolo Antonello and Florian Mussgnug have termed "postmodern *impegno*" where the contemporary vogue for stylistic virtuosity – including the use of pastiche, abundant citation, semiotic playfulness, imagistic saturation, and decorative exuberance – can coexist with an ethics of political engagement in the arts.[3] As such, Sorrentino's achievement harks back to the *cinema* politico films of Francesco Rosi, Elio Petri, and Paolo and Vittorio Taviani in the 1960s, 1970s, and early 1980s, whose penchant for spectacle and stylistic departure from the naturalism of neorealist cinematography can be seen as important harbingers of *Il Divo*'s "postmodernized engagement with civic concerns."[4] In the cases of Petri, the Tavianis, and now Sorrentino, it is irony that opens the breach between the filmmakers' spectacular formal values and their denunciation of social ills, where stylistic bravura foregrounds the films' artifice while preserving the cognitive and moral relevance of its "signifieds."

Sorrentino's ironic take on his representational task in *Il Divo* is evident from the moment that his film's subtitle – *The Spectacular Life of Giulio Andreotti* – appears on screen. The incongruity of pairing *this* adjective with *this* particular proper noun reveals the magnitude of Sorrentino's challenge – to transform the man variously nicknamed "the hunchback, Moloch, the fox, the salamander, eternity, the man of gloom" into the hero of triumphant spectacle. At first glance, nothing could be less cinematic, less prone to fulfilling the medium's need for movement (*kine*), emotion, and glitz, than the portrait of this geriatric, physically inert, verbally inexpressive, funereal figure of state.[5] And no scene is more illustrative of this paradox than the one of the celebration thrown by Paolo Pomicino, the minister of the exchequer, to inaugurate Andreotti's seventh term as premier.[6] The festivities are in full swing, with frenzied dancing to the throbbing beat of Caribbean drummers, and everyone is in Dionysian motion, from the grey-haired members of Giulio's inner circle to the scantily clad *cubiste* shimmying on pedestals lining the walls. As the camera makes its way through the rooms of bouncing and gyrating revellers, like a late-arriving guest who surveys the scene before deciding whom to approach and what attitude to strike, it enters an unexpected zone of order and calm – Giulio is sitting in statuary stillness, receiving a series of well-wishers who wait patiently in line to pay their respects. The contrast between the dancers' up-to-date exertions and this solemn rite of feudal obeisance could not be more stark. Giulio's very presence in such a festive space is rich with incongruity – the New Age freedom so exuberantly announced by these uninhibited revellers is effectively annulled by this ceremony of allegiance to the man who incarnates and underwrites the status quo.

The political/cultural irony enacted on the dance floor will be reinforced in a later gala celebration, choreographed this time in a manner far more sedate and age appropriate for Giulio's generation. Observing the dancing couples from the sidelines, Giulio is approached by a woman who bluntly inquires: "Have you ever danced, President?" As if pondering the same question, but from the detached, anti-literal perspective of

Sorrentino's *Il Divo* 141

This group has gathered to be photographed as members of Andreotti's government upon his election to a seventh term as prime minister.

the ironist, Giulio answers without a moment's hesitation, "All my life, *signora*." For the man who lives life at one remove, whose literal existence is a mere facade behind which the hidden operations of power and influence can be wielded, dancing can only be experienced *as* metaphor. For Giulio, the physical act of the dance is meaningful solely in that it points beyond itself to the one "signified" that fuels his existence: the power to lead the ritualized, synchronized, and shifting movements of political alliances across the ballroom floor of national life.

The film's Giulio is not always motionless, however – with the curved shoulders of the hunchback but the straight lower spine of the martinet, he walks robotically forward or backward with hardly a sideways glance. These movements are structured within the choreography of another dance, one that plays a strategic part in the corporeal dimension of Sorrentino's satire: the tightly constrained steps of Giulio's early morning constitutional down Via del Corso, surrounded by a police escort whose gait is closely matched with the prime minister's own. Not to be overlooked is the musical score to which this dance is performed – the hymn-like melody of Fauré's Pavane pour Orchestra Op. 50, accompanied by a chorus of celestial sweetness that elevates this ritual to the level of a religious procession, as if Giulio were the icon to be paraded through the streets on his saint's day.[7]

The quietness of this scene, along with all of those set in Giulio's household, is played off against the frenzied busyness and kinetic energy that his presence seems to trigger in others. Activity swirls around him – he is the calm within the vortex of public affairs that stretch from 1992 to 1996, and it is in this ironic counterpoint that Sorrentino confronts the enigma at the core of his protagonist's career: to what can we attribute this unprepossessing character's inordinate power and influence over the political life of his country?

Sorrentino's film, I would argue, is nothing more than an enactment of that question at the level of form. *Il Divo*'s cinematic ingenuity – its ability to commandeer such a plenitude of signs at the service of Andreottian representation – works as an analogy to the power mechanisms put in place by the story's own protagonist. The film's stylistic virtuosity – its flamboyant camerawork, performative excess, over-the-top musical score, obtrusive editing, theatrical lighting, dazzling set design – call such attention to *Il Divo*'s formal surface that its object of representation ceases to be Andreotti himself, and becomes instead the imaginative processes set in motion by the very idea of representing Andreotti on screen. It's as if Sorrentino were saying, "Watch me think *cinematically* about Andreotti, look what the medium-specific language of film allows me to say about him," and conversely, "Look at how Andreotti pushes me to expand my own powers of cinematic inventiveness."

Sorrentino's struggle to forge an adequate representational approach to Andreotti parallels the attempts of the characters within the film to overcome the protagonist's steely reserve. "I have to tell you that I will never understand you. I don't know you," sighs Vincenzo Scotti, the minister of the interior whose report on Salvo Lima's murder is met by Giulio's bizarre riff on his cousin Teresa's hypochondria. Franco Evangelisti, Giulio's devoted right-hand man, offers his boss a gift only to be greeted with an ingratitude verging on cruelty. Livia, Giulio's strong and sympathetic wife, seems incapable of connecting with her husband on the level of sentiment – a failure poignantly revealed as the couple watches television and Renato Zero's romantic crooning impels the woman to gaze lovingly upon her spouse to the lyrics of "I migliori anni della nostra vita" (The Best Years of Our Life).[8] Giulio returns her gaze for the briefest instant before reverting to his habitual state of emotional withdrawal, and Livia finally looks away, her face grim with disappointment. Toward the end of the film, in what promises to be a moment of climactic self-revelation, Giulio offers to share his darkest secret with Francesco Cossiga.[9] After exquisitely preparing his interlocutor (and us) for the removal of the mask that had shielded him from any form of knowability up until now, he reveals his secret to be a teenage crush on Mary Gassman, the sister of the actor Vittorio – an infatuation that ended after adolescence. In Giulio's flirtation with self-disclosure during his tête-à-tête with Cossiga, we realize that our desire for true intimacy with the protagonist will never reach consummation – that we, like Cossiga, will never experience the unmasking that *il divo's* teasing promise had so coyly intimated, and so maddeningly withheld.

But this scene is not entirely without hints of what lies underneath the façade of impassivity. In a telling moment of reminiscence, Giulio asks Cossiga:

> Do you remember Nenni, enthusiastic, passionate? He used to say, "I head a commission and I will balance the Railroad budget." I answered: "In the insane asylum, those who don't say that they're Napoleon say that they'll balance the Railroad budget." We hated each other, Nenni and I. But how much esteem, how much reciprocal respect!

Nenni is the anti-ironist, for whom the will to committed action translates into declarative sentences, and the present indicative of political power leads to future-tense verbs of decisive deeds. Giulio, the ironist, living at one remove from the language of action, signals his will to obstruct its workings by denying the real-world referentiality of Nenni's speech – speech that can only point to the hallucinated "signifieds" of the mentally deranged.

Giulio's psychological impenetrability takes the outward form of a rigid and hidebound physique. His face has a heavy fleshiness that seems to prohibit expressivity, as if the weight of the skin alone would require a superhuman effort to break a smile or dissolve into tears (he admits to having done the latter three whole times in his life). His body seems to be enclosed in a suit of armour that steels him against not only external assault but also errant humanizing impulses from within. Such is his temperamental and physical reserve that Giulio's closest associates are reduced to deciphering small hand movements in order to understand the thought behind his gestural innuendoes. "If he twiddles his thumbs, it means that you are saying something intelligent. If he twirls his wedding ring, it means that he disagrees with what you're saying. If he begins to tap his fingertips together at regular intervals, it means that within five minutes, you will be told to leave." This is the lesson that Signora Enea, Giulio's secretary, imparts to the unnamed character played by Fanny Ardant who awaits an audience with him and longs for behavioural directives. "And when his eyes suddenly dilate, what does it mean?" the lady asks, to which not even the wise and experienced Enea can supply an answer. "I don't know. No one knows." As the metaphoric windows of the soul, dilated eyes should reveal an over-abundance of meaning, but Giulio's hold no such signifying promise. The hands may enact responses of a purely situational sort, but the kind of consequential truths conveyed by the eyes will remain forever beyond interpretive reach.

Giulio's opaque persona does not lead Sorrentino to give up trying to represent the man's enigma, however. On the contrary, the filmmaker revels in its challenge to his ingenuity, and its dare to the cinematic medium through which that challenge must be met. Giulio's personal inscrutability means that Sorrentino must entrust the signifying task to what Pudovkin called film's "plastic material," or, in T.S. Eliot's terms, the filmmaker must find medium-specific "objective correlatives" for Giulio's inner state.[10] Hence the work of representing Giulio must be displaced onto the externals of mise-en-scène, lighting, music, camerawork, and editing – a requirement that Sorrentino fulfils by making *Il Divo* a series of stagings of brilliant visual and musical set pieces that serve to externalize and dramatize what would otherwise elude representation. Thus *Il Divo* consists of an unusually high number of short scenes that function like modular units, whose position within the temporal sequence could change without causing any appreciable difference in the film's overall structure. This procession of short scenes serves not only to give quick movement to a portrait that is inherently static and therefore lacking in cinematic interest, but also foregrounds the prodigious effort of mounting this spectacle, and with it the "primacy of style" and the "strong staging" that have become Sorrentino's authorial trademark.[11]

The setting most illustrative of Giulio's state is the domestic one, enshrouded in darkness, confined by the geometry of corridors and doorways, heavy with the funereal furnishings so dear to the bourgeoisie of the century previous to his own.[12] A number of individual instances of virtuoso staging punctuate the film, and deserve special mention. The arrival of the "brutta corrente" (bad current) of Giulio's henchmen, including Paolo Pomicino, Vittorio Sbardella, Cardinale Angelini, and Giuseppe Ciarrapico, is performed as a series of automobile ads, where gleaming top-of-the-line vehicles disgorge important-looking men, met by a pair of stunning female associates (in the case of Pomicino) or by a valet who opens the doors, and all recorded by a slow-motion camera to give *gravitas* to the proceedings.[13] Sorrentino's camera has a distinct fondness for corridors – the lugubrious one where Giulio paces with insomnia as dark-hued statues look on, the bright and gleaming one of the "Transatlantico," outside the Chamber of Deputies, where

Pomicino slides exuberantly from one end to the other, and where an empty skateboard ominously careens before morphing into the image of Giovanni Falcone's incinerated and plunging vehicle of death.

Giulio's diplomatic visit to Moscow is characterized by two bravura set designs – one in the guest bedroom, presided over by a huge portrait of Marx, and one shot outdoors in a scenario that could come straight from a winter greeting card, with huge snowflakes falling on a white-blanketed urban background as Giulio takes a stroll, tightly bundled up in fur-trimmed Russian finery. In another set piece fraught with satiric innuendo, Sorrentino stages the dinner where Giulio's disciples will "nominate" him to run for the presidency as a Last Supper. Absent is the Judah figure, Sbardello, who has already defected to the enemy faction, but Giulio's acceptance of the mantle of leadership smacks less of a vocation for Christian martyrdom than of a belief in his divine right to power.

Perhaps most illustrative of Sorrentino's focus on stagecraft is the scene of Giulio's fabled kiss with Mafia boss Salvatore Riina. This formulaic sealing-of-a-pact is set in an incongruously modernist interior, decorated with furnishings of the cleanest design and works of art of impeccable taste, as the two men enact the solemnities of an ancient rite. When Giulio rises to meet the approaching Riina, the prime minister's face superimposes itself over a contemporary painting of a huge anthropological mask, with obvious relevance to his own facial immobility.

In Sorrentino's displacement of the signifying task from the object of representation to the "plastic material" of the film medium itself, staging was not the only focus of his attention. Music played a vital role in maintaining the ironic breach between the staid and sombre Giulio and the flamboyant cinematic vehicle on which he is borne. The blend of Europop (Cassius, Trio, Barbara Morgenstern and Robert Lippok), classical (Fauré, Vivaldi, Saint-Saëns), romanatic retro (Bruno Martino, Renato Zero), and electronic/orchestral (Teho Teardo) creates a musical overlay that refuses "background" status, engaging the film's visual and dramatic elements in a dynamic interchange. Such eclecticism and jarring musical choices recall Pasolini's "contaminated" use of music to challenge conventional matchings of image and sound. Sorrentino has frequently referred to *Il Divo* as a rock opera – a term whose inappropriateness to the Andreottian subject matter sums up the incongruous relationship between music and image that drives the entire film.[14] Early in *Il Divo*, for example, the montage of assassinations is accompanied by the silly sonorities of "Toop, toop"; somewhat later, the apostles toast their leader as they plot his political apotheosis to the sentimental stanzas of "La prima cosa bella" (The first beautiful thing); the kiss exchanged between Andreotti and Riina is accompanied by the crooning lyrics of "E la chiamano Estate"(And they call her summer); and the final shot of the courtroom that awaits the verdict on Giulio's Mafia connection is followed by the rock beat and inane lyrics of "Da da da/ Iche lieb dich nicht du liebst nic nicht/Aha aha aha."

In addition to set design and musical interventions, Sorrentino's formalism involves the emergence of an iconic language that takes on a life of its own. The replay of the skateboard and Falcone's plunging car, the recurrence of the solemn procession down Via del Corso, the reappearance of Moro in captivity, are but some examples of this trademark device. Most obvious is the glass of effervescent aspirin with which several scenes begin, as Giulio stands alone in his kitchen or participates in group festivities while other characters fill their glasses with wine to begin the meal or to drink a toast. This tonic then sets Giulio apart – he must treat his headaches as others treat themselves to a beverage of alcoholic refreshment with the pleasure and conviviality that such drinking evokes.

Of utmost significance is the fact that Sorrentino connects Giulio's headaches to his political longevity. "They predicted my death," he says of his rivals. "I survived. It was they who died. In exchange, I have struggled against atrocious headaches for my entire life." The adjective "atrocious" returns us to the confessional scene with which this chapter began, where Giulio defended his "irony" as one of the "atrocious cures for death." Giulio's irony and his headaches are thus linked – they both derive from the logic of power that requires death-dealing strategies for survival. If irony is what keeps Giulio detached both from his own mortal existence and from the lethal measures he must take to stave off political death, then the headache is the price he must pay for such self distancing, the *emicrania*, or the pain in one half of the head, that symbolizes the self-division of the ironist.

From the very opening scene, where Giulio recounts his survival at the expense of others and his life of chronic migraines, Sorrentino announces that this is *his* Andreotti, an extravagant invention, part caricature and part hallucination.[15] Like Fellini, whose auteurship was built into the very language of his film's titles (*Fellini Satyricon, Fellini Roma, Fellini Casanova*), Sorrentino announces from the start that this Andreotti is the figment of his imaginative process as governed by the creative possibilities available to the plastic material of film. Illuminated amidst the darkness, speaking directly to us as he lifts his face into the camera's full view, Giulio recounts that he is undergoing acupuncture treatment, as evidenced by the cluster of needles protruding weirdly from his forehead. At the meta-level of the film's reflection on its own workings, the needles act as devices for holding in place the mask that has moulded Toni Servillo's face into a caricature of Andreotti, and we realize that Sorrentino's Giulio is being "assembled" before our very eyes. At the same time, however, the film cleaves closely enough to historically verifiable (and recent) facts to make this Giulio recognizable as the public figure with whom we are all familiar. Sorrentino does not follow the rules of the game that Petri, for example, plays in *Todo modo* (in accordance with Sciascia's own lead), where well-known political figures are cloaked in fictitious names and represented by generic embodiments of power. Sorrentino, like Moretti in *Il Caimano*, plays a more daring game, directly naming and pointedly caricaturizing the butt of his satire – who was at the time of the film's making and first screenings a living and still politically influential figure – while at the same time announcing his freedom to take radical authorial liberties with his film's referent.

This game of referential ambiguity becomes immediately evident in the use of captions, which are common markers of documentary intent, grounding the work in the precise time-space coordinates of a factual and verifiable historicity. But the pretence of investigative seriousness is immediately undercut by the playfulness of Sorrentino's captions – the upside-down hanging corpse of Roberto Calvi is accompanied by a correspondingly upside-down caption, which turns right side up as the photogram rotates 180 degrees to its proper position. Similarly, the caption identifying Michele Sindona, poisoned in his jail cell, is shown backwards until the camera circles around the dying man so that we can read his name from left to right. Throughout the film, captions dance about the screen in a kind of free-floating semiotic abandon. Words, like images, have come untethered from their "signifieds." By transforming the convention of the caption – hitherto understood as an indicator of its film's unproblematic and unequivocal referentiality – into one more sign to be manipulated at will, Sorrentino asserts his ambiguous relationship to the truth-claims of the documentary genre and its offshoot in the films of *cinema politico*.

What this means is that the viewer of *Il Divo* is constantly shuttling between two competing planes of signification – Sorrentino's as he weaves this extravagant and fanciful portrait of the most influential figure in post-war Italian history, and the spectator's own knowledge of Andreotti as gleaned from six decades of current events. The viewing experience of *Il Divo* thus involves a recognition in the etymological sense – a re-cognition, or a re-knowing, filtered thought the prism of Sorrentino's extravagant auteurship. The film's penchant for enumeration is eloquent in this regard. *Il Divo* abounds in lists: the violent deaths that make up Sorrentino's initial montage (Pecorelli, Calvi, Sindona, Dalla Chiesa, Ambrosoli, Falcone); the accusations by the journalist, Scalfari, in mid-film that produced the "È un caso?"(Is it by chance?) litany of scandals connected to Andreotti, including not only the above-listed examples but also the killings of Pisciotta and Giuliano; the chain of suicides following upon the Tangentopoli investigations; the intrigues of P2 and Licio Gelli; the charges of collusion with the Mafia; and the series of questions posed at trials to which Giulio answers, "I don't recall." Whereas the public that has lived through the Andreottian era has experienced these allegations incrementally, scattered over the past several decades, the film reports them as a lump sum, and thus not only reactivates the memory within the collective Italian consciousness, but does so in an aggregate whose sheer volume is incriminating. In other words, the film's allusions to this itemized list of egregious wrongdoing amounts to an archive – the counterpart to the archive that Giulio himself keeps in order to intimidate and silence those who would threaten his hold on power. Explaining in voice-over why he never presses charges for libel, Giulio offers the following rationale: "I have a large archive, given that I don't have much fantasy. And every time that I speak of this archive, whoever must be quiet, stays quiet, as if by magic." The source of the protagonist's power, this documented memory of incriminating information about potential detractors thus finds in Sorrentino's film an equivalent "dossier" of facts, not secret like Giulio's but open and accessible to the public, which has already been apprised of them over the years. It is in assembling this counter-archive that Sorrentino delivers the full brunt of his film's satiric blow, for in so doing he contests and defeats the protagonist's career-long effort to bridle his critics and to obstruct the workings of an open and democratic society in its pursuit of justice. The very making of this filmic counter-archive is therefore performative in that it undoes the injunction to silence that Andreotti's archive was designed to instil. The resulting sense of plenitude, of unlimited semiosis released by this process, reflects and exalts the emancipatory power of successful satire.

However, with the exception of two oneiric sequences – that of the fabled kiss exchanged with Riina and that of Giulio's confession, addressed to an imagined Livia – Sorrentino never makes an explicit pronouncement regarding Giulo's guilt.[16] What he offers us, instead, is an inferential strategy based on purely cinematic means – a strategy I would label "guilt by montage." In the virtuoso sequence that cross-cuts between the assassination of Salvo Lima and the horse race attended by Giulio, the strategic juxtaposition of the prime minister's exhortation "Vai" (Go!) addressed to his favoured horse, and the killer's burst of gunfire, offers a strong suggestion of the link between Andreottian cause and homicidal effect. At the very same time, Sorrentino undercuts the charge of culpability implicit in this use of parallel montage by introducing a gesture that is as subtle as it is significant. Cross-cutting between the finale of the horse race and the fall of Lima, Sorrentino shows Giulio twisting his wedding ring in a clear indication of disagreement and displeasure, according to Signora Enea's earlier dictionary of gestures. The cinematographic verdict on Giulio's guilt remains open.

There is one violent death, however, for which Sorrentino directly implicates Giulio, and he does so by imputing to his protagonist a conscience racked by guilt.[17] When Don Mario, his priest-confessor, asks him if he feels qualms about the immediately preceding murder of Lima, Giulio says no, "I suffer for Moro." And it is to Moro that the film entrusts its decisive judgment of Giulio. Throughout *Il Divo*, Moro has spoken in voice-over. "What to remember of you, Honorable Andreotti? It's not my intention to evoke a grey career. This is not the crime. What to remember of you? A cold, impenetrable director, without doubts, without palpitations, without a modicum of human pity," he had said over the visuals of Giulio in the snowy Moscow landscape. "You will pass without leaving a trace, you will pass to the sad chronicle that suits you especially now," he predicted in voice-over as Giulio paced the corridors in the throes of insomnia. "My blood will fall on you," the voice-over later foretells, in a variant of the biblical charge of deicide that is laden with Christian Democratic irony. These three instances of vocal commentary by Moro are superimposed over scenes of Giulio in solitude, followed by a cut to Sorrentino's simulation of the infamous photograph of the prisoner posed before the banner of the Red Brigades in the narrow cell of his fifty-five-day captivity. The nightmarish recurrence of this image places us in the "prison cell" of Giulio's own mind – a mind haunted by the spectre of the colleague whose sacrifice to the cause of political expedience weighs so heavily on the protagonist's conscience.

For Giulio, the ghost of Moro closes up the ironic distance between himself and the events of lived experience – Moro forces him to take possession of his actions and their consequences. Whereas Giulio has been his own "narrator" throughout the film, speaking in voice-over and constantly reinforcing the critical distance that irony has afforded him, it is Moro who becomes the final narrator, uttering a concluding judgment that collapses the distance between the ironist and his deeds. As Giulio sits in the courtroom and the camera closes in on him,

This is the voice-over summation of Andreotti's career as delivered by Aldo Moro against the backdrop of the courtroom where the protagonist awaits the outcome of his trail.

transitioning from colour into black and white (signaling the refusal of moral shadings), we hear Moro's condemnation of him in a diatribe that warrants quoting at length.

> Andreotti remained indifferent, livid, absent, closed in his somber dream of glory. He had to move forward his reactionary design ... In the presence of all this, what did the incurable pain of the old bride [Moro's widow], the destruction of a family, matter? What did all this matter for Andreotti, once he had conquered the power to do evil as he had always done evil throughout his life? All this meant nothing.

The last word on Giulio is therefore left to Moro – a character who speaks from beyond the grave, having experienced the extreme logic of Giulio's own "cure for death." At this point, Sorrentino's camera momentarily assumes a position on the judge's bench, looking back at Giulio and thereby adopting a judicial subjectivity that we as spectators are invited to share.[18] With this final shot, Sorrentino aligns the camera's view with the words of Moro, who by now has seized control of Giulio's narrative and replaced the protagonist's ironic, guilt-denying voice with the value-laden and morally charged one of his most illustrious victim. In other words, the breach between actions and their moral consequences made possible by Giulio's ironic self-distancing is healed by the intervention of Moro, who makes the signifier "Giulio" a legible sign – one that overtly broadcasts its burden of guilt.

But *Il Divo*'s final verdict rests on a judgment call of another sort: one involving the extent to which Sorrentino's Giulio may be seen to coincide with history's Andreotti. By posing that question to viewers, and thereby engaging us in an interpretive process fraught with moral implications, *Il Divo* marks a new phase in the Italian cinema of *impegno*, consciously situating itself in a state of "afterness" with respect to the mimetic film language used by the likes of Rossellini, De Sica, Visconti, Rosi et al., while foregrounding the Italian national story, no matter how enigmatically represented. Perhaps we could argue that the film's moral force derives precisely from that enigma – the space between Sorrentino's Giulio and history's Andreotti is the space that we must now inhabit as spectators and citizens, charged with the responsibility for rendering judgment on a history that is still playing itself out in the present tense of Italian life.

Chapter Ten

Liberating the Left: Toward a Humanist Language of Engagement for a Post-political Age in Roberto Andò's *Viva la libertà* (Long Live Freedom), 2013

Direction: Roberto Andò. *Screenplay, based on the novel* Il trono vuoto *by Roberto Andò*: Angelo Pasquini, Roberto Andò. *Cinematography*: Maurizio Calvesi. *Editing*: Clelio Benevento. *Costumes*: Lina Nerli Taviani. *Sets*: Giovanni Carluccio. *Cast*: Toni Servillo (Enrico Oliveri/Giovanni Ernani), Valerio Mastrandrea (Andrea Bottini), Valeria Bruni Tedeschi (Danielle), Michela Cescon (Anna), Gianrico Tedeschi (Furlan), Eric Nguyen (Mung), Andrea Renzi (De Bellis), Judith Davis (Mara), Brice Fournier (Bertrand), Massimo De Francovich (Presidente), Renato Scarpa (Arrighi), Anna Bonaiuto (Evelina Pileggi), Stella Kent (Hélène).

Synopsis: This is a story of twin brothers, Enrico Olivieri and Giovanni Ernani (their last names differ because Giovanni has replaced his with the title of a beloved Verdi opera), whose adult paths intersect at two moments of great personal and political consequence. In the first instance, Giovanni steals the beautiful and alluring Danielle from his brother's arms. This devastates Enrico, and the brothers will remain estranged, as a result, for the next twenty-five years. During this time, Enrico shuts down emotionally, abandons his artistic passions (literature and cinema), and enters the highly disciplined, ideologically rigid terrain of the political left, where he ascends to the heights of party leadership in the role of secretary. When Enrico takes a plunge in national opinion polls, dashing his party's electoral hopes, he mysteriously disappears, prompting the brilliant expedient on the part of his assistant, Andrea Bottini, to secretly replace the secretary with his twin brother. Bottini manages to track down Giovanni as an outpatient of a psychiatric facility, where the latter had been confined after a career as a philosopher whose extremely unconventional views had ill adapted him to life on the "outside." In the hope that Giovanni's medications will restrain his behavioural extremes, Bottini installs him in his brother's role, where the imposter flourishes, winning mass support for his free-spirited, and deeply humanistic political vision. Because Giovanni must fill in not only for Enrico's "day job" but also take up residence in his brother's household, a strong emotional tie develops with the latter's wife, who has suffered from her husband's abandonment. In the meantime, Enrico has fled to Paris, where he has taken refuge in the home of Danielle, now married to the Asian ex-pat filmmaker Mung, an idol of the cultural avant-garde. While in France, Enrico's tender side is awakened by the couple's warm and precocious young daughter Hélène. With Danielle, who is working at a film shoot as the "continuity secretary," Enrico travels to the Camargue region in southern France, where he is recruited to replace the film's assistant set designer, who had taken ill, and where he has a fleeting affair with the young and voluptuous Mara. Enrico catches wind of headline news about Giovanni's success in garnering resounding public support for the party of the left back in Italy. The twins' story reaches its climax when Enrico decides to return to Rome, and Giovanni simultaneously disappears from view. After a sleepless night of searching for the latter in vain, Bottini returns to the office to find the party leader back at work. But the identity of the man seated behind the desk remains shrouded in ambiguity.

Early on in Roberto Andò's novel *Il trono vuoto* (The Empty Throne), which serves as the basis for the film *Viva la libertà* (Long Live Freedom), directed by the author himself, leaders of the major opposition party hold an emergency meeting in the wake of the sudden and mysterious disappearance of their secretary, Enrico Oliveri. While most party members are distraught at this turn of events, some see it as a blessing in disguise, given Oliveri's recent nosedive in public opinion polls. At the close of the meeting, a committee member gives voice to the group's confusion in strikingly literary terms: "One can't tell if it's a comedy or a tragedy."[1] To these options, a colleague adds a third, definitive possibility, "[It's] a farce." For Andò, instead, another literary genre commands centre stage in *Il trono vuoto* – that of the novel, both as the object of much self-conscious reflection within the text and as the blueprint for *Viva la libertà*, whose very filming is anticipated in the story's plot.

Though Andò's decision to give separate titles to the novel and film indicates a desire that the two works stand on their own, they exist in a symbiotic relationship so intense and profound that, like the relationship between the twin brothers on which the narrative is based, the full cultural and political impact of his achievement cannot be understood by considering them in isolation. Instead, the novel and the film complete each other – their juxtaposition sets in motion a series of anticipations and fulfilments that make the process of cinematic adaptation into a model for the building of a humanist discourse for a post-ideological age.

Central to an understanding of the synergy between novel and film is the career path of the protagonist, Enrico Oliveri, who had given up a youthful vocation for literature and a passion for filmmaking to enter the arena of politics. The commingling of these three spheres produces a series of passages in the novel of considerable interpretive note, and the result is a plea for a new understanding of political engagement that combines the imaginative freedom of literature with the performative outreach of film. In other words, the story is about the emergence of a new, post-ideological *homo politicus*, whose birth as traced in the pages of Andò's novel will come to its fullest fruition in the frames of the film.

In narrative terms, Andò's aim requires splitting the main character in two, invoking the ancient topos of brothers identical in appearance but antithetical in temperament, harking back at least as far as Plautus's *Menaechmi* and echoing throughout literary history.[2] Within this particular brothers' plot, Giovanni represents the extreme version of what Enrico would have become had he not repressed all his creative impulses and emotional vibrancy in the wake of his failed romance with Danielle. Just as Giovanni had replaced Enrico as the object of Danielle's affection twenty-five years prior to the action of the film, so will he replace his brother again, this time as the head of Italy's major progressive party, capable of winning the public's support by forging a political style diametrically opposed to the tired sloganeering and claustrophobic interparty manoeuvrings that to date had characterized the left. This infusion of energy into the political scene comes from a powerful source: Giovanni's background as a free-thinker, who spontaneously counters the cynical, sclerotic, and narrowly technical approach of his peers with culturally rich and value-laden appeals to a public hungry for alternatives.[3] When pressed by colleagues to state his views on allying with the centrist party to form an electoral majority, Giovanni answers by humming a refrain from Verdi's *La forza del destino* and walking out of the room reciting lines from haiku. Outside party headquarters, the same question is posed by a waiting throng of journalists, to whom Giovanni replies that the only possible alliance "is with the conscience of the people." With this evolving and increasingly eclectic response Giovanni rejects the conventional rules of political engagement, coining instead a language of cultural pastiche and moral accountability that completely disarms his interlocutors. Whether it be the invocation of Hegel in an interview for *Corriere della sera* or advice to his party nemesis (articulated in the novel, p. 152) to study the strategies of self-invention espoused by "la cultura Punk," Giovanni is able to wield his wide-ranging erudition to waylay his would-be detractors. These ingenious rhetorical strategies amount to a sweeping indictment of contemporary political culture, with particular emphasis on its failure of imagination.

Not least among the cultural influences to play a prominent role in Giovanni's galvanizing effect on others is music, his signature art form. His virtuoso performance of Schubert's Sonata in A major one midnight enchants Enrico's wife Anna and awakens in her longings that will eventually culminate in an embrace by the sea. "The frenzied rock of Chuck Berry" (in the novel, p. 89) fuels the exuberant gyrations of Giovanni and fellow dancers during one of his regular visits to the recreation room of the asylum after being discharged. And of course, there is the aria from *La forza del destino* that Giovanni hums rather than answer a question about his willingness to forfeit the integrity of party by allying with the centrists. That Giovanni has traded the last name "Oliveri" for "Ernani" – the title of a Verdi opera – is of obvious consequence for the way in which this character will bring music to bear on his campaign to forge a national popular language of consensus. Verdi's association with an art form capable of inspiring a will to activism in the name of a liberation ideology needs no belabouring here. Of equal importance is the performativity at the source of opera's power to move hearts and minds through the combined forces of music, the poetic word, and dramaturgy. These forces alone would be insufficient, of course, were they not enacted in the flesh-and-blood persons of performers, as witnessed by an audience made receptive to the creator's vision by the power of spectacle. In this light, Andò's adaptation of his own novel to the screen begins to make sense. The film is, of course, a performance of the text, a physical realization of it, though without the common experience of time and space shared by actors and audience, made possible by the material conditions of live staging. Nonetheless, seeing Toni Servillo's on-screen persona give his body and voice over to Giovanni's fervent delivery of his words turns speech into speech acts, saying into doing, in a secularized incarnational process by which an idea becomes flesh.

Andò's cinematic adaptation of his novel is especially attuned to Giovanni's personal triumph over the written word. Throughout *Viva la libertà*, Giovanni is filmed before backdrops festooned with slogans,

Against this backdrop littered with tired verbiage, Giovanni supplies the missing element for the awakening of *homo politicus*. The English translation of the on-screen text is "There's a word that is particularly dear to me."

against which he performs his exuberant *libertà*. Every time we observe Giovanni in political settings – in the meeting room of the party leadership, in an auditorium for an address to the party faithful, in a great outdoor campaign rally – we are invited to measure the power of this orator's performance against the anemia of the catchphrases inscribed everywhere. In the party's hermetically sealed meeting room walled off by plexiglass panels imprinted with terms such as "youth, immigration, action, research, project, employment, school, opportunity," Giovanni defies the talking points built on this lexicon and, as mentioned above, answers a question about a cynical political manoeuvre by humming the overture to *La forza del destino*. But it is in his first formal address to the party faithful that he shows his determination to break free of the language that has failed to fire the imagination and win the consensus of a populace hungry for change. Walking into the auditorium, Giovanni removes his trench coat as if preparing for battle, and standing in front of a screen emblazoned with the title "The challenge of growth" he delivers his own, completely unrelated response – "Today I'm speaking about the catastrophe" – signaling his intent to leave the comfort zone of conventional oratory and propel his listeners into a radically new terrain of political communication.[4] Later in the film, at a huge outdoor rally, he will appear on a platform backed by a billboard full of the usual buzzwords and some new ones, only to explicitly denounce the poverty of such sloganeering. "There is a word that is particularly dear to me. It's not here. Passion." And with this he liquidates the catalogue of assorted issues, the parataxis of party thinking, the pragmatic items of the leftist agenda, to craft a syntactic flow of compelling concerns and moral urgencies, borrowed verbatim from Brecht's poem "To One Who Hesitates." In other words, Giovanni refuses to stay "on message," especially when that message does nothing to address the wellsprings of popular discontent or to strike the longed-for notes of utopian desire.

In performing his flamboyant *libertà*, Toni Servillo's Giovanni walks a fine line between displaying full control of his charade and teetering on the brink of madness. When the character first realizes that he's been mistaken for Enrico, he wears the amused look of self-satisfaction that indicates his mastery of the simulator's art. But when his faithful factotum Bottini guarantees Enrico's wife Anna that "there's some method to his madness," we sense that the young man may not really be so sure. Serving as the stand-in for our own position as viewers, Bottini rides a roller-coaster of reactions from angst to admiration and back, as the private chorus of Giovanni's act. The performer's first public appearance in his brother's guise signals the pattern of anxiety followed by relief that his behaviour will trigger throughout the film. It is the morning of his first day "on the job," and the security guards, along with Bottini, have gathered in front of the Oliveri apartment building. "Is the secretary back?" asks one of the men, to whom Bottini answers, in a tone more hopeful than convinced, "Of course." When Giovanni descends the stairs, head down, to the background strains of *La forza del destino*, the awaiting men snap to attention, but when the impersonator lifts his head to the light, Bottini and another agent register their concern. Once Giovanni reaches for his glasses (one of Enrico's trademarks) and puts them on, he dissipates any doubts about his ability to take on the role, prompting Bottini to relax, while another agent chirps, "Welcome back, Your Honor." The shift from anxiety to relief is musically accompanied by the move from a minor to a major key in the *Forza del destino* musical backdrop. In a voice seemingly accustomed to wielding authority, Giovanni announces "Now we can go," and he enters the chauffeur-driven car with his bodyguards as if he had done so every day of his professional life. This brief scene, so minimalist in word and gesture, reveals the totality of Giovanni's "entrance into character" – his power to conjure up an alternative persona, to imagine a radically different mode of being, and to "body forth" that understanding through the nuances of gesture and speech. At the meta-level of Tony Servillo's performance, the audience's awareness of this actor's much deserved renown – his seeming ubiquity and his astonishing versatility – is set in motion by scenes such as these.[5]

Bottini's assurance that Giovanni is in control of his charade will be put to the test throughout the film as the impostor manages to keep us, along with his factotum, off balance, feeding our fear that his *libertà* will take him across the boundary between eccentric genius and insanity. This angst is reinforced by the medical certificate, read by Bottini early in the film, to the effect that "Mr. Giovanni Ernani no longer presents forms of interpretive delirium of reality, and therefore he will be released from this facility. We consider essential the continuation of the treatment with Lemidal, which should be taken in the same daily doses as administered in the Institute." At this point, the viewer may well imagine any number of dire scenarios – what if the prescription runs out, what if he takes the wrong pill, what if he simply refuses to submit to any further pharmacological control?

But it soon becomes clear that Giovanni's "interpretive delirium of reality" is infinitely preferable to the realist interpretive stance that has kept the left in a permanent state of opposition to the powers that be. Bottini's shy confession that he would "vote" for Giovanni over Enrico makes clear his own sense that the former's delirium is not a pathology at all, but the very tonic needed to revive the party's fortunes. Bottini's own transformation under the influence of Giovanni, whose euphoria becomes contagious – granting the younger man licence to relinquish his inhibitions, to entertain utopian dreams, and even to muss up his own hair – enacts in miniature the enlivening effect that Giovanni is having on the Italian body politic as a whole. Indeed, it is difficult to overcome the suspicion that Giovanni's institutionalization was not the result of pathology but of the threat he posed to the status quo, delivered in the philosophical treatise that he published entitled *L'illusione di vivere* (The Illusion of Living), whose contents we never learn but whose critique of the dominant ideology we can all too easily infer.[6]

If Giovanni's eccentricities are an act, geared toward safeguarding his *libertà* from the constrictions of social norms, those eccentricities are not confined to the realm of the verbal. In this regard, Giovanni's obsessive-compulsive habit of walking along the lines of floor patterns had been worrisome to observers such as Bottini. But the assistant's concerns upon witnessing this strange footwork are soon allayed when Giovanni's eccentric gait gives way to the steps of a torrid tango, glimpsed behind the closed doors of the room in which he is meeting with the female chancellor of Germany, who is a most willing partner in this pas de deux. The lady, wearing a fetching pink suit and matching high heels, has clearly anticipated a diplomatic encounter with a frisson of romance. As Bottini eavesdrops through a keyhole, his eyes first alight on two pairs of shoes, neatly arranged on the floor, while two pairs of bare feet execute intricate dance steps nearby. Convinced that his boss's eccentric behaviour, far from leading to disaster, is yielding surprising and successful results, Bottini himself experiments with walking along the lines of the floor as he withdraws from his place of surveillance.

In another scene of equally disastrous potential, Giovanni is ushered into the *mappamondo* (world map or globe) room of the Quirinale, where he proceeds to play a game of catch-me-if-you-can with the president, darting behind and around the two huge spheres that give the room its name.[7] The camera, sometimes following him in his movements and sometimes assuming the point of view of the president, who is trying to locate Giovanni amidst the globes, is clearly participating in the gamesmanship of this whimsical scene. Giovanni accompanies his antics with variations on lines from *Hamlet* – "To be or not to be, better to be as if we had already disappeared, or to disappear completely to return to be." With this last phrase, he essentially captures the entire plot of the film, and its recipe for political renewal – Enrico Oliveri must disappear so that he can return as the new *homo politicus*, modelled on Giovanni's example.

The title of Andò's adaptation, *Viva la libertà*, is a multiple indicator of how the film will liberate the power of the written word of the novel, activating its potential to reach audiences and leading them on the path of *impegno*. At the ideological level, the film's title refers to the emancipation from fear – "the fear of existing" in Giovanni's words, and its corollary, the fear of winning. Enrico's life, up to the point of his self-banishment, displayed such fear in his obedience to fixed programs, to narrow platforms, and to the rigid principles of logic that had keep the left perennially on this side of power. But the film's title also has a submerged structural meaning, available only upon recourse to the novel, in a mise-en-abyme of considerable complexity and depth. Within the novel, the film that is being shot by Danielle's troupe involves the story of Maxime, Annette, and Paul, members of a chamber music trio with the improbable name "Viva la libertà." When asked about this strange title, Maxime explains: "It contains the secret of playing together, of making music, at least for us ... To hold high the banner of freedom within [the confines of our] bond, I believe that this is the mystery of the interpretation, to find one's own freedom within the constriction of the musical score" (169).

The logic behind the trio's title "Viva la libertà" within the novel comes to have ever-expanding meanings, extending from the aesthetic principle of freedom of performance within the bounds of a musical score, to the political principle of creativity within the limits of party protocol, to the relationship between the twin brothers' temperaments, whose impulses toward unruly creativity, on the one hand, and rigid discipline, on the other, finally converge to form a harmonious composite whole.[8] By choosing to give his film the name of the trio within the novel, Andò makes this the key to the "mystery of the interpretation" (in Maxime's terms) of the entirety of the story. While it is obvious that Enrico and his party need Giovanni's example of exuberant freedom to be "reborn," Giovanni in turn needs the prefabricated structure of another man's accountability to social and political norms in order to work his magic. Without the "musical score" of his brother's political celebrity, without the strictures imposed by the role into which Giovanni was suddenly cast, he could not have demonstrated his bravura talents and resurrected the party that had been waning under Enrico's leadership. Without the script of Enrico's life that he had been recruited to enact, we can imagine Giovanni isolated within his post-asylum existence, writing sequels to *L'illusione di vivere*, to be read by the exclusive membership of his cult following. The brothers emerge as the yin and yang of a composite unit, the complementary parts of a totality that had been torn apart by the rivalry over Danielle, and that will be recomposed according to the terms of the story's happy ending. That ending will be anticipated by Danielle herself, who tells Enrico, "I loved you both. I loved your right eye and his left one," in a formulation that blends the brothers into a single corporate whole.

Given the all-important themes of doubling and splitting on which the novel is based, it should come as no surprise that the mirror would emerge as an important imagistic device throughout the cinematic version. Within the first two minutes of the film, Enrico withdraws to a restroom to monitor his image in a mirror, and the party's poll ratings on his iPad. After the disastrous meeting of the party's national assembly, he contemplates his reflection again as he undresses for bed in his sterile apartment. Later in the film, the the mirror moves beyond the function of mere self-reflection to assume a host of more complex meanings. In a fleeting montage, Enrico uneasily contemplates the spectacle of twin girls in a café, chewing in unison, then gazes upon a newspaper with a photograph of Giovanni under the headline "Never [have there been] such clear words: 'The only possible alliance is with the conscience of the people,'" followed by a cut to the Olivieri apartment where Giovanni, dressed in one of Enrico's smart suits, admires himself in a mirror. The progression of these three editorially conjoined scenes is important, for it runs the gamut from uncanny self-recognition and self-entrapment in the condition of twinship to a discovery of the emancipating possibilities of such a condition. While the specularity of the twin girls in the cafe obviously causes Enrico discomfort, the mirroring effect of Giovanni's newspaper photograph, like the reflection in the Olivieri's apartment mirror, offers the possibility of becoming another, of inhabiting an alternative identity, with all of the *libertà* that such an option entails. The mirror becomes a medium for self-distancing, for seeing the self as an object of another's consciousness, and therefore as an occasion for creative reinvention. Both the newspaper photograph-as-mirror and the looking glass in the Olivieri's apartment reflect back to their respective observers the virtue of incorporating the specular other into the self. That mutual insight comes to fruition as the brothers' identities merge to form the unitary protagonist of the film's final frames.

Leading up to this ending is an intricate sequence that requires close analysis if we are to fathom "the mystery of the interpretation" of the film as a whole. Just as suddenly as he had appeared on Danielle's doorstep toward the beginning of the film, so Enrico will steal away in the night to return to Rome, leaving only a cursory note to explain his motives. In the throes of insomnia, Danielle wanders the house to find the note, whose contents we hear recited by Enrico in voice-over. In the note, he expresses his pleasure in reconnecting with her and in observing her role as continuity secretary of the film production, requiring her to "protect the order of events from senselessness." As we listen to Enrico's voice-over commentary, fleeting images on screen illustrate his inner thoughts as he speeds away from the Camargue. First we are shown an overhead shot of twin boys clad in matching pajamas, lying in bed, one positioned upside down with respect to the other, before the frame rotates 180 degrees clockwise so that the boys switch places with respect to their original on-screen alignment. Enrico's voice-over comment on Danielle's role as continuity secretary of the film-shoot-within-the-film occurs here – she is the *filo conduttore* (the connecting thread) that allows him, retroactively, to see the order of his life's course. Most importantly, the progression of these shots offers a shorthand version of Enrico's newfound understanding with regard to the brothers' plot. The camera movement that reverses the twin boys' alignment in the first frames of the sequence anticipates Giovanni's replacement of Enrico in Danielle's affections. Enrico's return in adulthood to Danielle and the delicate suggestion of the new insight gained by reconnecting with her after so many years leads him to imagine a scenario for fraternal reconciliation. That hope is

The enigmatic nature of the secretary's smile maintains the ambiguity of the character's identity and the open-endedness of the film as a whole.

inscribed in the final shot of the sequence, with the twin boys lying awake, now side by side.

This glimpse into Enrico's reverie is followed by a series of intercuts between his journey from the Camargue back to Rome and Giovanni's simultaneous cab ride through the city, past the Colosseum to Piazza del Popolo. At one point during this parallel montage sequence Enrico removes his glasses, making it difficult for viewers to determine which of the twins is being shown in any given shot. Our confusion as spectators is shared by Bottini in the very last episode of the film, when he shows up for work the morning after searching in vain for Giovanni, who had disappeared the previous night. While he is relieved to see the secretary seated at his usual desk, something strikes Bottini as slighty off – an impression reinforced by his boss's summary of all that had taken place during his absence. "Pascal bet on the existence of God on the basis of probability. We politicians bet on the sense of history. You preferred to bet on a madman." As Bottini turns to leave, however, the secretary hums a few bars from *La forza del destino*, prompting the younger man to peek back through the semi-closed door and survey the seated figure, panning from head to toe to note the impeccable grooming, smart apparel, and elegant footwear associated with Enrico. The secretary, conscious of Bottini's gaze, turns toward him with a look of statuary solemnity. The camera fixes on him in close-up, so that we, along with Bottini, can study the slow ripening of his expression into one of suppressed merriment. The secretary does not break into a wide-open grin, but keeps his lips closed as their corners slowly arc upwards until the teeth barely come into view, and his eyes begin to twinkle. Accompanying this subtle movement of the facial muscles, the orchestral strains of *La forza del destino* interrupt the silence of the scene to announce the symbolic co-presence of Giovanni in the film's final frames. That the secretary does not burst out laughing, and refrains from assuming the exaggerated features of the mask of comedy, is important here. The smile, the sartorial details, and the musical commentary maintain the ambiguity of the film's conclusion – which of the brothers is occupying the party leader's place?[9]

The film's lack of closure signals a striking departure from the novel, which offers a realistic scenario of Enrico's return to assume the position of power made possible by Giovanni's interventions, while the latter withdraws to his old quarters in the half-way house. But the film stops short of such a clear-cut ending, leaving us to wonder, as we join Bottini in contemplating the enigmatic smile of his boss. The gentleness of the protagonist's hilarity is significant – he is not laughing *at* Bottini, just as the film is not laughing at us. It is letting us in on a secret, regarding not the literal identity of who is wielding power, but what makes one deserving of such a privilege. That the concluding image of the man behind the desk is a composite figure raises the film's finale to the level of allegory: the new *homo politicus* combines the yin and yang of the two brothers, the anarchic exuberance of the one and the disciplined accountability to sociopolitical norms of the other, "freedom within the constrictions of the musical score."

The final words of the film belong to Enrico/Giovanni as he dismisses Bottini for the day, noting that the young man is tired and needs to get some rest. "We have many things to do," the secretary states, in a conclusion that is also a new beginning. Without prescribing a concrete agenda, without specifying the items of the to-do list for the revived party of the left, the film is nonetheless a call to action.[10] The first-person plural of the secretary's address extends far beyond the confines of the "*io*" and "*tu*" of this immediate exchange. It expands to embrace an entire political class that must radically rethink its identity, jettisoning the cynical strategies of inter-party manoeuvrings cloaked in false pieties and empty sloganeering, in order to adopt a new language – one of conscience, dignity, commitment, passion corresponding to the heartfelt, value-laden, ethically charged vision of "the political" proposed by Giovanni. It is the humanist cultural matrix – the verses by Brecht, the sonata by Schubert, the lines by Shakespeare – that gets beyond the clichés of politics as usual, disarms the cynics, and reaches out to a public hungry for a new vision of the *res publica*. And it is Giovanni who releases the closet humanism of Enrico, whose "fear of existing," like his party's fear of winning, had prevented him from using the power of his own cultural erudition to connect with the humanity of his constituents. And finally, it is cinema, with its appeal as spectacle, that can release the power of the written word, endowing Andò's novel with the flesh-and-blood performativity that can reach a mass public in the arduous and all-important task of liberating the left.

Chapter Eleven

The Pontiff and the Shrink: Nanni Moretti's *Habemus Papam* (We Have a Pope), 2011

Direction: Nanni Moretti. *Subject and screenplay*: Nanni Moretti, Francesco Piccolo, Federica Pontremoli. *Cinematography*: Alessandro Pesci. *Music*: Franco Piersanti. *Editing*: Esmeralda Calabria. *Sets*: Paola Bizzarri. *Costumes*: Lina Nerli Taviani. *Cast*: Michel Piccoli (Melville), Nanni Moretti (Giovanni Brezzi, psychoanalyst), Renato Scarpa (Cardinal Gregori), Jerzy Stuhr (Vatican spokesman), Margherita Buy (psychoanalyst).

Synopsis: After a prologue consisting of archival footage documenting the funeral of John Paul II, Moretti recreates the pageantry of the conclave that will elect the pope's fictitious successor. An impasse emerges after several votes fail to produce a consensus, and on the following round a dark horse, Cardinal Melville of France, is finally elected pope. Totally unprepared for this result, Melville is stunned but reluctantly accepts the charge. When the announcement is to be made from the balcony that overlooks St. Peter's Square, a primal scream echoes through the corridors as the pope-elect gives vent to his anguish and refuses to appear before the crowd. The crisis prompts Vatican officials to call in the help of a psychoanalyst, Giovanni Brezzi (played by Moretti himself). Forbidden from using any of the techniques of his profession, and forced to interview Melville in the presence of a gaggle of cardinals, the therapist is able to make no progress in treating his patient's anxieties. A decision is made to secretly send Melville to a therapist outside Vatican grounds, and he is ferried off for a session with the ex-wife of Brezzi, who is herself a psychologist but holds to a different diagnostic procedure based on the tenet that all problems stem from "deficit di accudimento" (insufficient parenting). As Melville exits her office building, a moment of distraction on the part of his guards allows him to escape and disappear into the depths of the city. There follow three days of freedom in which the neo-pope is able to have direct contact with life outside the Vatican bubble. His most consequential encounter is with a theatre troupe that is rehearsing Chekov's *The Seagull*, a play whose lines Melville knows by heart, having harboured dreams of an acting career in his youth. In the meantime, Vatican officials are staging an elaborate charade to mask Melville's absence, insisting that he has withdrawn to his papal apartment for a time of reflection. He is finally tracked down in the theatre during opening night of the Chekov play and whisked back to the Vatican, where he is expected to address the crowd in St. Peter's Square. As the cardinals gather for this triumphal moment, and the people wait in feverish excitement below, Melville finally appears on the balcony, only to announce his refusal to accept the papal charge.

Given the tumultuous events that overtook the Vatican in February 2013 with the abdication of Benedict XVI, it's tempting to wonder if Moretti had some deep insight into the unrest in the soul of the pope when he made *Habemus papam* (We Have a Pope). The 2011 film offers an uncanny preview of those events in the story of an elderly French cardinal named Melville who wins the vote of the Vatican conclave but ultimately declines the office.[1] Considering the history of factionalism, financial corruption, administrative ineptitude, and sexual abuse cover-up that plagued the Vatican at the time, what is striking about Moretti's film is its restraint – its modesty and reticence in refusing to privilege these concerns.[2] In effect, Moretti de-politicizes and de-theologizes his character's choice to reject the papal mantel, and he does so by a process of subtraction, focusing our energies on the inner struggle of a desperate soul caught in the throes of a decision that is existential in nature. To the degree that *We Have a Pope* delivers a critique of the church, Moretti's target is limited to the institution's secrecy and detachment from the lives of ordinary men and women. The satiric bite of the film is further softened by the good-natured humour and even affection that suffuses its vignettes of cardinals and assorted other Vatican personnel.[3] But the church is not the sole butt of Moretti's critique. The Vatican must share the film's satiric focus with psychoanalysis, the lay institution that promises an alternative answer to the health of the soul, understood here in the ancient Greek sense of *psyche*. Within the film, "the talking cure" is personified by Moretti, self-cast as the psychiatrist, Giovanni Brezzi, called in to counsel the panic-stricken pope-elect. Reminded by the head cardinal that "the soul and the subconscious do not coexist," Brezzi is denied all the tools of his trade, forbidden to inquire about sexual fantasies, mother-son relationships, frustration or dreams, in his sessions with the traumatized neo-pope. Hamstrung by such prohibitions, the psychiatrist is reduced to the most whimsical of power displays – he ends up organizing a volleyball tournament among the college of cardinals. With this comedic masterstroke, Moretti manages to target both the clergy and the shrink, lampooning the competitiveness of the former, whose rivalries must be channelled through sporting activities, and the control mania of the latter, who takes the lead in orchestrating them.

The purpose of Moretti's "soft" satire in *Habemus Papam* is ultimately to sideline the political and theological issues raised by Melville's abdication in order to clear the stage for the film's core drama, which is ethical and existential in nature. But in order to gain the full measure of this film's engagement with the tormented subjectivity of its protagonist, we must take a step back and locate *Habemus Papam* within the context of an evolving filmography, whose representational energies up to then had centred around the on-screen persona of Moretti himself.[4] Until the 2006 film *Il caimano*, Moretti's work had traced the fortunes of his own generational cohort, with the filmmaker in the starring role of Michele Apicella, a thinly veiled surrogate of the autobiographical self. Taller, hairier, and more eccentric than his peers, Moretti's body-on-screen gave hyperbolic expression to the culture for which he stood, making him the tenured spokesman of his generation, the *uomo-simbolo* (man-symbol) of his age. Throughout his corpus of films, Moretti's protagonism had embraced several of the life choices – slacker, teacher, communist party leader, writer/director – that his generation faced in the years following the turmoil of 1968. Of particular interest for our current purposes is the 1985 film *La messa è finita* (The Mass Is Ended), in which Moretti plays the role of clergyman Don Giulio, a variant of the Michele Apicella persona – restless, driven, angry, and unconventional – an inveterate idealist whose utopian dreams leave him acutely vulnerable to disappointment.

We should specify at the outset that Don Giulio's drama in *La messa e finita* never involves the matter of faith, and his adherence to the doctrine of *caritas* is unwavering. Its basis is the theological virtue most tied to right actions in this world, the horizontal bonds that link him to his fellow humans rather than the vertical movement along the axis of transcendence. Herein lies the continuity between the 1968 utopian social project, featured and often spoofed, in Moretti's earlier films and the Christian communitarian dream of *La messa è finita*.

Throughout the film, it is the sacrament of marriage that enacts the religious ideal of *comunitas* in microcosmic form. *La messa e finita* begins and concludes with nuptial celebrations, but within the body of the film, marriages fall apart or fail to materialize, and Don Giulio's hope in the greater possibilities for human connectedness deteriorates to the point of utter collapse. But the bleakness of the film's commentary is tempered by a set of striking stylistic and narrative moves at its finale. After presiding over the wedding ceremony that closes the film, Don Giulio announces his resignation from his parish in Rome. Yet this does not signal his intention to abandon the priesthood. His plans, instead, are to withdraw to a parish in the Tierra del Fuego, "where the people need a friend." At the stylistic level, the film itself undergoes its own form of withdrawal – from a realistic representational mode into the realm of Don Giulio's wish-fulfilment fantasy, characterized by the daydream of ballroom dancing, a motif that traverses Moretti's filmography as the moving image of harmonious coupledom.

It will take twenty-six years for Moretti to revisit the church as a subject for his art, and much will have changed in that quarter century to affect its representation within a rich and evolving filmography. The post-1968 social concerns that found their theological expression in Don Giulio's pursuit of *caritas* will be replaced by the existential preoccupations of the pope-elect, Melville, who will follow the path of *humilitas*. As in *La messa è finita*, *Habemus Papam* involves no crisis of religious belief. Melville's first response to the psychiatric inquiry about his mental state is the emphatic, "I have no problems of faith." Like Don Giulio, the protagonist of *Habemus Papam* is most worried about the relationship between religious belief and right action in the world – in the case of the latter film, he is daunted by the responsibility for leading a congregation of one billion souls. The weight of his office is literalized in the words that Melville uses to announce his renunciation of the papacy at film's end: "I was chosen, but instead of giving me force and awareness, it crushes me."

The violence of this last phrase is rendered plastically through costuming and mise-en-scène. When Melville first dons the papal mantle he seems strangled by it, and once fully robed he seems unable to stand erect under the sheer physical burden of his new attire. The monumental spaces and overwrought wall coverings of the Vatican rooms are of such a colossal scale that they dwarf Melville's not-insubstantial frame as he makes his solitary way through their expanse.[5] In fact, the central irony of Melville's elevation to the highest office in Christendom is that it shrinks his personhood to nothingness. For him, the papal election means the dissolving of identity – a prospect that emerges in his nightmare of phantasmagoric withdrawal on the part of all those who knew him in his pre-pontifical state. "They began to disappear, they weren't there anymore," he sighs. "So many people whom I knew, they weren't there anymore, *tutto* [everything] has disappeared." This *tutto* is the condition of selfhood, the identity built over a lifetime of cumulative events and encounters. From the moment of his election, that human being in all the richness of his past, his privacy and mystery, no longer exists – what remains is only that which is visible to the public eye, that which can live in absolute transparency in fulfilment of the papal role. When a hotel clerk opines that the Vatican is withholding the name of the new pope because he has died, that supposition contains its own kernel of truth. The private Melville has indeed been laid to rest.

In the film's early moments, Moretti's camera spares no efforts to document the magnificent control and beautifully orchestrated workings of Vatican machinery, revelling in the solemn procession, the chanting of prayers, and the ascent of the marble staircase that leads the cardinals to the Sistine Chapel. But an electrical blackout creates the first hitch in the proceedings, the first lapse in the obsessive protocol of Vatican workings and, in particular, the all-important task of determining papal succession. This momentary power failure will be the harbinger of the personal crisis unleashed by this tightly controlled electoral process

When pressed to explain his crisis, Melville comes up with a litany of negatives: he searches within to find his God-given capacities for leadership "and I don't find anything"; he looks for the expression of a past self and "everything has disappeared, I don't remember anything"; he admits that his head is too full, but he doesn't know of what. The loss of selfhood experienced by the neo-pope is paralleled by the viewers' lack of knowledge regarding his character. Moretti provides no background information about the film's protagonist, who thus emerges as a cipher, a blank slate, devoid of personal history. All we learn is that he harboured theatrical ambitions, which were thwarted by his failure to gain entrance to drama school. In a therapy session with Brezzi's wife, also a psychiatrist, Melville's frustrated career dreams give rise to an elaborate fiction that he invents when asked about his line of work: "What is my job? I'm an actor!" With this utterance, his face lights up for the first time in the film – his expression becomes animated, revealing a hidden wellspring of psychic energy that infuses his entire being with buoyant life. In perpetrating this fiction, Melville rewrites his life story, imagining an alternative autobiography that allows him to wrest control of the selfhood now denied him as pope. By creating the figment of an acting career in his therapy session and by revealing the liberating effect of this imagined calling, Melville sets up the ideal against which the papal election fills him with angst. Papal identity is intensely performative (as we'll see later on), but it abolishes the vital distinction between self and role on which the actor's craft depends. Unlike Pirandello's profoundly tragic view of the life-as-theatre metaphor, requiring elaborate social masking and the impossibility of authentic human interconnection, Melville considers the gap between the person and the role to be essential for safeguarding and sustaining the private self. But the papacy brooks no such distinction. "How dare you?" objects Cardinal Gregori when Brezzi offers a diagnosis of Melville's psychic malaise. "I'm speaking of the man, not the pope," the psychiatrist counters. "But they are the same thing," the prelate insists.

Once Melville gives voice to his acting ambitions, the film bifurcates into parallel forms of stage craft, cross-cutting between the Vatican theatrics to conceal Melville's panic-stricken state from the public and the activities of the theatre troupe preparing a performance of Chekhov's *The Seagull*. Melville is inexorably drawn to the latter – having accidentally bumped into the group during a hotel stay, he tags along with them to dinner and attends a rehearsal of the play. It is in these scenes that Melville is happiest. He is welcomed into the collective with open arms and finally settles into a role for which he feels entirely qualified. He becomes the troupe's dialogue coach, thanks to his prior familiarity with Chekhov's work during his youthful flirtation with a career on stage. The theatre ensemble serves as a utopian community, evidenced in their spontaneous incorporation of Melville into their ranks and their compassion for a fellow actor who is hospitalized with a nervous breakdown and who, upon his return to the troupe on opening night, is met with warmth and grace.[6] Toward the end of *Habemus Papam*, Melville is tracked down in the theatre where *The Seagull* is being performed. When the audience is suddenly invaded by an army of cardinals, Swiss Guards, and nuns, all of whom turn their attention to Melville sitting alone in a box, it becomes clear that the pope-elect has become the unwilling star of the show; his story has upstaged the play.

Of equal interest to the theatrical theme of *Habemus Papam* is the Vatican charade mounted to conceal the fact that Melville has escaped his confines to wander the streets of Rome. In order to convince the cardinals, and by extension the public at large, that the pope is living secluded in his apartment, a member of the Swiss Guard has been asked to occupy the rooms and to promenade behind the curtains, rustling them at intervals, to ensure onlookers that the Holy Father is there. Despite the humour of this performance, it sends a disturbing message about the nature of Melville's pontifical role. For one thing, it underlines the fact that the neo-pope himself was elected merely to put on an act. As the dark horse of the conclave, he was chosen to break the impasse created by the competition among the better-known contenders for office. It was his relative obscurity, the result of a lackluster past career, and not any record of administrative prowess, theological expertise, or reputation for holiness that recommended him for elevation to the highest rank in Christendom.[7] Accordingly, the dumbshow performed by a member of the Swiss Guard enacts, in a low comic register, Melville's own existential doubts about his job qualifications. "I don't know if I'm up to this," frets the young Guard who has been cast as the papal understudy, and who is little reassured by the spokesman's characterization of the role as "pretty easy ... Only a shadow must be seen." This staging of a phantom papacy, these fleeting appearances as a silhouette during the day and a ghostly apparition at night, are all that is needed to convey a pontifical presence to the world.

Among Moretti's most striking moves in *Habemus Papam* is the choice to withhold judgment on his tormented protagonist. In his unwillingness to moralize, in his refusal to condemn Melville's decision as the product of cowardice or spiritual sloth, the filmmaker's approach flies in the face of the cultural conditioning that Italians would bring to a story of papal abdication. Moretti's tolerance of his protagonist's doubts is the antithesis of the most authoritative treatment accorded to this subject matter within the Italian context: Dante's portrait of Celestine V, the thirteenth century neo-pope who "fece il gran rifiuto" (made the great refusal; *Inf.* 3, 1.60) by abandoning the position after only five months in office. Dante makes no secret of his contempt for this character, consigning him to the "vestibule" of Inferno among the "neutrals," those who "lived without infamy and without praise," a condition so base that not even Hell proper will receive them within its confines. "Naked, bitten by horse flies and wasps / faces streaked with blood mixed with tears that are gathered by loathsome worms at their feet," these sinners parade behind "a whirling banner that rushes forward with such speed as to seem unworthy of any fixed place." While Dante the pilgrim fixates on the plight of these sinners, Virgil pronounces them undeserving of further notice: "non ragioniam di lor," he counsels, "ma guarda e passa" (let's not speak of them, but look and pass by).

Moretti, instead, deems papal abdication supremely worthy of "ragionamento," brushing aside the dismissal of it on Christian-moral grounds, and subjecting the issue to the most sympathetic and humane investigations. But Dante is not the only literary model against which Moretti is reacting in *Habemus Papam*. The very name of the film's protagonist invites us to compare this character's abdication with that of another renowned figure, Herman Melville's Bartleby, for whom the line "I would prefer not to" had become a kind of mantra, a manifesto of selfhood within the workplace and beyond.[8] By alluding to Melville's recalcitrant scrivener, Moretti offers an important insight into the specificity of his own protagonist's motivations in making the *gran rifiuto*.[9] Throughout the short story, Bartleby's escalating series of refusals culminates in a refusal of life itself, a definitive withdrawal from the arena of the living, while the Melville of *Habemus Papam* instead makes his *gran rifiuto* in the name of prolonging life, in this case, the life of the private self, whose extinction would have been guaranteed by his acceptance of the papal charge.

Throughout *Habemus Papam*, Melville has been hopelessly inarticulate about his state of mind, unable to give words to the morass of thoughts plaguing him in this time of crisis, understood in the literal, etymological sense of "decision-making." Words come easily to him in only three instances: when he recites entire passages from *The Seagull*, when he talks to himself on a crowded bus in preparation for his inaugural address as pope, and when that speech is finally delivered. It is in the fullness of this public monologue that his astonishing eloquence, withheld until now, is revealed. This is his great star performance, his apotheosis as actor, and it hinges on the existential choice to renounce the office that would require the breakdown of the distinction between the private self and public role on which acting depends.

It is during his odyssey through Rome disguised as a layman that the theological rationale of his abdication takes shape. In his wanderings, Melville chances upon a small parish church in which a young priest is giving an impassioned sermon to a congregation of one worshipper, but the sparseness of the audience does not dampen his fervour as he preaches the virtue of humility. This is the lesson Melville will enact before the tens of thousands crowded into St. Peter's square when he announces his *gran rifiuto*. In so doing, he will carry out his own *imitatio Christi* – his own descent into humility – an analogy suggested by the theologically charged number of days – three, to be exact – separating his election from his renunciation of the papal charge. The Christological model of Crucifixion, the Harrowing of Hell, and Resurrection over a three-day period find their existential equivalent in the death and recovery of personhood experienced by Melville during the course of the film. Far from a blasphemous Christology, I see Melville's abdication as a profoundly authentic commitment to the ideal of humility. In this, I read the film's counterargument to the Dantesque condemnation of Celestine V "per viltà" (from cowardice).[10]

At the level of film language, Moretti enacts the protagonist's own choice of *humilitas* over the grandeur of papal power by subordinating its visual magnificence to the simplest and most fundamental unit of cinematic expressivity – the facial close-up. For all of the fascination

Moretti's *Habemus Papam* 173

Melville's face registers his reaction as he absorbs the impact of the ballot count that builds to a crescendo in his favour.

of Vatican splendour and all of the curiosity aroused and fulfilled by this behind-the-scenes glimpse of spaces and events otherwise concealed from public view, it is the face of Melville that commands centre stage. Every time we catch sight of that visage in close-up, we are seized by a particular form of attentiveness that requires us to read the disposition of facial features, their nuances and shifts, for the slightest clue to Melville's inner state.[11] Film in this sense becomes the art of "micro-physiognomy," as Hungarian theorist Béla Balázs wrote in 1941: "In the close-up, the smallest wrinkle of the face is transformed into a fundamental line of character, every fleeting vibration of a muscle has its pathos that is striking and that is an index of great interior events."[12] The medium-specific power of the cinema inheres not only in its microscopic access to the face, but in its ability to record the fluidity of expressive changes. "An expression does not need to be finished when the next one comes along, and very slowly absorbs it," Balázs continues. "In this binding of visual continuity, the previous expression and the one to follow are already in the present one, thus showing us not only single states of mind, but even the mysterious process of their development."[13]

The protagonist's face becomes a screen within the screen, the privileged surface on which the conflict between the external pressure of events and the character's private impulses plays itself out. What complicates our reading of the face, of course, is its double function as window and mask, whose very ambiguity resides at the source of its signifying power, as Noa Steimatsky argues in her seminal study *The Face on Film*.[14] Of the utmost relevance to a reading of *Habemus Papam* is Steimatsky's analysis of the mechanisms by which the language of cinema activates the power of the face, isolating it from the flow of images via the close-up. In so doing, she reveals how the film steps back from the progression of frames used to advance the plot – where images serve a purely communicative function – allowing the face to come into its own, to be contemplated as an end itself, apart from any utilitarian narrative purpose, as the object of curiosity and wonder.[15] In Steimatsky's view, the facial close-up is a liberating gesture, freeing the image from bondage to its syntactic/semiotic relationship to the image chain, and making possible an alternative form of looking, one that restores the image to its primordial, iconic status and that exerts a deeply irrational and hypnotic hold over the viewer according to Pasolini's ground-breaking essay "Cinema di poesia."[16] This means, according to Steimatsky, that the close-up connects us with the auratic nature of the image, its primordial status as a function of the sacred.[17] As such, the facial close-up assumes hyperbolic proportions and offers the sense of unbounded plenitude – it exceeds the limits of the frame, and shrinks the distance between spectator and screen. By offering us intimate visual access to another human face, the close-up poses the great question of subjectivity itself, challenging us to acknowledge and welcome its mystery.

By liberating the face from its communicative function in the advancement of plot, the facial close-up performs, at the level of film language, Melville's own emancipation from the events that would seal his destiny as pope. Just as the close-up escapes the signifying entrapment of the image chain, Melville has freed himself from the order of papal succession. It is the essential unruliness of the face as image, its indeterminacy, its power to take on "a life of its own"[18] once projected on screen, that provides Moretti with the medium for his message. That message uses the embodiment of the highest authority within the Catholic world to pose questions of enormous consequence in terms neither theological nor political, but ontological, and humanist in nature.

We have travelled a great distance from the altar of the parish church where Don Giulio announced his resignation in Moretti's 1985 *La messa è finita*. Within the fiction of that earlier film, the Morettian character's retreat from the world did not presage a similar retreat at the level of

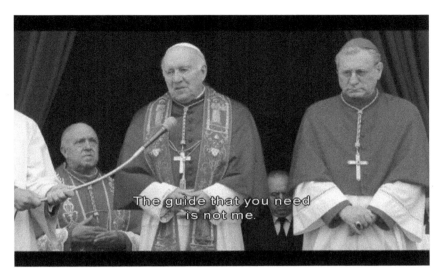

In his first and only public address as pope, Melville announces what Dante would have called the "gran rifiuto" (the great refusal).

the filmography, which would continue to make the author's on-screen persona its central concern. That all changed in 2006 with *Il camaino* (The Caiman) and, most momentously for us, with *Habemus Papam*, where Moretti relegated his character to the margins of the work, perhaps in tacit acknowledgment of the fact that it was time for his generation to renounce its illusion of power and control. By withdrawing to the sidelines, Moretti is clearing the stage for a very different kind of cinema – one that takes on the issue of subjectivity no longer limited to the personal and idiosyncratic terms of his earlier work, but considered now in the more universal terms personified by Melville, who remains, significantly, a cipher. Moretti's use of the facial close-up is thus grounded in paradox: while it is the cinematic device that brings us closest to the subjectivity of a character, *Habemus Papam* never penetrates the mystery of its protagonist's inner life. With immense delicacy and tact, the film acknowledges the incommunicability of the essential self, the unrepresentability of our interior being. It is in this sense that Moretti's film displays its own profound *humilitas*, bowing to the grandeur of that mystery, respecting the privacy of the man who chose to vacate the papal balcony, and by extension the stage of the public world, in order to preserve the integrity of his inner life. Though

Melville's abdication should not surprise us, given his staunch resistance to the pressures upon him throughout the story, the gentleness of Moretti's touch, with its lovely comedic interludes and its whimsical plot twists, leaves us unprepared for the absolute starkness of the film's conclusion. Unlike the ending of *La messa è finita*, which tempers the disappointment of Don Giulio's resignation by offering a flight into musical comedy, the final frames of *Habemus Papam* offer no such cushions against the existential force of its message.

The image of the empty balcony that has hovered over the film since Melville's early refusal to emerge onto it and give the crowd in St. Peter's Square the opportunity to meet their newest pope finds its dire fulfilment in the film's final frames, with the yawning expanse of blackness behind the balustrade, flanked by dark-red curtains that emphasize the emptiness of the papal stage.[19] The principal action of the entire film has been bracketed by these two scenes of vacancy, whose implications extend beyond the confines of the church to embrace the crisis of leadership in Italy and abroad.[20] Transitioning from the balcony now devoid of Melville to the dumbstruck crowd in Piazza San Pietro to the black screen, accompanied by the musical soundtrack of "Miserere" (have mercy on us), the film leaves us to ponder, along with the throng of faithful in the square waiting to greet their new pope, what such an absence portends for us all.

PART FIVE

Women

Chapter Twelve

"It Ended the Way It Should Have Ended": Francesca Comencini's *Lo spazio bianco* (The White Space), 2009

Direction: Francesca Comencini. *Subject*: The same-titled novel by Valeria Parrella (2008). *Screenplay*: Francesca Comencini, Federica Pontremoli. *Cinematography*: Luca Bigazzi. *Editing*: Massimo Fiocchi. *Music*: Nicola Tescari. *Sets*: Paola Comencini. *Costumes*: Francesca Vecchi, Roberta Vecchi. *Cast*: Margherita Buy (Maria), Gaetano Bruno (Dr. Giovanni Berti), Giovanni Ludeno (Fabrizio), Antonia Truppo (Mina), Guido Caprino (Pietro), Salvatore Cantalupo (Gaetano), Maria Paiato (judge).

Synopsis: Set in contemporary Naples, *Lo spazio bianco* tells the story of Maria, a no-longer-young single woman who teaches Italian in a night school for adults seeking to earn their middle school diplomas. A random encounter with a man named Pietro, a single father, leads to a brief affair, but Maria's ensuing pregnancy drives away this commitment-averse lover, leaving the protagonist to decide that she will bear the responsibility for this child alone. In her sixth month of pregnancy, Maria gives birth – an event that turns her life into an anxious vigil in the neonatal intensive care unit, awaiting a verdict on the viability of her daughter's hold on life. During this time, she is emotionally supported by her devoted friend Fabrizio, by a young doctor with whom she forges a love relationship, and by her neighbour, a female judge who has been separated from her husband and children in order to preside over a highly fraught criminal trial. But most decisive are the bonds that Maria forms with the other mothers in the neonatal unit, once she has overcome her own temperamental reserve and her

---

This chapter is an updated version of "Unnatural Childbirth: Naples, the Neo-natal Intensive Care Unit, and the Blank Space of Possibility in Francesca Comencini's *Lo spazio bianco*," in *Italian Motherhood on Screen*, ed. Giovanna Faleschini Lerner and M. Elena Damelio (New York: Palgrave Macmillan, 2017).

cultural distance from women lacking the educational advantages and socio-economic means that she enjoys. Developing in tandem with her baby's progress toward viability are her night-school students' preparations for the exam that will determine their success in earning the coveted diploma. The decisive moments in these parallel plots converge as Maria rushes from the exam site, where she is able to rescue a flailing student from writer's block, to the hospital, where she is able to hold her baby, newly liberated from the incubator and finally able to breathe on her own.

In the opening episode of Francesca Comencini's 2010 film, the protagonist Maria has a chance meeting with a former lover whom she had obviously not seen for some time. "Yes, I stayed in Naples," she remarks. "I like Naples, I made it, see?" From this sliver of dialogue, we glean some vital background information: that Maria is a relative newcomer to the city, and that her adjustment to Neapolitan life has not been easy. At this point, her ex-lover produces a photograph of his six-month old daughter, causing a moment of confusion in the spectator, who is led to wonder if Maria was the baby's mother and had abandoned the child in early infancy. Subsequent dialogue dispels this misunderstanding; nonetheless, it sets up a vital connection between Naples, new parenthood, and the photographic representation of incipient life.[1]

During the course of the film, based on Valeria Parrella's 2008 novel of the same title, Maria will give birth to her own child, Irene, delivered in the sixth month of pregnancy and confined to a neonatal intensive care unit for the fifty days necessary to determine the infant's viability.[2] Comencini's adaptation of the novel makes Naples a focal point of its signifying technique, appropriating a time-honoured topos – the city's link with triumphant procreativity – and exploits the profound irony of the fact that the protagonist's pregnancy is anything but triumphant, and more importantly, anything but natural in its final months. In so doing, the filmmaker both invokes and complicates an Italian iconography that feminizes the metaphor of the body politic, according to a figurative history dating back at least as far as Virgil's representation of Roma as an empress wearing a crown in the shape of a walled city, echoed by Cesare Ripa's famous 1593 emblem of Italia as a queen, and her many subsequent incarnations across the centuries.[3] Naples partakes of this iconographic tradition with a characteristic flair: the baroque excess of Neapolitan popular culture makes the feminized signifier in and of itself insufficient to represent the city's plenitude. Corporeal depictions of Neapolitan collective identity require a body that harbours within it new life.

Though Comencini's choice of setting was determined by Parrella's novel, and by the filmmaker's own stated association of the city with the theme of *sopravvivenza* (survival),[4] the Neapolitan location places *Lo spazio bianco* within a genealogy of films that align the city with the pregnant body. Roberto Rossellini's *Journey to Italy* (1954) immediately comes to mind, as does Vittorio De Sica's *Yesterday, Today and Tomorrow* (1963). In the former, the cold and repressed British tourist Katherine Joyce undergoes a profound emotional awakening upon exposure to the raw passions and exuberant vitality of the city, which makes a fetish of its dead (the charnel house of Le Fontanelle) while proudly exhibiting the bringers of new life (the multitudes of pregnant women who crowd its public spaces). It is the spectacle of the Pompeian couple, eternally frozen in a desperate embrace, that triggers Katherine's emotional breakdown and inspires the following diagnosis of her own marriage's decline: "Maybe what is wrong is that we didn't have a child."

The Neapolitan cult of procreativity finds no more flamboyant enactment than the "Adelina" episode of De Sica's *Yesterday, Today and Tomorrow*, where the fulsome body of Sophia Loren becomes the personification of an entire community as it delights in the serial pregnancies that prevent her character from going to jail (expectant mothers are exempt from serving time). In keeping with the upbeat cinematic culture of "Il Boom," Italy's Economic Miracle of the late 1950s and 1960s, Adelina's dire socio-economic situation gives birth to a boisterous musical comedy, crowned by a rousing production number in which the protagonist parades down the streets of the old city to the anthem "*Tien la panza*" (She has a belly) accompanied by a chorus of neighbours, and bevies of small children, who rejoice in her triumphant maternity.

In Comencini's film, instead, a street in the old city becomes the setting for Maria's collapse and the prolongation of her pregnancy by artificial means in the neonatal intensive care unit of a Neapolitan hospital. The iconic link between the city and the pregnant body becomes denaturalized – technology intrudes to challenge the stereotypical association of Naples with easy and abundant procreativity. Maria accompanies the announcement of her out-of-wedlock pregnancy to her friend and confidant Fabrizio with a sonogram – harbinger of the technological interventions necessary to keep the fetus viable. As in the film's opening scene, which established the nexus between new parenthood, Naples, and the representation of incipient life, here too Maria invokes the theme of *napolitanietà*. This time, however, she does so as a way of

The scene in which Maria confides her out-of-wedlock pregnancy to her friend Fabrizio revolves around the ultrasound images of the fetus that foreshadow the film's final scene of her baby's emergence into the world of full-fledged photographic representation.

absolving her lover of responsibility for her plight. "I knew that this city would screw me," she quips,[5] prompting Fabrizio's wry response, "Now even you blame Naples," suggesting that Maria is not alone in endowing the city with the power to sew chaos in its residents' lives. In a feeble attempt to relieve his friend's distress, Fabrizio remarks of the image in the sonogram, "It's really a pretty baby," but Maria immediately calls his bluff: "It's only a shadow." Fabrizio's comeback, "It's a pretty shadow," drives home a sobering truth – the sonogram, at this stage, can only mark the shadowy beginning of a long and precarious journey toward medical viability and technological visibility. The difference between this embryonic mark of pregnancy and the fully realized photograph of the six-month-old displayed by Maria's ex-lover in the film's first scene is a measure of the challenge the filmmaker faces in forging a cinematic language adequate to the task of bringing this "pretty shadow" into the world of possible neonatal imagery.

Given Comencini's acute cinematic self-consciousness about filming the story of Maria's anomalous pregnancy, it should come as no surprise that movie-going itself would be elevated to a place of primary thematic concern. As Maria explains to Fabrizio, cinema has become her hedge against the emptiness of her solo life. In order to while away the afternoon hours before proceeding to the night school where she teaches Italian to adults seeking their middle school diplomas, Maria goes to the movies, and it is there that her affair with Pietro, the co-author of her precarious pregnancy, has its start. Himself a single parent who is spending an afternoon babysitting his infant in a movie theatre, Pietro is forced to leave in mid-screening when his child's squalling becomes a public nuisance. At the conclusion of the show Maria encounters Pietro outside the theatre and urges him to see its second half. Asked how the story ends, Maria replies, "Well. Not well in the sense that everyone lived happily ever after. It ended the way it should have ended." Pietro, baffled by her response, can only think in terms of a conventional romantic denouement: "They stayed together?" he guesses. "No." "He went away?" "No." Refusing to spoil the plot, she invites him to see the second half for himself, "even tomorrow." Though Pietro takes her up on the invitation, he nonetheless will never learn the film's outcome, because he and Maria will spend their time in the movie theatre initiating their own love story, literally blocking the camera's access to the inner screen as they passionately kiss in the foreground of the frame. Like Pietro, all we will ever know about the film-within-the-film is what Maria had previously reported: that its ending involved neither of the alternatives expected of a conventional romance plot: the lovers' union or their splitting apart.

This indeterminacy, of course, is what will define Comencini's "outer film." Pietro's exit from the love story does, in fact, adhere to the unhappy ending that he proposes as the second possibility for the conclusion of the "inner film," but it will emerge as immaterial to the real substance of *Lo spazio bianco*, which covers the interval between a premature birth and the moment when an infant exits the mechanized womb of the neonatal intensive care unit as a sustainable life form. Within that blank space, another life will also take definitive shape – that of Maria *mater*, who will evolve from a state of shock, confusion, and ambivalence to one of growing preparedness and confidence in her own maternal strength. *Lo spazio bianco*, then, is the space of possibility and hope afforded by the technology of artificial gestation on the one hand, and by freedom from the strictures of the conventional love plot on the other. In other words, the title points toward a space beyond the either/or of happily-ever-after or abject abandonment – a space for a new kind of narrative that "ended as it should have ended."

The novelty of *Lo spazio bianco* extends beyond generic confines to include a rewriting of Naples itself, understood as a topos in the literal sense – as a place that conjures up a welter of popular associations beyond those connected with procreativity.[6] First and foremost is the expectation of Neapolitan backwardness, Bourbonic inefficiency, and general civic dysfunction – all of which are powerfully contradicted by the state-of-the-art workings of the neonatal intensive care unit and the robust institutional health of the hospital as a whole. While Maria ascends for occasional cigarette breaks to the rooftop terrace of the building, where the lovely Vesuvian skyline seems to reinforce traditional views of Naples as a picturesque outpost immune to the incursions of progress, her experience within the hospital places the city firmly in the flow of twenty-first-century scientific advances. Comencini's insistence on documenting Neapolitan cultural modernity emerges in the settings of two important scenes, one located in a gallery of contemporary art and the other in a musical venue featuring the avantgarde solo performance of Maria's ex-lover.

It is the protagonist's engagement with the city of Naples in vocational terms that gives the title to both Parrella's novel and Comencini's film. Maria makes her living as a teacher of literacy for adults who had to leave school prematurely, and for whom the preparation course leading to the proficiency exam constitutes its own form of artificial gestation portending a second birth – this time into the world of increased cultural and economic possibility. In completing the essay portion of the test, Gaetano, one of the most promising students of the class, encounters writer's block. Maria, who is proctoring the exam, sidles up to him and offers a hint about how to proceed. "Leave a blank space and start all over, writing what you want." With this, she liberates him from the spatial strictures of conventional essay form and allows him to write his own text for a "new present."

In adapting Parrella's text to the screen, Comencini has sharpened the running parallelism between the preparation for the literacy exam and the development of Maria's child in the intensive care unit. The shared issue of time limits – the countdown to the exam date, on the one hand, and the day when Irene will be disconnected from the breathing tubes to test if her lungs can function on their own – structures the progress of both narrative strands. Unlike the text, in which the administering of the literacy exam is reported in an epilogue, the film stages both climactic events on the same day, and Maria is torn between her needs to be present at both. Hoping that Irene's "test" will take place first thing in the morning so that she can attend her students' exam on time, she is distraught to learn that another infant's emergency has delayed the timing of her daughter's breathing trial. Rushing to the location of the exam, she is onsite just long enough to rescue Gaetano from his paralysis before a text message calls her back to the hospital, where she arrives to cradle Irene in her lap, freed from life support and breathing on her own. The camera allows us to linger momentarily upon the unencumbered image of this beautiful infant before she is enfolded in Maria's arms and the nurse draws a white curtain in front of mother and child to protect the intimacy of this scene from further optical intrusion. At this point, the screen fades to white and the film's title receives its final and definitive cinematic rendering.

Significantly, this is not the first time that Comencini had used the fade-to-white editorial device in the film. An earlier instance of its use had preceded Maria's introduction into the neonatal intensive care unit as she scrubbed up in preparation for entering that sterile environment.[7] This striking technique for turning the entire screen into a *spazio bianco* (white or blank space) thus serves to bracket the narrative present of Maria's incubator-side vigil, and suggests that within these brackets a text of possibility, like the blank space on Gaetano's page, can be written.[8] That text will have nothing to do with the conventional scenario for cinematic romance that had been ruled out by Maria's cryptic response to Pietro's questions about the ending of the film-within-the-film at the start of their affair. Throughout Maria's *spazio bianco* experience within the neonatal care unit, the spectre of Pietro progressively shrinks in size, in paradoxical contrast to the enormity of the hold that the miniscule figure of Irene has on the protagonist's consciousness. "Now he is far away, tiny tiny, tinier than Irene," Maria confides to Fabrizio, "as if he had deflated, melted into a puddle." That puddle of murkiness, that dark tangle of emotions caused by the botched love story, has been replaced by a clean page onto which Maria is now able to inscribe a new narrative, unbound by conventional strictures of genre and emotional clichés that have been rendered obsolete by the unprecedented experience of artificial gestation and the new evolutionary relationships it brings into the realm of possibility.[9]

Whiteness also prevails within the precincts of the neonatal intensive care unit itself, in the ubiquitous curtains that envelope each cubicle, surrounding the incubator and its margins with an illusion of privacy. That illusion marks the attempt to offset the traumatic reality of a pregnancy turned inside out, where the private, opaque, and internal tissues of the uterine walls are usurped by the transparent, porous, and synthetic materials of their high-tech replacement. The nature of the gestational experience as one of unalloyed interiority and intimacy has now been rendered external, public, and mechanized. The categories of "inside" and "outside" have undergone a monstrous inversion. Blood vessels have been replaced by synthetic tubes, the placenta by a network of electrodes whose signals are translated into numbers to be broadcast on monitors for public consumption. Mina, the most loquacious and down to earth of the mothers in this neonatal community, gives voice to the shocking and profoundly estranging experience of such high-tech gestation – she compares it to a horror film. Later, when Maria asks Fabrizio his impression upon visiting the unit for the first time, his answer is succinct: "It's truly torture." Significantly, this conversation takes place in a setting far removed from the hospital grounds – in the above-mentioned avant-garde art gallery, a context that puts a premium on unconventional modes of looking. Maria's very strategy for framing her query is telling: "Come sembravamo di là del vetro?" (How did we seem on the other side of the glass?), she asks, in a formulation that makes of the "vetro" an aperture in the existential wall separating the world of natural processes from that of their artificial inversion.

When viewed "di là dal vetro," the workings of the neonatal intensive care unit are obscene in the etymological sense (from the Greek term for "offstage," meaning something that should not be seen). The violation of pregnancy's intimate and private course is nowhere more dramatically portrayed than in the episode held on "visitor's day" when friends and relatives are invited to witness the mechanisms and effects of mechanically prolonged gestations. Comencini films this sequence as a comic sketch, devoid of dialogue and accompanied by upbeat music appropriate to the forced gaiety of the occasion. The display of each child, in succession, to the audience "di là dal vetro" becomes a grotesque spectacle – one in which Maria will take no part. Rather than wheel Irene's incubator toward the "vetro" for public viewing, she and Mina, choose to hide themselves and their babies under tent-like coverings, sealed in a pact of invisibility, bound by their efforts to disappear from this awkward voyeuristic scenario.

Comencini's enactment of Maria's desire to protect her tiny daughter from probing eyes has significant meta-cinematic implications for the filmmaker's own wielding of the camera to show us what we should not be able to see. She is acutely sensitive to the ethical problem of filming an inside-out pregnancy, of exploiting the visual access to fetal development that artificial gestation affords, and of capitalizing on the prurient curiosity that such high-tech human drama can arouse. Comencini's camerawork must achieve a delicate balance between discretion and revelation, and it does so by appropriating Maria's own subjectivity as she tentatively takes in the spectacle of her premature daughter for the first time. A curtain is drawn open and the neonatologist announces, "Here is your daughter." As he explains the baby's condition and prognosis, the camera begins a long, slow pan, moving from right to left, following the pathway of tubes leading from a bottle of IV fluid down into the incubator, past the metal carapace around the baby's torso, up a series of tubes to another IV bottle, and then to a monitor dense with numbers, symbols, and lines. During this journey, all the camera has shown us of the baby is a fleeting view of the top of her head, bristling with black hairs, and the hint of an ear. At this point, the doctor and his team exit the cubicle, and Comencini's camera remains with Maria, filming her in profile against fleeting glimpses of the baby's leg, followed by a shot of a tiny arm. From the "pretty shadow" as Fabrizio had remarked of the sonogram, the baby has become a fragmented and unreadable image, a composite of hair, wrinkled skin, metallic casing, and plastic tubes that Comencini, with delicacy and tact, refuses to probe. In a later scene, we get a full-body view of the baby from an extreme aerial height, as Maria imagines the incubator in its nocturnal solitude. The oneiric quality of the scene and the camera's distance from its object afford us no access to the baby as an intelligible image. In a later scene, the only sustained close-up we get of the infant before the film's final frames involves an extremely blurry shot of the baby's head with breathing apparatus protruding from her mouth. The opportunity for mothers to directly observe the gestational process from outside the maternal body is seen as an ironic privilege by Mina, who expresses her views in a formulation rife with meaning for Comencini's own project in filming the story of a pregnancy turned inside out. "Other mothers have to content themselves with sonograms, but we see everything live," she muses, and in so doing calls attention to the visual invasiveness of the very film we are watching.

Comencini's reticence in portraying this inside-out pregnancy may be seen as a reaction to the intrusiveness of the filmic medium in a medical setting, evoking Benjamin's comparison of the cameraman to the surgeon in "The Work of Art in the Age of Mechanical Reproduction." Referring to the writings of otolaryngologist Luc Durtain, Benjamin compares the "specific technical sleights of hand" of the surgeon to the boldness of the cinematographer's "thoroughgoing permeation of reality with mechanical equipment."[10] While Benjamin celebrates the cinema's ability to surgically penetrate into the hidden recesses of the real, Comencini balks at such voyeuristic intrusiveness when the body part is a pregnant womb, albeit an artificial one. What Comencini shares with Benjamin in his canonical essay is a profound ambivalence about the technology of artistic reproduction itself. For Benjamin, of course, cinema both usurps the "aura" of the work of art and exponentially increases the human faculties of visual and acoustic apperception. For

Comencini, photographic technology, while seen as invasive, cannot be separated from the crucial role played by the technological sphere within the story of Irene's miraculous survival.

Throughout the early days of Maria's incubator-side vigil, her struggle to maintain a modicum of privacy had led her to reject emotional contact with the other mothers in the unit, and to refuse the staff's request that she make public the name of her child. Maria spends her time enclosed in her cubicle, reading – an activity that in and of itself separates her from the relatively uneducated majority of her cohort. At one point early on, an outburst of emotionalism on Mina's part sends Maria even further into her cocoon of solitude. There is a moment, however, that marks a significant breakthrough in her willingness to emerge from isolation. The young doctor (who will ultimately become Maria's new lover) urges her to place a name tag on the front of the incubator, and he employs a clever rhetorical device in the attempt to convince her. "Writing her name here is like putting it above the doorbell. It means that the house is inhabited, that there's someone home." With this analogy, the doctor gives Maria a metaphoric alternative to that of the inside-out womb. "It's a little as if we found ourselves in an empty room," he continues, "in which we can't say what will happen." The "empty room" is another version of "lo spazio bianco," the blank page on which a text of possibilities is yet to be written. What clinches Maria's acceptance of the doctor's plea to name her child and "go public" with it is his declaration that "your daughter has a very strong constitution." With this vote of confidence in the baby's viability, Maria responds, "Write Irene on it," referring to the incubator tag. Of signal importance is the fact that Irene was the name of Maria's mother, and in giving it to her fragile child, she is inserting this new young life into a feminine genealogy with all the hope of sustainability that such a lineage entails. With this breakthrough, Maria enters slowly into the community of mothers who share her plight, agreeing to join them at lunch, helping the distraught Rosa to read the fetal monitor, shopping with Mina for baby clothes, participating in the exercise of "music therapy," and daydreaming about her cohorts performance of an interpretive dance on the hospital floor.[11]

In her growing willingness to bond with the mothers in her unit, Maria reverses the condition of estrangement that had characterized her relationship to Neapolitan forms of family life. Throughout much of the film, she had been consigned to a position of watching others engaged in familial routines. Two scenes offer striking examples of Maria's outsider status within the Neapolitan context. Living in the city's upper reaches, she commutes downtown on a cable car that affords her a montage of glimpses into the lives of those whose balconies and windows border its tracks. A series of shots pass by on-screen, intercut with images of Maria observing from within the vehicle: a boy walks from the balcony into a kitchen to join his father at the table; a middle-aged woman, coffee cup in hand, stands at a window; an elderly man plays cards; a young woman with luxurious black hair smokes on a balcony; a woman sits at a table preparing food; two girls play cat's cradle. It is of the utmost importance that this sequence, which foregrounds the mobilized gaze and the technique of montage at the heart of cinematic language, leads Maria to a movie theatre. Adding to the importance of this juxtaposition is Maria's Freudian slip at the box office, where she mistakenly orders two tickets in a none-too-subtle revelation of her desire for companionship. And of course, it will be this screening that provides the impetus for the affair with Pietro. Significant, too, is the fact that the funicular ride recurs toward the end of the film, just after Maria telephones Fabrizio to say that Irene's breathing trial is scheduled for the next day and that she is ready to take on the full-fledged responsibilities of motherhood. During the second, though shorter, montage sequence viewed from the window of the cable car, glimpses of the same households recur, but the intercuts to Maria's face show her more engaged. In one shot she is smiling, and in another the stillness that has characterized these inserts is broken by a rotation of her face, at first partially concealed, toward the camera into a full three-quarter view.[12]

There is another character in the film of singular importance in that she, like Maria, lives in Naples as an outsider, and like Maria, struggles with her maternal role. This woman (added to the cast of characters included in Parrella's text) is a judge whose choice to preside over an anti-Camorra trial in Naples required her to leave behind a husband and three children in the north.[13] Living on the same floor as Maria, the judge is insulated by a permanent entourage of bodyguards, but the two women do manage to have a rooftop dialogue of considerable consequence to the film's ethical concerns. The pretext for engaging Maria in conversation is that the judge has found a way to combat the scourge of ants that have invaded the building. "Don't give up," she had told Maria earlier in the film, and in its most general sense, this exhortation applies to the judge's own decision to join the struggle against organized crime, though it means sacrificing her role as wife and mother. For Maria, the battle cry will sound the opposite summons – to embrace her new maternal role, to resist surrendering to the difficulties of single motherhood, and to accept the possibility that her child will be impaired. Toward the end of the film, a TV news flash reveals the unfortunate denouement of the judge's subplot with the report that she has been removed from the trial – a defeat for both her commitment to the anti-Camorra cause and her decision to place the demands of social justice above those of her domestic life. In metaphoric terms, we could see the three years that she had devoted to preparing for the trial as a prolonged period of gestation, ending in an ideologically fraught miscarriage.

Since pregnancy and birth shape the temporal confines of *Lo spazio bianco*, time itself becomes a central philosophical preoccupation of both novel and film. Early in Parrella's text, the first-person narrator introduces an oxymoronic formulation for the process unfolding over the course of her vigil. She attributes a double and contradictory set of terms to Irene's condition: comparing it to a game of toss-up: "It's as if someone had tossed a coin in the air, and sooner or later it had to land, heads or tails. For forty days, the same coin, *morendo-nascendo* [dying-being born]" (11). Only at the end of forty days, when the breathing tubes are removed, will one of the two gerunds prevail in describing the process that had taken place over the proceeding weeks. In the meantime, Maria inhabits the "suspended life" (31) of those consigned to Dante's *Inferno*, living in "quell'aura sanza tempo tinta" (that air without the tint of time; *Inf.* 3, l. 29). "I didn't wear a watch, none of us did" (39); "Our time, dilated and still, did not respect the frenetic hours of the others" (45). In Frank Kermode's lexicon, Maria is living in a condition of *chronos*, of simple duration, of undifferentiated temporal succession.[14] The passage of time is marked by repetition and waiting, of ritual handwashing, of commuting to and from the hospital, of the regular rhythms recorded on the fetal monitor. What Maria craves, in Kermode's terms, is the experience of eventful time, moments organized according to a hierarchy of importance: *kairos*. In Comencini's film, the hunger for eventfulness expressed in the novel is intensified, and it has an occasional dark underside. At a certain point, Maria confides to one of the night school students, Luisa, that she longs for something decisive to happen. This confession is immediately followed by a hospital scene in which a fetus is rushed to intensive care – the result of a late-term abortion. In another scene, Irene's fetal monitors begin to sound an alarm, and Maria hesitates before reporting this ominous development to the hospital staff. Here, her longing for *kairos*, for a definitive turn in events, has led to a sinister if entirely understandable impulse to "intervene" by inaction in the face of a medical crisis.

Kairos, in its fervently awaited and potentially most hopeful form, comes on the day of Irene's scheduled "second birth," when the breathing tubes are removed and she passes the test of viability. As the mother-daughter narrative reaches this joyous conclusion, we are

This shot of mother and child immediately before the white curtain shields them from view takes us back to the album of sonograms when Irene was a mere "shadow," and reminds us, in the process, of the momentous journey that has brought her into the world of full-fledged photographic representation.

reminded of Maria's answer to Pietro's question about the end of the "inner film" that marked the beginning of their affair: "finiva come doveva finire" (it ended the way it should have ended). At this early point in her own plot, Maria could hardly have imagined the narrative and ethical force of the auxiliary verb *doveva* (it should have) that will come to describe the novelty of her own story's resistance to the conventions of romance. The *dovere* of Comencini's film inheres in its commitment to the blank space of opportunity made possible by the removal of Pietro from the plot, and its restructuring around the mother-daughter scenario. The utter irrelevance of the failed love story to the film's denouement is displayed in the final seconds of *Lo spazio bianco*, where the spectacle of white curtains drawn around the image of mother and child presents a telling alternative to the freeze-frame ending that a more conventional filmmaker would have supplied. Comencini's decision, instead, to shelter this tender scene of bonding from our prolonged gaze brings closure to the film's running theme of privacy, and restores the intimacy lost during the ordeal of artificial gestation that had brought mother and child to this fortunate pass.

Of crucial importance to the film's final moments is the absence of dialogue and the resounding musical soundtrack of Nina Simone's "I Wish I Knew How It Would Feel to Be Free." Though the lyrics speak of a slave's unrealized dream of emancipation, the song's foregrounding of that wish focuses our attention on the many levels of freedom that are indeed achieved by the film's conclusion. Most consequentially, Irene has been liberated from the tubes and wires that bound her tiny form within the confines of the incubator. At the same time, Gaetano has been freed from the strict rules of the exam format by leaving a blank space that allows him to finish his essay in the "new present." In terms of Maria's sentimental life, the plot's freedom from the strictures of romance opens up a future unencumbered by any ongoing saga of paternal negligence or the quest for a substitute Pietro – options that would divert Maria's energies from pursuing a materially and emotionally independent ménage à deux. The image of Naples, which has exerted a kind of protagonism throughout the film, is freed from its iconic connection with easy fertility, traditional family structure, and general socio-economic backwardness. In its relationship to the literary source, Comencini's film has asserted its freedom to add characters (the judge in particular), shift emphases, and make the medium-specific changes necessary to give the novel a "second birth" in film. At the technical level, the film has liberated itself from the kind of clinical voyeurism and documentary invasiveness that a drama set in a neonatal intensive care unit would normally invite, insisting instead on preserving the privacy of that anomalous maternal condition.

"Bene" (well), Maria had said in response to Pietro's question about the ending of the specular film-within-the-film that had spawned their affair. "[It did not end well] in the sense that everyone lived happily ever after," she clarified. "It ended as it should have ended." The outer film, too, will end well, not in the formulaic "happily-ever-after" sense, but in its very indeterminacy, its offer of a clean page on which Maria can write the script of her "new present." In both its content and its cinematic form, *Lo spazio bianco* may be viewed as the preparation course for Maria's test of maternal readiness and Irene's test of viability, as both mother and child learn to breathe on their own.

Chapter Thirteen

Comic Relief: Riccardo Milani's *Ma cosa ci dice il cervello* (Don't Stop Me Now), 2019

Direction: Riccardo Milani. *Screenplay*: Furio Andreotti, Giulia Calenda, Paola Cortellesi, Riccardo Milani. *Cinematography*: Saverio Guarna. *Editing*: Patrizia Cesesani, Francesco Renda. *Costumes*: Alberto Moretti. *Music*: Andrea Guerra. *Cast*: Paola Cortellesi (Giovanna), Stefano Fresi (Roberto), Tomas Arana (Eden Bauer), Teco Celio (Gerard Colasante), Remo Girone (Comandante D'Alessandro), Vinicio Marchioni (Marco), Lucia Mascino (Francesca), Claudia Pandolfi (Tamara), Giampaolo Morelli (Enrico), Emanuele Armani (Edoardo), Carla Signoris (Agata), Chiara Luzzi (Martina).

Synopsis: Set for the most part in contemporary Rome, the film centres on the conflicting claims placed on Giovanna Salvatori by her professional life and her domestic role. Separated from her husband Enrico, Giovanna leads a household consisting of her precocious ten-year-old daughter Martina and her own mother Agata – a caricature of the age-denying, hypersexualized older woman. Giovanna's work/life balance is made even more complex by the contradiction internal to her professional identity. Ostensibly an accountant within Il Ministero, the generic government bureaucracy, she is in reality a secret agent for the Department of Security. The intense demands of her job require her to shut out all possibility of an active social life, and to outsource her parental duties to her mother, who is anything but matronly but who takes on the grandmaternal task with conviction. This difficult status quo is upended by two plot developments. Professionally, Giovanna is sent on a mission to thwart a plan by the villainous Eden Bauer, a would-be sower of mass destruction, and privately, she is invited to attend the reunion of a close group of friends from her high school days. In recounting their life stories during the twenty-four years since graduation, the four friends (Tamara, a flight attendant; Francesca, a physician; Marco, a children's soccer coach; and Roberto, a teacher of literature) profess satisfaction with their career choices but express dismay over incidents of incivility on the part of the passengers, patients, children's parents, and pupils whom they respectively seek to serve. Giovanna furtively takes it upon herself to "re-educate" these uncouth clients of her friends' professional activities, and she commandeers the resources of the Secret Service to that end. Once discovered, her antics are punished by a temporary suspension from the workplace, during which time she joins her former high school friends to relive the vacation in Seville that they had undertaken decades earlier. The result is the rekindling of Giovanna's high-school crush on Roberto, as the two of them succeed in tracking down Eden Bauer and bringing him to justice.

Ma cosa ci dice il cervello is the fourth film made by director Riccardo Milani and his wife, actress Paola Cortellesi, who plays the starring role. After the resounding success of *Come un gatto in tangenziale* (Like a Cat on a Highway, 2017), a satire aimed at a think tank that offered a well-intentioned but hopelessly abstract approach to the urgent problem of class inequality, *Ma cosa ci dice il cervello* differs in the scale of the social issues it confronts. The newer film is concerned with a less visible zone of civil malfunction: the "daily injustices"[1] that mar the smooth functioning of communal life, from bullying in schools to rude behaviour in traffic jams, with assorted other examples of bad behaviour thrown into the mix.

In fulfilling the film's social agenda, Milani is especially determined to reach a mass audience, to overcome "the detachment of a great part of the populace with respect to forms of art, culture, spectacle. Cinema in this regard can and must take the responsibility to speak to people without alienating them."[2] Based on the assumption that a cinema of civic engagement will have only limited audience appeal, Milani vows to "bridge the gap that exists now with the public" because the film medium "can give a cultural push with respect to a [given] moment, a [given] situation of the country." In *Come un gatto in tangenziale*, that "cultural push" was delivered via a pointed critique of class inequality cloaked in comedic garb. In *Ma cosa ci dice il cervello*, while the social stakes are lower (everyday incivilities), the comic effects are considerably heightened, thanks to the work's exuberant pastiche of genres and the hilarious incongruities that follow.

The film's set-up immediately signals that we're about to watch a domestic sitcom, unfolding within the unremarkable walls of home, school, workplace, and leisure-time activities. Individual alarm clocks launch the three members of the Salvatori household into the whirlwind of morning activities necessary for each to assemble the self-image that she will present to the world. But already, a dissonant note enters this portrait of a normal household of routine – Grandma Agata dresses as a superannuated Barbie doll, while Giovanna, her forty-three-year-old daughter, dons the inconspicuous and bland attire of one who does not want to be noticed. Early in the film, Giovanna's quest for public invisibility will be on vivid display at a "meet-the-parents" event sponsored by the elementary school attended by her daughter, Martina. A parade of spectacular appearances aimed at delighting and dazzling the children includes a veterinarian mom who ends her performance by opening a basket full of puppies, an astronaut aunt who sports full flight gear, and a dad dressed as a medieval warrior who brandishes two blazing torches. When Giovanna is invited to speak in her drab attire, the announcement that she processes payrolls at the Ministero is met with predictable disappointment. In the ensuing silence, she struggles to engage the audience by embellishing her job description with further glamourous details – "I also calculate withholding taxes."[3] What we will learn in the wake of the film's central plot twist is that Giovanna's performance on this day was the most convincing performance of them all. Her enactment of mediocrity, of employment in the proverbial safe haven of dull and meaningless governmental agencies, will be radically overturned when her true working identity is exposed. And it is here that the collision of genres and this film's exuberant hybridity first come to the fore.

Far from the mere protagonist of a sitcom, Giovanna is someone who dons her bland public persona *as a mask*, a disguise to protect her actual identity, which will only emerge once she exits the elevator on the bottom-most floor of the Ministero, threads her way through the shabby corridors of the building's basement, and enters the brightly lit, high-tech wing of what will turn out to be the Italian secret service. In generic terms, the film has transitioned from sitcom to spy movie, and Giovanna has morphed into a superheroine as her self-effacing persona gives way to a full-fledged physical transformation: she walks at a brisk pace, her blank expression is replaced by a bright smile, and her posture becomes erect as she enters the inner sanctum, the nerve centre of the government's antiterrorist operations. It is here that her elevated position within the secret service hierarchy becomes clear – she is chosen for a mission to track down Eden Bauer, a world-class villain who is about to put the final touches on a weapon of mass destruction. The assignment requires Giovanna to leave right away for Marrakesh, whose very name conjures up the expectations for exoticism and intrigue associated with the cinema of spying. But her incongruous response to the assignment immediately derails these generic associations. "I have dance!" she blurts out, referring to her daughter's ballet lesson, scheduled for that afternoon. This jostling of generic registers is prolonged throughout the helicopter journey to Morocco as she trades cell phone messages with the "mamme seconda B" (the mothers of second graders, section B) who are organizing a birthday party for one of members of Martina's class.

Once she is on the ground on the outskirts of Marrakesh, her superheroine skills emerge in full force: she performs three identity changes (from the jumpsuited helicopter passenger to the smartly attired hotel receptionist to the shabbily dressed and fly-by-the-seat-of-her-pants tour guide), shows her total linguistic mastery of Arabic and English, and is able to adapt instantaneously to the breaking news coming from the command centre about the whereabouts of Bauer and his accomplice, the Belgian chemist Gerard Colasante. But quick thinking, polylingualism, and the fluid assumption of multiple identities hardly exhaust Giovanna's arsenal of superheroine traits. She is also a paragon of physical strength and agility, able to scale walls, leap from formidable heights, and sprint through crowded marketplaces with ease.

All this speaks to the wildly parodic nature of *Ma cosa ci dice il cervello*, with its echoes of the James Bond franchise, as well as the subgenre of the feminine superheroine, featuring such figures as Gal Gadot's Diana of *Wonder Woman* (2017) and Jennifer Garner's Sydney Bristow of the TV series *Alias* (2001–6). In considering parody as an interpretive key to *Ma cosa ci dice il cervello*, Linda Hutcheon's study of the parodic mode as "fundamentally double and divided" is of particular relevance.[4] "While the act and form of parody are those of incorporation," she observes, "its function is one of separation and contrast."[5] Both the incorporative and the contrastive elements in the relationship between *Ma cosa ci dice il cervello* and *Alias* are well worth exploring if we are to take the measure of the Italian film's place within the genre of female superheroism.[6]

Like Giovanna, Sydney Bristow hides her covert identity behind an elaborate facade: she is a part-time graduate student of literature and part-time bank employee (Credit Delphine). And like Giovanna, she is plurilingual (fluent in Chinese, among other languages), shows considerable athletic prowess, and loves a good disguise. The Italian film's debt to *Alias* is nowhere more obvious than in the staging of the women's first entrance into their respective spy agencies – both are scanned through a sophisticated security apparatus, and upon crossing the threshold adopt a body language of the utmost self-possession. But these surface qualities of resemblance give way to the "separation and contrast" that Hutcheon attributes to the parodic mode when two major factors are taken into consideration. First is Sydney's abundant use of lethal force, while the norms of comedy prevent Giovanna from causing undue physical harm to her opponents. Comedic conventions also dictate the second major departure of Giovanna's story from that of her American counterpart. Although both heroines are involved in love relationships that threaten to "blow their cover," Sydney's fiancé Danny is murdered early in the first episode because he has discovered his beloved's line of work. This means that the *Alias* series is rooted, from the very start, in the dichotomy between domestic happiness and female superheroics. *Ma cosa ci dice il cervello* instead firmly rejects *Alias*'s opening premise by ending its plot with Giovanna's comedic ultimatum to Roberto, who has just discovered her true identity, "Either I kill you, or I marry you."

In characterizing the parodic separation and contrast between these two narratives, a Hollywood label readily comes to mind. Sydney's tale would fall under the "hard-boiled" category, whereas Giovanna's version offers a "soft" rethinking of the sentimental/professional split. Ironically, it is Giovanna's estranged husband Enrico who writes the screenplay for reconciling the rival demands of domesticity and success on the job. "Stop living your [personal] life as if it were a cover," he advises her. "Daily life is your true life. Do things with your daughter. Make some friends. Get yourself a man." While this counsel holds out the hope for bringing Giovanna and Enrico back together – a possibility that hovers over the entire film but remains unrealized – it does indeed offer a prescription for the behavioural changes that will lead to the film's happy ending as prescribed by comedy in its classical sense (marriage and the resolution of the conflicts that had posed obstacles to the couple's union).

But the film's softening of such hard-boiled feminine superhero examples as *Alias* brings us back to the parodic nature of *Ma cosa ci dice il cervello*. It is worth revisiting Linda Hutcheon's claim that "while the act and form of parody are those of incorporation, its function is one of separation and contrast," especially in light of critiques such as that of Andrea Fornasiero, who blasts the film's spy segments as painful and amateurish, faulting "the spectacular insipience of the mise-en-scène" and describing the National Security set as one of "dazzling poverty, where the photography has no depth and the lines delivered by poor Remo Girone [in the role of the commander] are uttered with barely

Giovanna disguises herself as a tattoo artist in an attempt to avenge her pediatrician friend Francesca, who has suffered a dislocated shoulder in an attack by the irate mother of one of her patients.

concealed embarrassment."[7] Such a critical stance betrays a failure to recognize this work's nature as a multifaceted parody that pokes fun at an array of generic modes, foremost among them, of course, the spy film. Were *Ma cosa ci dice il cervello* operating entirely within the conventions of the thriller, Fornasiero's objections might have point, but given the film's good-humoured spoof of the genre, only the most tone-deaf critic could take its spy trappings seriously. It is the film's exuberant hybridity, its self-conscious pastiche of modes, that provides the parodic pleasures of Milani's achievement. In its sudden and frequent shifts of genres, ranging from sitcom to thriller to travelogue to sentimental romance and back, the filmmaker elicits viewers' awareness of the rules governing each, and the sense of mastery attendant upon such understandings.

Key to this strategy is the bravura of Paola Cortellesi's performance as Giovanna, who convincingly and joyously fulfils the differential requirements of each genre, enacting in her body language and facial eloquence the nuances of each. Within the narrative itself, the plot twists that require Giovanna to inhabit thirteen distinct personas in order to pull off her stunts –hotel receptionist, tour guide, baggage truck driver, tattoo artist, Snow White impersonator, transvestite clarinetist, soccer mom, food courier, flight attendant, ER doctor, taxi driver, security guard, electrician – reveal the multiple ways in which the film calls attention to its own theatricality, and that of its agile protagonist.

A second misreading of the film's parodic nature emerges in Fornasiero's attack on its geographic sweep:

> If the Moscow sequence is little more than a postcard of the Red Square, that of Marrakech passes quickly through the byways of the market, with the inevitable stereotypes of Arab merchants and Japanese tourists, while at Seville we come upon a sort of touristic album of Instagram, with the group of friends that take one selfie after another in front of various characteristic locations. As if this weren't enough, a car races through the landscape of the [Andalusian] windmills and not even a bull is lacking to chase the vehicle decorated in red.[8]

For viewers attuned to Milani's parodic take, this trafficking in clichés would come as no surprise, given the protagonist's amusing indifference to her exotic surroundings, and the film's impulse to poke fun at generic pretensions of all sorts (in this case, the earnestness of travelogues, or the ulterior motives of tourist industry propaganda). In *Ma cosa ci dice il cervello*, location is subservient to parody and not an end in itself (Marrakech veritably invites spy film scenarios, Moscow is prime territory for tales of international intrigue, and Seville, as tourist mecca, presents a perfect backdrop for travellers in search of romance). Surprisingly, the sequences set in these three exotic cities were filmed onsite rather than produced by CGI, or simulated on studio grounds. The result for the viewer is the pleasure of virtuoso overhead camerawork of the sort impossible in artificial locations, penetrating depth-of-field shots, and a sense of photographic authenticity that would not escape the discerning eye.

Of the utmost significance is the fact that the film's high degree of self-reflexivity is not limited to questions of genre. Milani's meta-cinematic awareness also extends to the very materiality of his medium, as displayed in one of the film's early scenes. A phone call inviting Giovanna to a reunion with high-school friends whom she hasn't seen in twenty-four years brings back warm memories of their tight-knit group, whose exploits were recorded by mid-1990s media formats that she had tucked away in a box above her wardrobe. As she sifts through the stash of memorabilia, the protagonist embarks on a journey in time that functions like a flashback, but with a striking difference. Rather than a straightforward return to the past by cinematic

Having lingered over the photos, audio tapes, and other memorabilia stored in a box stashed above her bedroom wardrobe, Giovanna sits surrounded by the vestiges of the mid-1990s media formats that have ushered her back into her high school past.

means, it is the individual items – period photographs, audio tapes, notations on the pages of her daily calendar for 1995 – that transport her back to that time. At this moment in *Ma cosa ci dice il cervello*, the film draws a clear distinction between its own status as a contemporary mass medium in digital form, and personal ways of recording experience by analogue means. Annotated calendars (short-hand versions of diaries), audio tapes, and photographs leave physical traces that can be touched or listened to (if obsolete playback devices remain, as in Giovanna's case) or read, and their materiality takes the observer back to the way in which an earlier generation represented itself to itself. This means that an entire cultural atmosphere, consigned to the archives of collective memory, can be momentarily retrieved and vicariously inhabited by observers in the here and now. For Giovanna, the effect is to plunge her into "deep memory," the state in which temporal distance collapses and the subject is again "back there," in this case, Seville, destination of the group's celebratory high school graduation trip. From this scene of reminiscence, the film cuts to the group's reunion in the narrative present, setting in motion the plot development that will culminate in a reprise of the legendary trip to Seville.

The role of analogue technology in galvanizing Giovanna's memories of her past throws into high relief the dominance of digital media in the world of the surrounding film. In her workplace, digitized communication is omnipresent – cell phone connectivity keeps Giovanna in touch with the command centre in her most harrowing situations abroad, where split-second manoeuvres require instructions from the boss, and once she is back on the home front, the most sophisticated spy technology enables her to construct rotating mug shots of her "targets" on screen. But it is social media that offer the most striking contrast to the material vestiges of the analogue past. The very shelf life of these last (tucked safely away in a miscellaneous box for the last twenty-four years), vs. the ephemeral passage of impulses on microchips (and their hackability) tells us much about their differential powers of engagement. In digital terms, the domestic Giovanna (as opposed to her secret professional self) does not exist, because she has no presence on social media. "I've been trying to find you. You're not on anything," Tamara reports in her first phone conversation with Giovanna after twenty-four years. "I don't do social media," she responds. And because Giovanna is not "on" anything, it took the most old-fashioned of methods to find her – Tamara just happened to bump into her mother, Agata, which enabled her to track down this long-lost friend.

Thanks to the group selfies that will proliferate throughout the rest of the film, Giovanna will be "on something" – she will begin to exist, according to the protocols of digital sociability. Significantly, the analogue photos of the group's 1995 trip to Seville will be restaged digitally in the film's narrative present, but this time without leaving the material traces that made those past images retrievable. But of all the social media items featured in the film, the meme of Roberto's physical assault by his student Edoardo is the most consequential, offering a record of the extremes to which violence against teachers may lead, and prompting Giovanna to avenge this outrage, along with the various other offences suffered by her friends. As if the shaming of Roberto within the schoolroom setting weren't enough, the internet platform enables the footage to reach a limitless audience, amplifying the impact of this grievous scenario on impressionable viewers eager to earn the kind of respect accorded Eduardo by his classmates within the video. A chilling statistic testifies to the sadistic allure of such incidents: the video garnered 188,786 views.

Roberto is not the only group member to be manhandled by an adversary. Francesca is subjected to an attack that dislocates her shoulder, Marco emerges from an altercation with a "soccer parent" with a pair of broken ribs, and Tamara is pushed by an irate customer, leading to a laceration of the forehead that produces a sizeable scar. Of considerable interest is the fact that these assaults are levelled against individuals engaged in serving others – Roberto as a teacher, Francesca as a pediatrician, Tamara as a flight attendant, and Marco as a children's sports coach – and that such offences do not remain at the level of verbal abuse. In the film, the affronts to civility take somatic form – they write themselves on the flesh and bones of their victims, leaving deleterious (and in Tamara's case, life-long) effects. This accumulation of damaged body parts – forehead, shoulder, rib cage, ankle – suggests a seemingly open-ended list that would come to disable the human organism in its entirety. It is here that the classical metaphor of the body politic comes into play, where the proper interrelationship of all physical parts is necessary for the health and stability of the corporate whole.[9] The injuries suffered by Giovanna's friends serve a synecdochal function – their little group constitutes a maimed social body, which in turn points beyond itself to an entire populace, afflicted by the malady of "bad manners and abuses of power, the passive acceptance of so many small [gestures] of incivility to which all of us ... have become inured."[10] In a witty editing move that reinforces the bodily metaphor underlying the film's social critique, the scene dedicated to the sagas of injuries sustained by Giovanna's friends is immediately followed by a montage of her rigorous training regimen, involving shooting practice, wrestling, boxing, wall scaling, all aimed at fortifying the secret agent's body against the kind of assaults expected in her line of work. Ironically, Giovanna remains unscathed despite the perils of the spy business, while her friends employed in the gentler professions experience the "daily injustices" visited upon them as bodily afflictions.

This is where the film's satiric element comes in. Until now, we have focused on parody as the key to interpreting the spy story in *Ma cosa ci dice il cervello*. But the film's overall social critique, its condemnation of incivility, places the film within the category of satire. Parody and satire are often conflated, but they should be distinguished, as Hutcheon does, by the "intramural" target (another style or work of art) in the former case, and the "extramural" target (social mores, public figures, institutions, etc.) in the latter.[11] The two modes often overlap, working in tandem to attack communal ills and promote corrective action in their regard. In *Ma cosa ci dice il cervello*, the spoof of the spy film is pressed into the service of combatting incivility – Giovanna uses her secret service training as a sleuth and a mistress of disguise to avenge the wrongs done to her friends, making parody the vehicle of satire at the level of plot.

Among the group members who suffer from this malignant social trend, it is Roberto, the high school teacher, who experiences the worst of the indignities meted out by the films' gallery of rogues. Unlike Tamara, Marco, and Francesca, he undergoes not one but two physical attacks – the first resulting in a fractured ankle and the second in a serious blow to the neck. The fact that he as a teacher is twice assaulted – that no institutional actions were taken to protect him after the first incident, and no punitive measures were exacted on the perpetrator – highlights the vulnerability of education to the viral spread of socially injurious conduct. The extensive footage accorded Roberto's plight, compared with the coverage of his friends' woes, makes it clear that the film is singling out education as the principal target of incivility's assault on the social body. Thanks to the cell phone video of Roberto's beating, this spectacle went viral, as mentioned above, reaching hundreds of thousands of viewers, some of whom no doubt found it entertaining and worthy of replication on their home turf.

The film's particular understanding of incivility is crucial here, and it hinges on the double valence of the Italian word's etymological root: *civiltà*, meaning both civility and civilization. In the film's hyperbolic language, bad manners, taken to their extreme, threaten the very fundamentals of civilized coexistence, as figured in the imagery of the wounded body politic. And it is Roberto's body, in its substantial size, which comes to subsume all of the other physical mishaps experienced by his friends, signifying the primacy of education as the target of the increasingly severe blows that *inciviltà* is inflicting on the health of Italian collective life.

The film's first explicit mention of the root word *civiltà* emerges in Roberto's explanation of his refusal to bow to Edoardo's demand for a passing grade. "I felt an overflow of civility" ("un rigurgito di civiltà"), he quipped, equating the term with professional integrity, especially with regard to the transmission and evaluation of knowledge. But the film's most vivid illustration of what is meant by *civiltà* arises in the clash between the *grand giugnol* of Edoardo's onslaught and the inscription on the whiteboard against which he slams his hapless teacher. Scribbled on the writing surface flanking the wounded man are the words "Kant and the Enlightenment," followed by the two lines the philosopher penned for his own tombstone: "The starry sky above me / the moral law within me." In the juxtaposition of Edoardo's barbaric deed and this manifesto of humanist values, the film delivers its own pedagogical message without engaging in didactic overkill. In the very few words scrawled on the whiteboard, the film appropriates Kant's invocation of the human being's place between heaven and earth, and the reflection of the cosmic order in the soul's moral life, to render its verdict on Edoardo's despicable act.

Roberto's hospitalization at the hands of the class bully leads to a grim witticism about the rampant nature of assaults on educators. When Giovanna asks a nurse for directions to her friend's ward, identifying him as Roberto Desideri, *professore*, she is told that the designation "teacher" is not enough. So numerous are these patients that the hospital staff members "divide them by subject matter." But the film's most powerful way of privileging education as the guardian of *civiltà* and the bulwark against its erosion is the narrative structure itself. In other words, the plot bestows its simplest and most time-honoured reward on the film's standard bearer of educational values: Roberto gets the girl.

He does so in unlikely fulfilment of the advice offered Giovanna by her ex-husband early in the story to "get [herself] a man" – unlikely because of a physical attribute that has made Roberto the brunt of several uncomfortable jokes throughout the film. He is obese, and his introduction in the film's present tense stands in the starkest contrast to his friends' fond memories of this former athlete's perfect physique. Roberto's belated entrance into the group's reunion scene, shot in slow motion and proceeded by a soundtrack of sentimental pop lyrics, is met by facial expressions of utmost disbelief.[12] "I'm still me," he feels the need to say upon registering the shock on the faces of the friends who had not seen him in twenty-four years, prompting him to tell the first in the series of self-deprecating "fat" jokes that he will utter throughout the rest of the film.

Roberto's connection to a firm inner core, and his willingness to speak out publicly on behalf of his ideals despite his vulnerability to abuse, is what draws Giovanna to him as she struggles with her own outward penchant for shape-shifting, unsure of what lies within. On a minor scale, his refusal to accept the "daily injustices" meted out to him has emboldened Giovanna to follow suit by confronting the rude drivers she encounters in her morning commute, for starters. But most consequentially, it is Roberto's moral courage that inspires her to forego outward appearances and choose a mate in keeping with her own inner promptings. Or to put it in pop-cultural terms, in choosing Roberto she has strayed as far as possible from the stereotypical Prince Charming who awakens his Sleeping Beauty – to mention one of Giovanna's more striking disguises – with a kiss. And if Giovanna's mother Agata is an accurate barometer of social expectations, then the older woman's disappointment upon meeting her future son-in-law says everything about her daughter's willingness to flout convention in marrying this overweight, under-appreciated high school teacher, especially in view of her previous marriage to the dashing jet fighter pilot husband whom she had chosen to leave. It is also worth noting that the conventional happy ending of the handsome couple embarking on a future of wedded bliss is further eroded by Giovanna's refusal to honour the patriarchal underpinnings of this cliché. For one thing, it is she who proposes marriage in the memorable ultimatum "Either I kill you or I marry you," in wording that spells out who will be in charge of this union and whose profession will prevail in the conduct of their married life.

The film's convention-defying denouement leads us back to parody, understood as a blend of incorporative and contrastive elements involving the imitation of a previous art work or style while simultaneously asserting its separation from that earlier mode.[13] The feminist, anti-fairytale spoof of the "happily ever after" formula needs no belabouring here, and it leads us to the broader issue of the film's formal identity in relation to the several genres that jostle and collide within its bounds: most obviously those of the sitcom and the thriller, but also the romantic comedy and the travelogue. It is therefore tempting to see Giovanna's assumption of myriad guises as the enactment of the film's own multi-generic form. And if we were to extend this parallel, then her opting for a quirky marriage, in keeping with her own innermost promptings, would correspond to the film's privileging of its core impulse, personified by Roberto – that of social enlightenment by means of humour and bold personal example. While this soon-to-be-married couple will surely not face a fairytale future, Milani's formula for a generic mix with a satiric bite may indeed offer a path forward for a cinema of social critique that succeeds in garnering wide public appeal. In this sense, the English title *Don't Stop Me Now* could well refer to the momentum that Milani's approach may gather within the expansive and dynamic sphere of Italian film comedy in the new millennium.

PART SIX

In a Category unto Itself

Chapter Fourteen

Hidden Beneath the "Blah Blah Blah": Paolo Sorrentino's *La grande bellezza* (The Great Beauty), 2013

Direction: Paolo Sorrentino. *Screenplay*: Paolo Sorrentino, Umberto Contarello. *Cinematography*: Luca Bigazzi. *Editing*: Cristiano Travaglioli. *Music*: Lele Marchitelli. *Sets*: Stefania Cella. *Costumes*: Daniela Ciancio. *Cast*: Toni Servillo (Jep Gambardella), Carlo Verdone (Romano), Sabrina Ferilli (Ramona), Carlo Buccirosso (Lello Cava), Iaia Forte (Trumeau), Pamela Villoresi (Viola), Galatea Ranzi (Stefania), Franco Graziosi (Conte Colonna), Giorgio Pasotti (Stefano), Massimo Popolizio (Alfio Bracco), Sonia Gessner (Contessa Colonna), Anna Della Rosa (Bloodless Girl), Luca Marinelli (Andrea), Serena Grandi (Lorena), Guisi Merli (Suor Maria), Dario Cantarelli (Suor Maria's assistant), Anita Kravos (Talia Concept), Roberto Herlitzka (Cardinal Bellucci).

Synopsis: After a prologue featuring a Japanese tourist who is literally overcome (perhaps mortally) by the beauty of Rome, the film introduces us to Jep Gambardella in the throes of an orgiastic party to celebrate his sixty-fifth birthday. Journalist, socialite, and washed-up novelist, Jep has never been able to replicate the success of his first book, *The Human Apparatus*, published at the age of twenty-six and winner of widespread acclaim. At the party, we meet a series of characters with whom Jeb will be involved throughout the film: Stefania, a latter-day Marxist who flaunts her ideological commitment in the face of her politically disengaged friends; Lello della Cava, a toy maker, and his free-wheeling wife Trumeau; Viola, a widow whose extreme wealth and social privilege are powerless to stave off the impending tragedy of her suicidal son, Andrea; Lorena, an obese, over-the-hill sex goddess who is addicted to cocaine; Jep's editor Dadina, whose emotional and cultural insightfulness are inversely proportional to her stature as a dwarf; and Romano, a middle-aged writer pursuing a doomed infatuation with a cruel and exploitative younger woman. The film follows Jep through a maze of social events, journalistic appointments, and chance encounters, punctuated by strolls along the streets, piazzas, and spectacular vistas of Rome during nocturnal hours or at daybreak. Among the most memorable episodes are the interview with the performance artist Talia Concept, who hurls herself naked into the abutment of an ancient aqueduct; the spectacle of a young girl, Carmellina, who produces a stunning abstract mural by throwing pails of paint against a huge canvas in a paroxysm of violence and anger; a disappointing tryst with the beautiful but infuriatingly narcissistic Orietta; a visit to a traveling Botox clinic; a funeral in which Jep puts on a virtuoso show of feigned bereavement; and a tour through the hidden palaces, gardens, and art collections of Rome's aristocracy. A succession of losses, including the death of Ramona, an aging stripper with whom Jep has shared an unlikely, platonic affection, and the decision of his dear friend Romano to leave the city, shakes the protagonist out of his existential paralysis. But it is two other events that ultimately serve to rekindle his creative life – a return in memory to his first love, Elisa, triggered by the news of her recent passing, and an acquaintance with a decrepit missionary nun, Suor Maria, who imparts the deceptively simple lesson that "roots are important." With the convergence of these two narrative threads, Jep is ready to write the novel that recounts the story of the film we just saw.

There is no small irony in the fact that it is the very unbeautiful Suor Maria, the 104-year-old missionary nun, shrivelled, shrunken, and toothless, who holds the interpretive key to the great beauty of Sorrentino's film. When asked to speak for herself, rather than let her spokesman field all the questions addressed to her, she replies succinctly, "I married poverty. And you don't recount poverty. You live it." With this terse response, the nun liquidates the film's previous one hour and fifty-four minutes of "blah-blah-blah," as Jeb himself put it in his concluding monologue when he spoke of the "lean and constant flashes of beauty" hidden under the "chatter and the noise ... [and] under the cover of the embarrassment of being in the world, blah-blah-blah." If authentic living precludes its recounting (in Suor Maria's terms), and if true beauty is concealed by the surface noise and clutter of life (in Jep's final formulation), where does that leave the arts? This, I propose, is the central question of Sorrentino's complex, multilayered film, which surveys artistic and architectural trends from antiquity to postmodernity at the level of content, but which ultimately pivots around the relationship between word and image or, more broadly, between literary and cinematic expressivity, at the level of form.

Jep's vocation as a writer obviously pushes literariness to the foreground of the film, contributing much to the "blah-blah-blah" that critics, along with the protagonist himself, have readily acknowledged. Celine supplies the epigraph, while the names of Proust, Ammaniti, Pirandello, Flaubert, D'Annunzio, Turgenev, Dostoevsky, and Breton are sprinkled throughout the film's dialogues. Several reviewers of *La grande bellezza* have faulted the pretentiousness of Jep, who "oozes bad literature from every pore," and the script that reads "as if the screenwriter were not at the service of the director but in competition with him."[1] But such criticism is deaf to the film's satiric thrust, which targets the "blah-blah-blah" of its characters as part of a broader critique of Rome's intellectual elite, infatuated with its own sophistication, living in a rarefied and hermetically sealed cultural environment.[2] Jep's balcony, site of orgiastic partying, sedentary soirées, and much solitary voyeurism, is the perfect spatial analogy for this self-enclosed world. His long, rectangular, open-air perch offers visual access to three vistas: an upper balcony occupied by a mysterious character whom the protagonist admires from afar and who turns out to be a Mafia kingpin; a garden and cloister belonging to an adjacent religious institution; and a spectacular view of the Colosseum, to which Jep's jaded visitors remain indifferent. In a delicious twist, it is the Mafioso who delivers the decisive verdict on the inconsequentiality of Jeb's world. "I'm a working man, while you have fun with your artist friends. I keep this country going."

In one of the most un-fun soirées on his balcony, Jeb brutally attacks Stefania, a sanctimonious author of literature with a leftist slant, who has written eleven novels aimed at bringing about social change. After Stefania's extended riff on her lifelong "civic vocation," dating back to her days as a student activist and culminating in her current commitment to the feminist cause, Jep lets loose with a barrage of charges against her radical-chic hypocrisy. This debate makes everyone present very uncomfortable, and Dadina, Jep's editor, seeks to defuse and depersonalize the exchange by raising the discourse to a higher level and pointing out the literary issues underlying the clash. What it boils down to, in Dadina's view, is the difference between an authorial stance based on ideology and one rooted in genuine feeling. Jep's embrace of the latter emerges clearly in his own advice to his dear friend Romano, who is struggling to adapt a D'Annunzio novel to the stage. "Try and write something of your own," Jep enjoins this would-be author – "a feeling, sorrow." Romano will eventually heed that advice toward the end of the film when he gives a public performance of a dramatic monologue steeped in a personal experience of sentiment and regret.

Because *La grande bellezza* is essentially the story of a writer's block, the awakening of Jep's creative imagination over the course of the narrative demands our closest critical attention.[3] His paralysis occasions repeated questioning by three of Jep's most trusted interlocutors – Dadina, Ramona, and Suor Maria – who wonder why he hasn't written another novel in forty years, after the prize-winning success of his first book, *The Human Apparatus*. His answers – that Rome is too distracting, that the people who surround him belong to the category of "fauna," that he has nothing more to say – dodge the deep personal issue underlying his creative impasse. If, according to Jep, literary greatness rests on genuine feeling, then we can attribute this writer's block to the drying up of the emotional wellspring that had previously nourished his art. Though we know little about his youthful novel beyond Stefania's self-righteous claim that it was "narrow-minded, frivolous, and as pretentious as its title," another character offers a precious insight into the impetus behind its writing. Orietta, a beautiful newcomer to Jep's social circle, and seductress of the first order, quotes lines from *The Human Apparatus* and opines that "you must have been in love when you wrote it." Whether or not this was just a ploy to get him into bed, it lays the groundwork for the linkage between eros and literary inspiration, preparing us for the news that will jump-start Jep's creative life. That news comes two scenes after the mechanical and unfulfilling tryst with Orietta, just as Jep arrives home to find a gentleman on his doorstep who identifies himself as Alfredo Marti, the husband of Elisa, Jep's sweetheart in adolescence. Jep's first response to this revelation is striking – "Did you have children?" To the news that the couple remained childless because Alfredo "couldn't," Jep remarks with gratuitous cruelty, "I, yes. I could." This cold-hearted remark is followed by Alberto's announcement that Elisa had died the previous day, prompting tears on the part of both men, filmed in close-up, and then framed in a beautifully composed long shot of them facing each other in symmetrically curved postures, positioned behind a curving baroque banister at floor level, and flanked to the left by a sweeping curved banister leading upwards. This intensely moving scenario is followed by a sequence that merits extended close analysis if we are to fathom the relationship between verbal and imagistic expressivity underlying the great beauty of Sorrentino's film.

A middle-age, white-clad nun cackles playfully and darts into a cloister, while the camera remains on a monument topped by the bust

Sorrentino's *La grande bellezza* 213

By locating Jep and Alfredo between the Guidi family monument at centre-left, and the white-clad nuns seen in the far distance at the top right of the frame, this composition offers a prime example of the interpretive richness of Sorrentino's art.

of a military man, supported by a pedestal displaying the following inscriptions:

Car. Benedetto Guidi
2-febbraio 1930
Giorgio Guidi
19-1-1891 5-4-1973
Valentina Guidi
maiden name Tailetti
3-7-1901 8-12-1989

Outside it is pouring, and two young nuns carrying umbrellas descend the staircase leading to the cloister. Jep and Alfredo, drenched in rain, stop during their own descent of the steps to converse. Within this sequence there is one particular photogram of surpassing importance to our analysis of Sorrentino's creative process. Shot from a distance, Jep and Alfredo are located to the left of the staircase, while the two young nuns are positioned to the right. In the foreground, to the far left, is the Guidi family monument.

The meaning of this composition is clear – the nuns have chosen to forego their place in such a genealogical chain, Alfredo and his wife were denied it by nature, and Jep was biologically equipped but not socially inclined, to take his part in a narrative of family succession. This mise-en-scène, so dense in its visual language and so fraught with significance for the immediately preceding dialogue about Alfredo and Elissa's childless marriage, has considerable theoretical implications for our understanding of this filmmaker's art. First of all, the verbal expressivity of the men's conversation has been matched (or perhaps exceeded) by the imagistic richness of this photogram, and yet the shot's full meaning depends upon a writing: the inscription of the Guidi family's names and dates. In this still image, any rivalry between word and image leads to a draw. More important, from a theoretical point of view, is the questionable legitimacy of basing a film interpretation on the stilling of a photogram that is supposed to be experienced in movement. If the theatrical viewer can only access this intricate mise-en-scène for the fraction of a second of its passage on screen, how can we give credence to an interpretation based on stop-action analysis of it? Yet this method is precisely what Roland Barthes defended in his essay "The Third Meaning" when he argued that "the filmic, very paradoxically, cannot be grasped in the film 'in situation,' 'in movement,' 'in its natural state,' but only in that major artefact, the still."[4] Barthes sees still-frame analysis as the emancipation of the medium from "the constraint of filmic time, which constraint is extremely powerful, continuing to form an obstacle to what might be called the adult birth of film."[5] If the "adult birth of film" requires viewing conditions unavailable to the theatrical spectator, then cinema can only reach its maturity through critical/scholarly means – an elitist conclusion that invites the uncomfortable question: What is cinema if not an audio-visual medium whose defining quality is its very accessibility to the masses?

In the case of *La grande bellezza*, I think that Sorrentino's film language, so dense as to require frame-by-frame analysis, skirts that thorny issue by shifting its focus away from the reception of his film to its inspiration. Since Jep and his entourage seem inordinately preoccupied by the workings of the creative imagination, it follows that the film itself would enact such content at the level of cinematic form. It is no coincidence that the news of Elisa's childless marriage and her death immediately precedes the striking tableau analysed above. Just as this revelation will trigger Jep's creative stirrings, so too does it challenge Sorrentino to exhibit his own powers of invention in cinematic terms. The theatrical viewer's inability to interpret the details of this photogram is immaterial to its function in Sorrentino's aesthetics. It is the creative energy that the filmmaker infused into this shot that matters, his own intense desire – like that of the medieval sculptor who places the image of an angel in the uppermost reaches of a cathedral ceiling, beyond the limits of mortal vision – to produce something of great beauty, for its own sake.

Of the utmost significance is the fact that the stirrings of Jep's literary imagination will be expressed in cinematic form throughout the course of the film, and it is only at the very end that Jeb entrusts to words his readiness to write the belated novel-to-be. The awakening of his imagination begins in the aftermath of his sixty-fifth birthday bash – a milestone and a stark reminder of the forty-year hiatus in the career so auspiciously begun with the prize-winning work of his youth. Resting in his bedroom after the all-night festivities, Jep glances at the ceiling and imagines it as a rippling body of water, as if he were projecting his own inner film of desired escape onto the screen of this plaster surface.[6] Later on, following the encounter with Elisa's husband, Jep resumes his marine reverie, only now this imaginary seascape is not empty, but populated by characters and enlivened by dramatic action, blending past and present, memory and contemporary angst. A speedboat pierces the calm waters off the rocky beach where a group of young women are sunning themselves. "Jep," they cry out in warning as the vessel heads toward the sixty-five-year-old protagonist, who is treading water. After the boat passes, he resurfaces as the young Jep, unscathed and triumphant, much to the joy of the girls on shore. Only one of them refrains from energetic applause and exclamations of relief. She is Elisa, beautiful and impassive, whose expression modulates into a smile as the camera slowly closes in on her.

Elisa will make two more appearances in flashback. Jep conjures her up the next time in a conversation with Ramona, the aging stripper with whom he has established a deep and abiding bond of affection, thanks to her unsullied innocence and her detachment from the world of his sophisticated friends. During an intimate conversation on Jep's balcony they exchange notes on their first amorous experiences. "On an island ... one summer ... at the lighthouse at night, I was eighteen, she twenty"; Jep then recounts his failed attempt to kiss her, but becomes tongue-tied as he tries to report what happened next. He twice utters the phrase "and then she said to me" slowly, followed by a long pause, before Ramona finally stops him, aware that Jep has entered the realm of deep memory, where temporal and spatial distances collapse and he is *back there* again, on the island in the summer of his eighteenth year in the presence of his first love. The flashbacks – brief, dimly lit close-ups of the attempted kiss in profile, and Elisa's face filmed frontally as she withdraws from him – are intercut with Jep's present-day visage, lost in memory as he tries and fails to bring verbal closure to his account. Of considerable importance is the musical soundtrack – "My Heart's in the Highlands," with the aura of sacrality conferred by the lyrics sung in an alto voice with an organ accompaniment.

Jep's partial memory, his inability to complete it in words, points to his continuing writer's block and anticipates the revelation of the great beauty that will arrive when he can finally overcome the obstacles to its full recovery. It is Ramona who propels him along the path to emotional and creative freedom in the next scene, when they lie in bed after a night of platonic closeness – antithesis of the empty and joyless sexuality of Jep's encounter with Orietta. Upon awakening, Jep comments on the beauty of their *not* making love, prompting Ramona's rejoinder, "it was beautiful *volersi bene*," using a verbal construction that has no English equivalent but connotes the form of love best captured in the Greek term *agape*, as opposed to *eros*. By way of reinforcing Ramona's sentiment, Jep's riposte builds on her word choice. "I forgot how it feels to *volersi bene*." Two other lines of dialogue in this scene reveal important bits of information: that Jep plans an outing for them to visit a "sea monster," and that Ramona is suffering from an unspecified disease whose treatment is costly and open ended. But this episode's most consequential moment comes when Jep invites Ramona to enter into his space of fantasy and to journey with him in its imaginary waters. Lying by her side on the bed, looking up at the ceiling, Jep asks if she too espies the sea on that plain plaster surface. By answering yes, she signals her acceptance of his wish that they connect at a level beyond that of mere surface communication. Strikingly, we spectators are not invited into their fantasy – this time, we do not see the lovely seascape Jep had projected onto his bedroom ceiling in previous scenes, and that Ramona now claims to perceive. We are excluded from the intimacy of this shared visionary experience, as if Jep's partnership with Ramona had now obviated the need to invite us into his inner world.

The privacy of their relationship reaches its most extreme form several scenes later, when we discover, in a brutally offhand way, that Ramona has died. Sorrentino's decision to omit Jep's experience during and after the loss of his soulmate leaves the viewer shocked and disorientated. The void surrounding Ramona's disappearance from the film, and its reticence about Jep's mourning, are especially jarring given the protagonist's theatrical performance of grief at the funeral of Viola's suicidal son Andrea, who meant relatively little to him. That performance had been meticulously choreographed in advance, when Jep took Ramona shopping for suitable mourning apparel and shared with her the cynical script he had in mind for his "grief-work" at the funeral. In the face of this hypocritical stagecraft, only silence and non-representation would be the appropriate response to the genuine bereavement occasioned by Ramona's loss. Here we might see another example of the clash between literary and filmic expressivity, where Jep's highly scripted performance at Andrea's funeral, his blah-blah-blah, is countered by a daring move of a quintessentially cinematic nature – the "editing out" of Ramona's demise and its consequences. In what may be taken as an oblique reference to Jep's sorrow, the film records his visit to the beached hulk of the Costa Concordia, image of his own shipwrecked emotions, and site of the "sea monster" whose spectacle he had promised to share with Ramona. Though her loss will play no further part in the film, it is clear that Jep's particular way of loving Ramona has propelled his creative imagination a good way toward the new novel heralded in the film's final frames.

Throughout *La grande bellezza*, other moments of genuine feeling emerge to advance Jep's progress toward the novel-to-be. One of the most striking occurs in the course of his journalistic work, while covering a photographic exhibit that harbours a lesson in autobiography with clear implications for the new writing project stirring within him. The exhibit involves a collection of selfies taken by a photographer every day of his life from adolescence to the present (his father had begun this practice from his child's birth until the age of fourteen, when the son himself took over), and the result is a daily record of his existence, captured in approximately fifteen thousand head shots of the exact same dimensions arranged chronologically. Jep is deeply moved by this spectacle, and he experiences the "flashes of beauty" that emanate from this site in distinct phases. Its first impact is architectural – the photo gallery is housed in an open-air structure, a partially enclosed circular space whose walls are divided into baroque niches, each of which contains the panels of photographs, and their totality creates the impression of mosaics when viewed from a distance. As the men approach the gallery, the photographer hangs back so that Jep can experience it in solitude, and the musical soundtrack that accompanies his viewing is the "Beatitudes," whose poignancy reveals the depth of feeling that this spectacle evokes. While the photographer's project is clearly the sign of an obsession, it is far from the narcissistic impulse that Jep had despised in Orietta with her nude selfies and her Facebook postings. Instead, it reflects a profound attempt to write a life story through a photographic means shorn of all vanity and hype. "Photography is an elegiac art, a twilight art," Susan Sontag had written. "Most subjects photographed are, just by virtue of being photographed, touched with

Against the poignant musical strains of the "Beatitudes," this scene invites the film-viewer to join Jep in the intensity of feeling inspired by his walk past the mosaic of daily photographs of a life that has reached middle age.

pathos."[7] That pathos becomes the very theme of this exhibit as it plays with time in a way that challenges the medium's promise to freeze a moment and render it permanent. Such permanence is undone by each immediately succeeding photograph, whose infinitesimal change from its predecessor may escape our notice, but whose position in an ongoing chain of daily photographs becomes a record of the aging process and a harbinger of its eventual end.

It is not only Jep's writing project that will benefit from his lingering over this striking exhibit. A powerful cinematic self-consciousness is also built into the episode, which allows Sorrentino to comment on the parallels between the exhibit's juxtaposition of still photos to simulate temporal movement, and his own medium's "dynamization of space" and "spatialization of time,"[8] to use Erwin Panofsky's famous definition of filmic art. The exhibit also calls attention to the special place of the facial close-up within the lexicon of cinematic expressivity.[9] Throughout the scene, the camera has cut between pans of the head shots in all their variety of expressions, and Jep's features in their rapt attention to the spectacle. In the final shot of Jep, the camera closes in on him to show a slight tremour of the lips as he struggles to contain the overwhelming emotion that he is experiencing, in an example of what Béla Balázs' called the "micro-physiognomy" of the human face to which film alone can give us privileged access.[10] The scene ends with a close-up of the photographer's visage – the "real-life" referent and goal of the fifteen thousand daily portraits of his life up to now. In this shot, the gaze of the photographer seems focused on no particular point – as if he were lost in a melancholy reflection on the "inventory of mortality"[11] to which this procession of images inexorably leads.

Over and against these precious moments of genuine emotion are the encounters with the vacuity of twenty-first-century Roman life – the blah-blah-blah of the soirées, the parties, the Botox clinic, the illusory giraffe, the recipes of the exorcist-turned-cardinal – that nourished Jep's writer's block. Chief among these foils to authentic feeling is the contemporary art scene, which supplies some of the film's most delicious targets for satire. Performance art comes in for special scrutiny in the episode of Talia Concept, who runs naked into the abutment of an ancient aqueduct and emerges with a bloody forehead before addressing the audience of rapt spectators with the punchline "I don't love you." This spectacle is followed by her interview with Jep, who has been commissioned by Dadina's magazine to cover the contemporary cultural scene, and who begins his questioning with a query about what inspires her art. "Vibrations. Extrasensory ones." When pushed to specify what she means by this, Talia rambles emptily before concluding that "artists don't need to explain jack shit." It becomes clear that her "vibrations" are transmitting two inter-related impulses – those of self-directed violence and hostility toward her public.

Violence also fuels the two paintings that are produced in real time at a party hosted by Rome's premier collector of modern art. The first is an unlikely portrait, the product of a knife-throwing display in which the weapons release blue paint upon impact with the panel behind Trumeau, the woman who dared to volunteer for this demonstration. The resulting outline of her body in blue paint is pronounced a "masterpiece" by one of the blithe observers of this hair-raising stunt. But the climactic enactment of artistic prowess is that of Carmellina, the little girl who has been dragooned into a performance that could best be described as *petit giugnol*. This child races back and forth between an assortment of paint cans and a huge white canvas, against which she hurls the paints and then smears them around with furious hand movements to produce a wild and glorious morass of colours. Her frenzied relay, accompanied by groans and tears, offers clear evidence of the suffering required to create this piece of work. Meanwhile, the adult onlookers remain in rapt stillness as they consume her exhibition of artistic fury while remaining unfazed by its human cost.

In one of the many examples of Sorrentino's stark juxtapositional strategy, where episodes are succeeded by their thematic and stylistic opposites, Carmellina's turbulent painting, and the violence that fueled all of the contemporary art featured in the film up to this point, give way to the surpassing serenity and classical aesthetics of a stroll through Rome's artistic past. Nothing could be more soothing and gratifying than this secret tour of palaces, gardens, paintings, and sculptures. While the contemporary art world was presented as the province of a hip, consumerist elite, these hidden treasures belong to a far more exclusive social caste – that of an inbred and aging aristocracy. A literal key is required for access to this hidden stash, and its custodian is Stefano, whose gait as tour guide is impaired by a limp – sign of the entropy of a class turned in on itself. Here the film ascends to a higher stylistic register, where dialogue is dispensed with and the soundtrack of the adagio movement in Bizet's symphony in C determines the camerawork and the movements of Stefano, Ramona, and Jep through this privileged domain. It is as if the representation of such artistic and architectural riches had issued its own cinematic challenge to Sorrentino, prompting him to use all of the medium's powers of lighting, mise-en-scène, and camerawork to do them justice. At the heart of the palace tour, after having witnessed the collection of classical statuary and such paintings as Raphael's *La fornarina*, the visitors encounter three elderly women playing cards in the brightly illuminated centre of a room surrounded by absolute darkness. These are the princesses, the aged and terminal proprietors of a glorious past, jealously guarded from the gaze of those descended from less lofty bloodlines than theirs.

This candle-lit tour of aristocratic spaces cannot help but evoke a similar sequence from *La dolce vita*, in which Marcello, Nico, and a group of revellers meander through the rooms of an abandoned villa belonging to a family of Rome's landed aristocracy. In fact, *La grande bellezza* abounds in such allusions to Fellini's ground-breaking film as the following: Jep's soirées, cynical and boozy versions of the evenings spent in Steiner's salon; the helicopter hovering above the Colosseum, a nod to Fellini's opening sequence in which Marcello and Paparazzo fly over ancient ruins on their way to the Vatican; Jep's bacchanals, echoes of the successive parties that end in the orgiastic finale of Marcello's self-debasement; Jep's offer to take Ramona to behold a sea monster, allusion to the creature that washes onshore to the amazement and disgust of Marcello and his fellow revellers; Elisa's final gaze upon Jep from a distance that seems more existential than spatial, a recall of the gap between Paola and Marcello that separates the protagonist from the possibility of redemption.

This list of parallels raises the crucial issue of Sorrentino's overall debt to Fellini[12] in *La grande bellezza*, whose very title, with its abstract noun, preceded by the definite article and adjective modifier, harks back to that of the 1959 film, with which it shares the episodic structure, the epic expanse (three hours in Fellini's film, two hours and fifty-two minutes in Sorrentino's), and the common narrative of an odyssey through Rome by a protagonist with serious authorial pretensions who must resort to journalism to make a living. It is significant that both protagonists hail from elsewhere (Jep grew up in or near Naples, Marcello in Rimini), and it is their outsider's relationship to Rome that becomes a major focus of each film.[13] In a formulation that links Jep inextricably to the city, Lorena cries out, "Best wishes Jep, best wishes Rome!" as she erupts from a cake during the raucous birthday celebration at the film's opening. In one of his soirées, Jep will proclaim that "the best people in Rome are tourists," and indeed, the film's prologue is dedicated to a group of Japanese sightseers one of whom was so overcome by a view of the city from the Gianicolo that he was literally felled by it. This perspective, both estranged and aesthetically engaged, will become Jep's during the course of the film as he eventually succeeds in overcoming his jadedness to experience those "flashes of beauty" that will coalesce into the novel that is percolating within him.

But the far more consequential Fellinian precedent for *La grande bellezza* is *8½* with Guido Anselmi, its washed-up filmmaker at the centre, stymied by the barrage of demands and expectations of those around him, and only able to access his own vein of creativity at the film's end. It would not be far-fetched to read *8½* as a simple quest for inspiration, signalled early on by Guido's daydream of his muse, the white-clad Claudia, who will hand him a cup filled with the rejuvenating waters of the spa, and who will return later on with a promise to bring "order and cleanliness" to his artistic process.[14] In a thematically important homage, Jep's deeply disappointed hopes for spiritual enlightenment from Cardinal Bellucci (prime contender for the papacy) echo those of Guido, whose two audiences with a cardinal visiting the spa end in pronouncements of the most irrelevant or exclusionist sort. These encounters with authoritative spokesmen for the church leave both men bereft of the tolerant and welcoming offers of *caritas* needed to fulfil their spiritual yearning.

But it is in structural terms that *8½* had its most powerful impact on *La grande bellezza*. Having fended off all of the external pressures to make a work of science fiction entirely against his nature, and having come to terms with the warring emotional claims on him from wife, mistress, friends, and actresses, Guido picks up the bullhorn at the end of *8½* and begins to direct the film that is true to his deepest inclinations. Succinctly stated, *8½* is the story of how he came to make the film we just saw. The end of *8½* is its beginning, in that Guido had to go through a crisis of personal and artistic identity in order to arrive at the point where he (as a fictionalized stand-in for Fellini) could direct the cinematic enactment of how he arrived there. In other words, he had to experience the *content* of his struggle before he could give it the artistic *form* of its filmic retelling. This is what I call a "Moebius strip narrative," where, just as the cut-out of a rectangle is twisted 180 degrees and the two ends are joined to form one continuous surface, so too do the narrative form and its content – its outside and inside – converge at the end of the story to account for the possibility of its artistic rendering.

La grande bellezza follows this same structural pattern, whose ending – Jep's command to "let the novel begin" – signals the commencement of the writing that will be the basis of the film we just saw.[15] To paraphrase, the content of *La grande bellezza* is the saga of the process Jep had to undergo in order to write the novel that will enable the film to take shape. There is a crucial difference however, between the Moebius structures of Fellini's and Sorrentino's plots. In the case of *8½*, the main character is a filmmaker, so that the medium with which the protagonist struggles at the level of content is identical to that which will express that content at the level of form. This is not the case with the protagonist of *La grande bellezza*, whose authorial vocation, though related to the medium of film, is nonetheless hardly identical with it. Jep's novel-writing could not smoothly map onto the beginning of Sorrentino's film the way that Guido's could onto Fellini's. For that to happen, written language would have to undergo a cinematic transfiguration.

And indeed, this is the very process that we have witnessed throughout the course of *La grande bellezza*, as Sorrentino has staged the progress from verbal to filmic expressivity in Jep's encounters with the great beauty beneath the blah-blah-blah of his life in contemporary Rome. But it is the final pronouncement made by Suor Maria, "roots are important," that penetrates to the core of the film's aesthetic vision. Uttered in the presence of the flock of flamingoes that has alighted on Jep's balcony, this phrase gives way to a whooshing sound with which Suor Maria alerts the birds that it's time for them to resume flight. Her abandonment of human speech for a natural language is striking in the context of Sorrentino's brazen artifice in this scene. But of course, the nun's Franciscan connection to nature is only made possible by computer-generated special effects, which point to the "roots" of cinematic language in illusionism, and in so doing recall the earlier scene of the giraffe, whose conjuror states three times, "It's just a trick." For Jep, Suor Maria's diet of roots not only counteracts Cardinal Bellucci's effete catalogue of recipes, it also returns Jep to the source of his imaginative life, "rooted" in the memory of Elisa on the island during the summer of his eighteenth year. Not surprisingly, the film's final flashback picks up where Jep's account of his romance with Elisa had broken off in conversation with Ramona about their first loves. Jep's thrice-repeated "and she said to me" in reporting that incident had reached a dead end in the earlier scene – he had been unable to bring verbal closure to a memory that lay at the root of his creative inspiration. In the wake of Jep's journey throughout the film – his closeness to and loss of Ramona, his survey of art forms both vapid and satisfying, his encounter with the silliness of the cardinal and the authenticity of Suor Maria – he can return to that locked memory and unleash it. Now he can fill in the blank after the suspended phrase "she said to me" with Elisa's last and only words in the film: "There's something I want to show you." As verbal language yields to visual imagery – as telling gives way to showing – she unbuttons her blouse and briefly bares her breasts before withdrawing up a stone path and seating herself on a rock positioned several yards beyond him. At this point, the sixty-five-year-old Jep takes the place of his eighteen-year-old self in the flashback, and delivers his concluding monologue, succeeded by a cut to Elisa, who turns toward the camera as the final incarnation of the great beauty announced in the written title that follows on screen.

But the film refuses to remain within the confines of Jep's story. *La grande bellezza* frees itself from its main character in the epilogue – an eight-and-a-half-minute final credit sequence, filmed from a sightseeing boat travelling the waters of the Tiber in a leisurely rhythm that simulates real time. With this, the framing of the film has come full circle, returning to the visitors' gaze of the prologue, and validating Jep's claim that "the best people in Rome are the tourists." At this point, Jep's narration is taken over by the city itself, and Rome becomes an object of pure aesthetic contemplation, expressed solely in images and music (the "Beatitudes"), freed from subservience to the bonds of plot and character, unshackled by the limits of narrative prose.

It is only from this ending that spectators can take the full measure of the film's great beauty. Sorrentino's fragmentary and wandering plot may seem to defy aesthetic standards of unity, clarity, and purpose until we evaluate, from the perspective of the ending, all of the symmetries, cross-references, visual and thematic patterns, and internal laws of logic that structure the film. Now its architectural integrity becomes clear as *La grande bellezza* encircles itself within the tourist's perspective – a perspective that began with the jarring, choppy footage of the prologue culminating in the tragedy of the Japanese visitor who will be felled by the beauty of the view from the Gianicolo. The epilogue, filmed from the sightseeing boat gliding slowly along the waters of the Tiber, instead stands as the soothing, continuous, and completely readable antidote to the film's fractured and incoherent start. Within this framework is embedded the story of one man, himself once a youthful visitor to the city whose powers to inspire creations of great beauty were lost on him until he was able to find his own rootedness in memory and genuine depth of feeling. As a stand-in for Sorrentino, who like his protagonist came to Rome from elsewhere, Jep enacts the filmmaker's own response to the city's powers of fascination and incentives to create. The gap between Jep's writerly vocation and Sorrentino's cinematic one allowed the filmmaker to foreground the specificity of his own medium in the dichotomy between the word and the image, the telling and the showing, the blah-blah-blah and the "flashes of beauty" hidden beneath it. But this opposition eventually gives way to unity as the characters' excessive verbiage and the surface clutter of their world serve as necessary threads in the composition of Sorrentino's grand cinematic tapestry. When Jep answers Suor Maria's question about his failure to write a second novel by explaining, "I was looking for the great beauty, and I didn't find it," we know that the film itself has consistently belied that claim at the level of form. But in order for us viewers to be able to rephrase Jep's statement in the affirmative – "I was looking for the great beauty, and I found it" – we must be ready to meet the film's formidable interpretive challenges, ranging from the analysis of individual photograms to the macroscopic structures of the film as a whole. Sorrentino's wager in making this complex, multilevelled work is that we will indeed take up his challenge to delve beneath the blah-blah-blah, and thus activate its great beauty on our own.

Notes

Introduction

1 Mino Argentieri, "Pasquale Scimeca e il mondo contadino del dopoguerra," *Cinemasessanta* 42 (March–April 2002): pp. 6–7. Unless otherwise noted, all translations of quotes from Italian texts are my own.
2 Gianni Quilici, "I cento passi," *La linea dell'occhio* 39 (Spring 2001): p. 5.
3 On the adherence of these two films to the paradigm of *cinema impegnato*, Gian Piero Brunetta comments that "it's as if Italian cinema still, and yet again, felt the need to respond to the call of *cinema civile* and to the need to recount the recent past to new generations with a lucid gaze at the present." See Brunetta, *Il cinema italiano contemporaneo: Da "La dolce vita" a "Cento chiodi"* (Bari: Laterza, 2007), p. 664.
4 Christian Uva, "Nuovo cinema Italia: Per una mappa della produzione contemporanea, tra tendenze formule e linguaggi," *The Italianist* 29 (2009): p. 306.
5 See the "Introduzione" of *Lo spazio del reale nel cinema italiano contemporaneo*, ed. Riccardo Guerrini, Giacomo Taglianti, and Francesco Zucconi (Genoa: Le Mani, 2009), p. 11 (emphasis in the original).
6 On the enormous impact of 9/11 on the language of cinema in particular, see Alessia Cervini, "Il cinema politico," in *Il cinema del nuovo millennio: Geografie, forme, autori,* ed. Alessia Cervini, pp. 19–36 (Rome: Carocci editore, 2020). "To understand what contemporary political cinema is," she writes, "it's necessary to see how it made that event its own, to invent a new cinematographic form just as unprecedented [as the event itself]" (p. 22).
7 For my extended analysis of this landmark film, see "*Caro diario* and the Cinematic Body of Nanni Moretti," chap. 15 in Millicent Marcus, *After Fellini: National Cinema in the Postmodern Age* (Baltimore: Johns Hopkins University Press, 2002), pp. 285–99.
8 Uva, "Nuovo cinema Italia," p. 307.

9 See Jean Baudrillard, *Simulations*, trans. Paul Foss, Paul Patton, and Philip Beitchman (New York: Semiotext(e),1983), p. 4.
10 See the Pierpaolo Antonello and Florian Mussgnug, eds., *Postmodern Impegno: Ethics and Commitment in Contemporary Italian Culture* (Oxford: Peter Lang, 2009), pp. 3–4.
11 See Antonello and Mussgnug, *Postmodern Impegno*, p. 9. For an extensive meditation on the ethical turn in the humanities, see Lawrence Buell, "Introduction: In Pursuit of Ethics," *PMLA* 114, no. 1 (January 1999): pp. 7–19.
12 Antonello and Mussgnug, *Postmodern Impegno*, p. 12. Antonello and Mussgnug go on to explain that this new approach to bettering our world arises from the micro-level of personal experience – concrete relationships with family, friends, neighbours, co-workers, community members, etc. – rather than from abstract, universalizing prescriptions for social change.
13 These are the words of Giovanna Taviani, quoted in Uva, "Nuovo cinema italiano," 308.
14 See Mario Sesti, *Nuovo cinema italiano: Gli autori, i film, le idee* (Rome: Teoria, 1994), p. 9; and Lino Miccichè, "Il lungo decennio grigio," in *Schermi opachi: Il cinema italiano degli anni '80*, ed. Lino Miccichè (Venice: Marsilio, 1998), p. 13.
15 See Franco Montini, "Una nuova generazione," in *La meglio gioventù: Nuovo cinema italiano 2000–2006*, ed. Vito Zagarrio (Venice: Marsilio, 2006), p. 23.
16 Ibid.
17 "Wu ming" is the Chinese term for "anonymous." In a similar spirit of internationalism, the group opted for English rather than Italian in its naming of the new Italian epic.
18 See *New Italian Epic: Letteratura, sguardo obliquo, ritorno al futuro*, Wu Ming I, *New Italian Epic 3.0, Memorandum 1993–2008* (Turin: Einaudi, 2009). Page references are included within parentheses in the text.
19 Though not based on a book, another of the films treated in my study, *La Mafia uccide solo d'estate*, also gave rise to an eponymous television series. Shown on RAI, it featured twenty-four episodes from 2016 to 2018.
20 Michael Z. Newman, "Intermediality and Transmedia Storytelling," 17 September 2012, https://www.c21uwm.com/2012/09/17/intermediality-and-transmedia-storytelling/.
21 I am grateful to Marta Boni for introducing me to this line of research. See her *Romanzo criminale: Transmedia and Beyond* (Venice: Ca' Foscari University Press, 2013) and "Mapping *Crime Novel*: An Epic Narrative Ecosystem?" *Series* 1, no. 1 (2015): 77–88. In my own chapter on *romanzo criminale* I will further develop the importance of Boni's work for an understanding of the film's transmedial life. On the subject of seriality, and its invitation to public participation through the creation of paratexts via social

networks, see Massimiliano Coviello, "Nuova serialità," in *Il cinema del nuovo millennio: Geografie, forme, autori*, ed. Alessia Cervini (Rome: Carocci editore, 2020), pp. 115–16.

22 According to Davide Gherardi, for example, both *Il Divo* and *Gomorra* herald "un ritorno alla dimensione dell'impegno cinematografico nel dibattito civile." See the introductory section of his essay "Giorgio Diritti e *Il vento fa il suo giro*," in *Italiana OFF: Pratiche e poetiche del cinema italiano periferico 2001–2008*, ed. Roy Menarini (Gorizia: Transmedia, 2008), p. 75.

23 Luca Malavasi, "Studio cubista di Andreotti," *Cineforum* 476 (2008): pp. 2–3.

24 A surprising choice, in light of the intention to privilege the local, home-grown nature of this film production. The logical explanation is the desire to attract not only domestic but international funding sources.

25 At least thirty as of 2013, with more in the works, according to Marco Cucco and Giuseppe Richeri in *Il mercato delle location cinematografiche* (Venice: Marsilia, 2013), p. 125.

26 For examples of critical attention to the advent of regional film commissions, and the cinematic trend toward localism in general, see Brunetta, *Il cinema italiano contemporaneo*, p. 685; Ofelia Catanea, "Perdersi: Geografie e spazi del nuovo cinema italiano," in *Gli invisibili: Esordi italiani del nuovo millennio*, ed. Vito Zagarrio (Torino: Kaplan, 2009), pp. 81–7; and an entire anthology dedicated to this subject matter, *Territori del cinema italiano: Produzione, diffusione, alfabetizzazione*, ed. Marco Maria Gazzano, Stefania Parigi, and Vito Zagarrio (Udine: Forum, 2013).

27 See Vito Zagarrio, "Benvenuto al Nord: L'immaginario delle Film Commission del settentrione," in Gazzano, Parigi, and Zagarrio, *Territori del cinema italiano*, p. 156.

28 See Cucco and Richeri, *Il mercato delle location cinematografiche*, p. 128.

29 See Anna Olivucci, "Una lupa distratta e venti gemelli affamati: Tra Stato centrale e politiche regionali di settore," in Gazzano, Parigi, and Zagarrio, *Territori del cinema italiano*, p. 87.

30 See Zagarrio, "Benvenuto al Nord," pp. 159, 165.

31 These are the words of a local high school principal, interviewed in *Focaccia Blues*.

32 See, for example, Ira Jaffe, *Slow Movies: Countering the Cinema of Action* (London: Wallflower, 2014); and Tigo de Luca and Nuno Barradas Jorge, eds., *Slow Cinema* (Edinburgh: Edinburgh University Press, 2016).

33 For the ground-breaking study regarding films in Italy of an environmentally charged nature, see Elena, *Italian Ecocinema: Beyond the Human* (Bloomington: Indiana University Press, 2019), winner of the Modern Language Association's Howard R. Marraro Prize in 2020. An important pioneer of ecocriticism within the Italian sphere is Serenella Iovino, author

and editor of numerous books dedicated to the subject. See, for example, *Ecocriticism and Italy: Ecology, Resistance, and Liberation* (London: Bloomsbury, 2016). A seminal contribution to the study of landscape within the language of Italian film is Sandro Bernardi's *Il paesaggio nel cinema italiano* (Venice: Marsilio, 2002).

34 Áine O'Healy notes that in the 1990s, when the migrant crisis was in full swing, relatively little cinematic attention was directed to this burning issue, whereas the first decade of the new millennium saw a dramatic increase in its filmic representation. See her *Migrant Anxieties: Italian Cinema in a Transnational Frame* (Bloomington: Indiana University Press, 2019), p. 2.

35 See Roberto De Gaetano, "Prefazione: L'immagine documentaria come domanda di senso," in *Per un cinema del reale: Forme e pratiche del documentario italiano contemporaneo,*" ed. Daniele Dottorini (Udine: Forum, 2013), p. 10. On the surge in documentary production, see Bruno Torri, "Ricambi generazionali (1943–2009)," in *Esordi italiani: Gli anni Dieci al cinema (2010–2015),* ed. Pedro Armocida (Venice: Marsilio, 2015), p. 36; and Vito Zagarrio, "La rivoluzione documentaria," in *Istantanee sul cinema italiano: Film, volti, idee del nuovo millennio,* ed. Franco Montini and Vito Zagarrio (Soveria Mannelli: Rubbettino, 2012), p. 164.

36 My data come from Daniele Dottorini in "Per un cinema del reale: Il documentario come laboratorio aperto," in *Per un cinema del reale,* p. 15. I have not been able to find statistics for more recent years, but the general tendency documented by Dottorini seems to be holding firm.

37 This compilation of documentary variants comes from Dottorini, ibid., p. 18, and Marco Bertozzi, "Di alcune tenendenze del documentario italiano nel terzo millennio," in *Il reale allo specchio: Il documentario italiano contemporaneo,* ed. Giovanni Spagnoletti (Venice: Marsilio, 2012), p. 18. As this proliferation of terms suggests, the definition of the term *documentary* itself is plagued by imprecision. In his 2020 essay on the subject, Dottorini asks point-blank: "What are we talking about? New documentary? Cinema of the real? Non-fiction film? Cinema of witness? The formulas follow each other one after the other ... What they have in common, if anything, is the awareness of the ethical and political necessity of 'thinking' an 'other cinema,' a sort of laboratory of forms that characterize an important part of contemporary film." See "Il 'cinema-senza-nome': Lo sguardo documentario del nuovo millennio," in *Il cinema del nuovo millennio,* p. 89.

38 See Bertozzi, "Di alcune tendenze del documentario italiano," p. 18.

39 See Uva, "Nuovo cinema Italia," p. 313. For recent English-language works dedicated to the subject of Italian film comedy see Rémi Fournier, *Comedy Italian Style: The Golden Age of Italian Film Comedies* (New York: Continuum, 2008); and Andrea Bini, *Male Anxiety and Psychopathology in*

Film: Comedy Italian Style (New York: Palgrave MacMillan, 2015). For coverage on one hundred Italian film comedies from 1932 to 1993, see Aldo Viganò, *Storia del cinema: Commedia italiana in cento film* (Genoa: Le Mani, 1995).
40 See Vito Zagarrio, "Il genere nel nuovo cinema italiano," in *Istantanee sul cinema italiano: Film, volti, idee del nuovo millennio*, ed. Franco Montini and Vito Zagarrio (Soveria Mannelli: Rubbettino, 2012), p. 53.
41 Ibid.
42 Ibid., pp. 53–4.
43 See Uva, "Nuovo cinema Italia," p. 313. For an extremely rigorous study devoted solely to the genre of *cinema natalizio*, see Alan O'Leary's *Fenomenologia del cinepanettone* (Soveria Mannelli: Rubbettino, 2013).
44 Uva, "Nuovo cinema Italia," p. 314.
45 See, for example, Flavias Brizio-Skov, ed., *Popular Italian Cinema: Culture and Politics in a Postwar Society* (London: I.B. Gauris, 2011), which includes chapters on the peplum, horror, the spaghetti western, comedy, and melodrama. Several Italian film histories dedicate chapters to genre cinema, among them Marcia Landy, *Italian Film* (Cambridge: Cambridge University Press, 2000); Mary Wood, *Italian Cinema* (Oxford: Berg, 2005); and Peter Bondanella and Federico Pacchioni, *A History of Italian Cinema*, 2nd ed. (New York: Bloomsbury, 2017). Catherina O'Rawe has written a number of important essays on various facets of Italian popular cinema.
46 Wood, *Italian Cinema*, p. 62.
47 Gianni Canova, *Cinemania: 10 anni 100 film: Il cinema italiano del nuovo millennio* (Venice: Marsilio, 2010), p. 9.
48 See Alessia Cervini, "Premessa," in *Il cinema del nuovo millennio*, p. 15.

Chapter 1

1 Filmmakers of the *cinema politico* genre included Paolo and Vittorio Taviani (*A Man for Burning*, 1962), Gillo Pontecorvo (*The Battle of Algiers*, 1966), Elio Petri (*Investigation of a Citizen above Suspicion*, 1970), and Marco Bellocchio (*China Is Near*, 1967) – members of a generation that took the neorealist legacy into more radical and didactic terrain. By the late 1970s, Rosi and the Tavianis adopted a "softer," variegated and lyrical approach to their filmmaking, adding complexity to ideological positions through characters whose inner lives as well as material circumstances dictated their actions. See, for example, Rosi's *Three Brothers* (1981) and the Tavianis' *Padre padrone* (1977).
2 Gaetana Marrone sees the decision to insert footage of the final frames of Rosi's work (frames that include the written inscription "The characters and events shown are imaginary. The social and environmental context

is real.") as a move on Giordana's part to highlight the referential force of his own film. See Marrone, *The Cinema of Francesco Rosi* (New York: Oxford University Press, 2020), p. 103.
3 The term *modelli imitabili* is Chiara Modonesi's. See her "Cento passi verso la libertà," *Acting* 1 (September 2000): p. 18. Tullio Masoni makes the ingenious argument that the citation of Rosi's *Le mani sulla città*, followed by the young crowd's preference for dancing over analysing the film, suggests the need to update the model of *cinema politico* for consumption by a new generation of viewers. See Masoni, "La Mafia, Pasolini, i Procol Harum," *Cineforum* 40 (November 2000): 62. Masoni goes on to claim that Giordana fails in this updating procedure – a position with which I take issue, as I will show in the following pages.
4 Marco Olivieri and Anna Paparcone make a strong argument for a psychoanalytic reading of Peppino's family dynamics in *Marco Tullio Giordana: Una poetica civile in forma di cinema* (Soveria Mannelli: Rubbettino, 2017), p. 92.
5 This scene has been singled out by a number of critics for special commendation, given the brilliance of its dramaturgy, the power of its iconography, and the subtlety of its psychological shadings. See, for example, Silvia Colombo's review in *Panoramiche/Panoramiques: Rivista di cinema* 27 (Fall 2000): p. 24; Emanuele D'Onofrio, *Film music, nazione e identità narrativa: Il cinema italiano contemporaneo rivisita gli anni settanta* (Reggio Calabria: Città del Sole, 2013), p. 199; Masoni, "La Mafia, Pasolini, i Procol Harum," p. 62; and for an especially detailed reading of the scene, Olivieri and Paparcone, *Marco Tullio Giordana*, pp. 92–4.
6 This image has prompted critics to advance a Christological reading of Peppino, and to see this moment in the film as a foreshadowing of his sacrificial destiny.
7 Pier Paolo Pasolini, *Poesie* (Milano: Garzanti, 1970), p. 125.
8 For a particularly insightful reading of this scene, see Daniela Bini, *Portrait of the Artist and His Mother in Twentieth-Century Italian Culture* (Madison: Fairleigh Dickinson University Press, 2021), pp. 73–4.
9 On the "paesaggio della fisiognomica," see Gianni Canova's analysis of *I cento passi* in *Cinemania: 10 anni 100 film: Il cinema italiano del Nuovo millennio* (Venice: Marsilio, 2010), p. 23.
10 Umberto Eco, *Apocalypse Postponed*, ed. Robert Lumley (Bloomington: Indiana University Press, 1994), p. 167.
11 For Giordana, writer and filmmaker of *Pasolini: Un delitto italiano*, the importance of the Pasolinian model can never be overestimated. See Olivieri and Paparcone, *Marco Tullio Giordana*, pp. 94–5.
12 See the review by Quilici, "I cento passi," in *La linea dell'occhio* 39, p. 5.
13 D'Onofrio's study of Giordana's musical soundtrack, on which my own subsequent remarks heavily rely, includes a refutation of the charge that

music serves only as an "agente emotivo," and thus vindicates the profoundly intellectual and cultural logic of the filmmaker's choice of songs. See his *Film music, nazione e identità narrative*, pp. 165–205.
14 Ibid., p. 187.
15 For this identification, see ibid., p. 189.
16 See ibid., pp. 193–4.
17 The phrase" Years of Lead" refers to the decade of violent attacks perpetrated by zealots on both the far right and the far left of the Italian political spectrum.
18 For in-depth analyses of these songs and their relevance to the film's narrative contexts, see ibid., pp. 196–8, 201–3, and 203–5 respectively.
19 On the thematic linkage between the popular song and the poem ("L'infinito") that the boy Peppino will recite to great family acclaim in the next scene, see ibid., pp. 176–7, and Marco Olivieri and Anna Paparcone, *Marco Tullio Giordana*, p. 87.
20 Giacomo Leopardi, *I canti di Giacomo Leopardi nelle traduzioni inglesi*, ed. G. Singh (Recanati: Centro Nazionale di Studi Leopardiani, 1990), pp. 162–3. Translation of the poem by R.C. Trevelyan.
21 In a highly nuanced discussion of the relationship between parody and satire, Linda Hutcheon characterizes the former as a double-edged instrument – a critique that can move bidirectionally, taking as its object a past work of art or aesthetic tradition but also providing a critical commentary on the current age. Peppino's "rewriting" of Dante would fall into Hutcheon's category of reverential parody – one that levels a withering satiric assault on the contemporary wielders of power. See Hutcheon, *A Theory of Parody: The Teachings of Twentieth-Century Art Forms* (New York: Methuen, 1985), pp. 57, 103ff.
22 This is a rough paraphrase of Ugo Foscolo's iconic lines in *Dei sepolchri*: "A egregie cose il forte animo accendono/l'urne de'forti" (ll.151–2).
23 See Modonesi, "Cento passi verso la libertà," p. 18.

Chapter 2

1 For a list of these films, see the introduction.
2 In so doing, Diliberto breathes new life into these static, easily overlooked fixtures of the urban landscape. For a superb analysis of the way in which the film revitalizes the history commemorated by traditional monuments, see Massimiliano L. Delfino, "A Cinematic Anti-Monument against Mafia Violence: P. Diliberto's *La mafia uccide solo d'estate*," in *Annali d'italianistica* 35 (2017): pp. 385–401, in which the author sums up the point of the father-son pilgrimage with the claim that "monuments thus become protagonists once again against the indifference and the decay with which they are associated in modern times" (397).

232 Notes to pages 40–6

3 Delfino's "A Cinematic Anti-Monument" is of particular relevance in this regard: "For Diliberto, through the monumental concretization of past bloodshed, perennial therapeutic sources open up in the wounded space of the city, and thus allow for a conscious civil re-appropriation of public space against indifference, forgetfulness and ignorance" (p. 397).
4 Delfino calls attention to this detail in ibid., p. 397n10.
5 Delfino, "A Cinematic Anti-Monument," p. 389.
6 Ibid.
7 On Pif's explanation for the logic of his title, see Alberto Crespi's review of the film in *L'Unità*, 25 November 2013.
8 Marco Dinoi, *Lo sguardo e l'evento: I media, la memoria, il cinema* (Florence: Le Lettere, 2008), p. 174; cited in Christian Uva, ed., *Strane storie: Il cinema e i misteri d'Italia* (Soveria Mannelli: Rubbettino, 2011), p. 14.
9 This is Christian Uva's term. See "I misteri d'Italia nel cinema. Strategie narrative e trame estetiche tra documento e finzione," in Uva, *Strane storie*, p. 16. For Alessia Cervini, it is the encounter between diverse media and the resulting interchange between "what we continue to call reality and what we think we understand as fiction" that resides at the heart of contemporary political cinema. See Cervini, "Il cinema politico," in *Il cinema del nuovo millennio: Geografie, forme, autori*, ed. Alessia Cervini (Rome: Carocci editore, 2020), p. 22.
10 Vittorio Fantuzzi, "Intervista a Paolo Benvenuti," in Paola Baroni and Paolo Benvenuti, *Segreti di Stato, dai documenti al film*, ed. Nicola Tranfaglia (Rome: Fandango, 2003), p. 104; cited in Uva, *Strane storie*, p. 13.
11 For his insights on the way in which these inserts place "Italian viewers at the very center of the fiction," see Delfino, "A Cinematic Anti-Monument," p. 394.
12 The five slain bodyguards were accorded a state funeral, while the obsequies for Borsellino were held privately at the request of his widow, Agnese, who asked that no politicians be present at the service.
13 This is Eric Santner's argument in "History beyond the Pleasure Principle: Some Thoughts on the Representation of Trauma," in *Probing the Limits of Representation: Nazism and the Final Solution*, ed. Saul Friedlander (Cambridge, MA: Harvard University Press, 1992), p. 144.
14 See Dana Renga, *Unfinished Business: Screening the Italian Mafia in the New Millennium* (Toronto: University of Toronto Press, 2013), especially pp. 6–16.
15 Uva, "I misteri d'Italia nel cinema," p. 27.
16 Antonio Pettierre finds much to admire, from a technical point of view, in Diliberto's debut as a filmmaker. See his review of the film at www.ondacinema.it/film/recensione/Mafia_uccide_solo_estate.html.
17 Pif appeared in "Le iene" on Italia 1 from 2000 to 2007 and in "Il testimone" on MTV and TV8 from 2007 to the present.

18 See Marzia Gandolfi's review of the film at www.mymovies.it/film/2013/solodestate.

Chapter 3

1 From the special feature "Dietro le quinte" (Behind the scenes) of the Warner Brothers DVD *Crime Novel* (2005).
2 See Gianni Canova, *Cinemania: 10 anni, cento film: Il cinema italiano del nuovo millennio* (Venice: Marsilio, 2010), p. 183.
3 From the "Dietro le quinte" special feature of the DVD.
4 For the phrase *gangerstistico-civile*, see Vincenzo Buccheri, "Gli anni '70, la politica, l'immaginario," in *Segnocinema* 25, no. 136 (November–December, 2005): p. 35. The "civile" component of the film was bolstered by Placido's expert preparation of the cast. The director turned the film's production into a collective project, investing actors with personal responsibility for conducting background work on the Banda della Magliana, on the historical period, on archival material documenting events of the time, and so on – and bringing the results of their research to the writing of the screenplay. See Daniela Turco and Bruno Roberti, eds., "Oltre lo schermo: Conversazione con Michele Placido," *Filmcritica* 561/562 (January/February 2006): pp. 39–40. Of particular interest is the fact that some of the cast members were too young to have had memories of living through the 1970s. "Regarding this entrance into Italian history," Placido mused, "it's a little as if history had become a body within the group of actors who had not lived it" (Turco and Bruno Roberti, "Oltre lo schermo," p. 40). On Pacido's expertise in eliciting the best possible performances from his cast, see Paolo D'Agostini, "Gli attori e la recitazione," in *La meglio gioventù: Nuovo cinema italiano 2000–2006*, ed. Vito Zagarrio (Venice: Marsilio, 2006), p. 66.
5 De Cataldo, who collaborated on the screenplay, objected to labelling *Romanzo criminale* a "film di genere," finding such categories "logore" (worn out). See Pierpaolo Antonello and Alan O'Leary, "Sotto il segno della metafora: Una conversazione con Giancarlo De Cataldo," *The Italianist* 29 (2009): p. 353.
6 For examples of critical objections to the film's treatment of "il reale storico" see Alberto Pesce, *Cinema italiano duemila: Primo decennio tra crisi e trasformazione* (Brescia: Liberedizione, 2013), p. 138; and Buccheri, "Gli anni '70, la politica, l'immaginario," p. 35. Canova, instead, vindicates the film's licence to "amplificare, alludere, suggerire, ipotizzare," given that it makes no claims to documentary reportage. See *Cinemania*, p. 183.
7 Marta Boni, "Mapping *Crime Novel*: An Epic Narrative Ecosystem?" *Series* 1, no. 1 (2015): p. 78. As noted in my introduction, I am indebted to Boni for her analysis of the film's afterlife in transmedial forms. She shared her

dissertation research with me in several extremely stimulating conversations. For her book-length study of the topic, see *Romanzo criminale: Transmedia and Beyond* (Venice: Ca' Foscari University Press, 2013).

8 The above synopsis paraphrases, in English, the definition of *romanzo* in the *Grande dizionario della lingua italiana*, vol. 17, ed. Salvatore Battaglia (Turin: UTET, 1994).

9 For Mikhail Bakhtin's seminal definition of the novel, which he defines over and against the static and rigidly codified nature of the epic, see the chapter "Epic and Novel: Toward a Methodology for the Study of the Novel," in *The Dialogic Imagination: Four Essays*, ed. Caryl Emerson and Michael Holquist, trans. Michael Holquist (Austin: University of Texas Press, 1981), pp. 3–40. The quotes from Bakhtin come from pp. 3 and 11 respectively

10 Sergio Citti, born in the shantytowns of Rome, was a novelist, screenwriter, filmmaker, and close collaborator of Pasolini.

11 From the DVD special feature "Dietro le quinte." Also included in this special feature are the remarks of actor Pierfrancesco Favino on the Pasolinian echoes in the film. For further examples of critical commentary on the subject, see Peter Bondanella and Federico Pacchioni, *A History of Italian Cinema*, 2nd ed. (New York: Bloomsbury, 2017), p. 510; and Flavio De Bernardinis's "Romanzo criminale" in *Segnocinema* 25 (November–December 2005): p. 35.

12 In this regard, De Cataldo's novel adheres closely to the vision articulated by the writers' collective Wu Ming, in the manifesto published in *New Italian Epic: Letteratura, sguardo obliquo, ritorno al futuro* (Turin: Einaudi, 2009). For an overview of the New Italian Epic, see the introduction to this volume.

13 This is the Italian remake of the American original, "You Were on My Mind," by We Five (1965). "Io ho in mente te" was released in 1966 by Equipe 84.

14 The theme of predestination figures prominently in the commentary of Placido and De Cataldi accompanying this scene of the DVD.

15 Referring to a local crook of no importance to the film's plot, singled out in this regard for his distinctly unappetizing name.

16 In the DVD commentary, Placido confesses to his use of poetic license in "adding" the dunes to the shoreline of Ostia, which is flat.

17 For an excellent overview of this genre, see Bondanella and Pacchioni, *A History of Italian Cinema*, pp. 475–514.

18 Allison Cooper sees this as an example of Freddo's deluded quest for ultimate freedom. See her "*Romanzi criminale*: Roma Caput Violandi," in "Italy's Other Mafias in Italian Film and Television: A Roundtable," ed. Alan O'Leary, *The Italianist Film Issue* 33, no. 2 (2013): p. 206.

19 For a superb analysis of the film's representation of *Romanità* and its link to themes of state surveillance as an instrument of its contemporary authoritarian aspirations, see Cooper, "*Romanzi criminale*: Roma Caput Violandi," pp. 204–6.

Chapter 4

1 See Emilio Cozzi, "La forma è sostanza: Intervista a Matteo Garrone," *Cineforum* 475 (1 June 2008): p. 16.
2 Ibid.
3 Pierpaolo De Sanctis, "Il crepuscolo della bellezza: Lo sguardo e il metodo di Matteo Garrone," in *Non solo* Gomorra: *Tutto il cinema di Matteo Garrone*, ed. Pierpaolo De Sanctis, Domenico Monetti, and Luca Pallanch (Cantalupo in Sabina: Edizioni Sabinae, 2008), p. 18.
4 For my thinking on film spectatorship as an embodied experience, and its phenomenological implications, I am indebted to conversations and correspondence with art historian and film scholar Hava Aldouby. It is she who called my attention to Sobchack's fundamental work, and in particular *Carnal Thoughts: Embodiment and Moving Image Culture* (Berkeley: University of California Press, 2004). "The Charge of the Real" is the title of chapter 11 of that work.
5 It should therefore come as no surprise that Garrone's next film, entitled *Reality* (2012), would explore this televisual phenomenon.
6 Understandably, these techniques have led critics to remark on the neorealist ancestry of Garrone's style. See Salvatore Salviano Miceli, "Il cinema antropocentrico di Matteo Garrone," in *Cinegomorra: Luci e ombre sul nuovo cinema italiano*, ed. Simone Isola (Rome: Sovera, 2010), p. 94; and Gianni Canova, *Cinemania: 10 anni, 100 film: Il cinema italiano dal nuovo millennio* (Venice: Marsilia, 2010), p. 253.
7 Elena Past dedicates considerable attention to the warm bonds that Garrone's film crew established with the on-location populace, and the resulting "hospitality" that the latter extended to their temporary "guests," sometimes with unintended consequences. Hence the vivid label "dirty cinema," understood as full immersion in the humus of a location, which Past attaches to this filmmaking approach. See *Italian Ecocinema: Beyond the Human* (Bloomington: Indiana University Press, 2019), pp. 75, 78, 80–1.
8 For the technologically pared-down nature of Garrone's cinematography, see Pierpaolo Antonello, who compares the film's style to that of the Dogma 95 directors in "Dispatches from Hell: Matteo Garrone's *Gomorrah*," in *Mafia Movies: A Reader*, 2nd ed., ed. Dana Renga (Toronto: University of Toronto Press, 2019), p. 296. On Garrone's exquisite receptivity to the cues provided by the setting and the actors themselves, see the

filmmaker's own comments in the interview with Simone Isola published in *Cinegomorra: Luci e ombre sul nuovo cinema italiano*, p. 97; and De Sanctis, "Il crepuscolo della bellezza," pp. 10–12.

9 Tullio Masoni, "Traccia di pietà nel regno del male. Matteo Garrone. *Gomorra*," *Cineforum*, no. 475 (2008): p. 7.

10 Silvia Carlorosi, alluding to Garrone's background as an artist, describes this mise-en-scène as a "visionary surrealistic painting," and goes on to suggest that the perceptual difficulty of this scene "is the formal aesthetic representation of the difficulty of focalizing the problem, the difficulty of seeing, understanding, and analysing such a complicated world as that of the Camorra." See "Epilogue: Neorealism, Cinema of Poetry, and Italian Contemporary Cinema," in *Global Neorealism: The Transnational History of a Film Style*, ed. Saverio Giovacchini and Robert Sklar (Jackson: University of Mississippi, 2012), p. 249. Gianni Canova, in *Cinemania: 10 anni, 100 film*, p. 253, notes the scene's affinities with science fiction.

11 As De Sanctis points out in "Il crepuscolo della bellezza," p. 15, the tanning salon is a postmodern variant of the barbershop scenario for conventional gangland settling of accounts.

12 Quoted in Masoni, "Traccie di pietà nel regno del male," p. 7.

13 See Carlorosi, "Epilogue," p. 249.

14 Much critical attention has been accorded to this aspect of the film. See, for example, Antonello, "Dispatches from Hell," pp. 298; John Jurgensen, "An Inside Look at the Real Wiseguys," *Wall Street Journal*, 6 February 2009, p. W4; Anthony Lane, "Gritty Cities," *The New Yorker*, 23 February 2009, p. 82; and Francesco Cattaneo, "L'insostenibile quotidianità del degrado," p. 9.

15 Cesare Zavattini was the scriptwriter of De Sica's signature neorealist films – *Shoeshine, Bicycle Thief, Umberto D* – and served as the a posteriori theorizer of neorealist aesthetics. For a synthesis of his writings on neorealism, see Zavattini, "A Thesis on Neo-Realism," in *Springtime in Italy: A Reader on Neo-Realism*, ed. David Overbey (Hamden, CT: Archon Books, 1978), pp. 67–78.

16 Cesare Zavattini, "Some Ideas on the Cinema," in *Film: A Montage of Theories*, ed. Richard Dyer MacCann (New York: Dutton, 1966), p. 221.

17 See Pierpaolo De Sanctis, "Da Saviano a Garrone," in *Non solo* Gomorra, p. 37. Massimo Gaudioso argues that the strategy of not representing the bosses makes them seem that much more formidable. See "L'uomo delle storie: Conversazione con Massimo Gaudioso a cura di Pierpaolo De Sanctis," in *Non solo* Gomorra, p. 124.

18 The Marco-Ciro plot line demonstrates a point made emphatically in Saviano's book (see his chapter entitled "Hollywood," pp. 266–82) and verbalized by Garrone in his interview with Maurizio Braucci, "*Gomorra*, il film,"

in *Non solo* Gomorra, pp. 74–5: that gangsters model their behaviour on cinematic representations of that behaviour.
19 Roberto Saviano, *Gomorra* (Milan: Mondadori, 2006). For the English edition, see *Gomorrah*, trans. Virginia Jewiss (New York: Picador, 2007),
20 See Garrone's comment on his decision to eliminate Saviano's "narrating I" in the interview with Simone Isola in *Cinegomorra*, p. 98. Significantly, Simone Villani remarks that the absence of a narrative voice "che stabilisce una rassicurante distanza culturale rispetto al narrato" renders the film more unconsumable than the novel. See "Garrone, *Gomorra*: Un nuovo modello di 'visibilità' per il cinema italiano?" in *Gli invisibili: Esordi italiani del nuovo millennio*, ed. Vito Zagarrio (Rome: Kaplan, 2009), p. 90.
21 Sobchack, *Carnal Thoughts*, p. 5.
22 Maurizio Braucci, "*Gomorra*, il film: Conversazione con Matteo Garrone a cura di Maurizio Braucci," in *Non solo* Gomorra, p. 69. For a rigorous analysis of Garrone's work with the image – going beyond its naturalistic representation, transforming it, "capturing its most intimate substance, its pure form" to arrive at "the object's most abstract value," in accordance with the poetic cinema of Pasolinian memory, see Silvia Carlorosi's "Epilogue," p. 250.
23 Cozzi, "La forma è sostanza," p. 17.
24 Ibid.
25 As Dana Renga points out in *Unfinished Business: Screening the Italian Mafia in the New Millennium* (Toronto: University of Toronto Press, 2013), p. 136, there is only a single character who appears in more than one plot strand: Maria, who figures importantly in both Don Ciro's and Totò's stories. Regarding the structure of otherwise unconnected episodes, Gaudioso recounts how Garrone and his fellow scriptwriters viewed episode films such as *Paisà* and *Short Cuts*, but decided not to embed *Gomorra*'s five plots within any overarching framing device. See "L'uomo delle storie: Conversazione con Massimo Gaudioso a cura di Pierpaolo De Sanctis," in *Non solo* Gomorra, p. 120.
26 See, for example, Saviano, *Gomorra*, p. 52.
27 In *Italian Ecocinema*, Elena Past provides extensive background material on Le Vele, locating it within the larger context of the "dirtiness," understood literally and figuratively, that she attributes to the geopolitical landscape of Naples and environs. See her pp. 66–9.
28 Anton Giulio Mancino, "Da Rosi a Garrone: L'ombra delle vele di Scampia," *Cineforum* 475 (1 June 2008): p. 12.
29 Antonella Sisto cites this scene as an example of the lack of an "outside" and the general "locationlessness" of the globalized condition in "*Gomorra*, aka *Gomorrah*: Italian Transnational Cinema," paper presented at the annual American Association for Italian Studies conference, New York, 2009.

30 Dana Renga devotes considerable attention to Maria, as the only female character to be developed in the film, and as an exemplar of the author's theory that women are the objects onto whom the culture displaces its inability to work through the collective trauma of organized crime via the mourning process. For Renga's extended analysis of Maria's role within the film, see *Unfinished Business*, pp. 136–45.

31 For Pasolini's influential formulation, see "Il 'Cinema di poesia,'" in *Empirismo eretico* (Milan: Garzanti, 1981), pp. 175–83. For the English translation of the essay, see *Heretical Empiricism*, ed. Louise K. Barnett, trans. Ben Lawton (Bloomington: Indiana University Press, 1988), pp.167–86. For Jean Mitry's related theory of the "semi-subjective image," see *Aesthetics and Psychology in the Cinema*, trans. Christopher King (Bloomington: Indiana University Press, 1997), pp. 214–19; and Gilles Deleuze, *Cinema I: The Movement Image*, trans. Barbara Habberjam and Hugh Tomlinson (Minneapolis: University of Minnesota Press, 1997), pp. 72–6. For the references to Mitry and Deleuze, and the concept of a continuum of positions between subjective and objective shots, I am indebted to my student Caleb Groos, whose research resulted in an honours thesis entitled "Pasolini: Free-Indirect Subjectivity in Cinema" (University of Texas at Austin, 1998).

32 See Michel Foucault, *Discipline and Punish: The Birth of the Prison*, trans. Alan Sheridan (New York: Random House, 1977), pp. 195–228. For calling my attention to the theory of the panopticon, I am grateful to my former student at the University of Texas Lawrence Tooley.

33 Dana Renga also remarks on this disquieting cut. See *Unfinished Business*, p. 138.

34 On the use of long shots in particular, and the function of space in general as a void to be filled by waste in connection with the Franco-Roberto plot line, see Simona Bondavalli, "Waste Management: Garbage Displacement and the Ethics of Mafia Representation in Matteo Garrone's *Gomorrah*," *California Italian Studies* 2, no. 1 (2011): 6.

35 Saviano, *Gomorra*, p. 318. Various critics have remarked on Garrone's retention of the Roberto character as Saviano's authorial surrogate within the film. See, for example, Antonello, "Dispatches from Hell," p. 295; and Bondavalli, "Waste Management," p. 3.

36 Bondavalli, "Waste Management," p. 13.

37 Saviano, *Gomorra*, p. 46.

38 In *Unfinished Business*, p. 139, Renga astutely contrasts the progressive isolation and immobilization of the persecuted woman to the ever-increasing mobility and criminal activity of the adolescent on his way to becoming "a made man."

39 Intriguingly, Garrone's inspiration for this mise-en-scène was the ending of Pasolini's *Che cosa sono le nuvole*, where the puppets played by Totò and

Ninetto Davoli are discarded as trash. See Cozzi, "La forma è sostanza," p. 17.
40 This phrase is a loose translation of the title of Francesco Cattaneo's article, "L'insostenible quotidianità del degrado," *Cineforum* 475 (1 June 2008): p. 10.

Chapter 5

1 On this unusual financial arrangement, see Elena Past, *Italian Ecocinema: Beyond the Human* (Bloomington: Indiana University Press, 2019), p. 87. This study, which includes an extended, in-depth analysis of Diritti's film, will be cited throughout my chapter for its deeply insightful and groundbreaking reading from an ecological, post-human perspective. On the film's atypical production mode, see also Morando Morandini, "... e prima o poi ritorna," *Cineforum* 465 (June 2007): p. 3; and Gianni Canova, *Cinemania: 10 anni 100 film: Il cinema italiano del nuovo millennio* (Venice: Marsilio, 2010), p. 187. The film's anomalous production practices extend to its mode of distribution, since these are governed by the "colossi" – RAI and Mediaset, according to Diritti, thus excluding such independent films as *Il vento fa il suo giro*. This means that the troupe's self-financed film was able to recoup its producers' investments only thanks to autonomous distribution efforts, which succeeded in garnering sufficient profits to offset expenses. The film enjoyed a cult following, exemplified by its year-long stint at the Cinema Mexico of Milan. See Past, *Italian Ecocinema*, p. 115; and Davide Gherardi, "L'anomala ventata: Il Vento e i suoi dintorni," in *Italiana OFF: Pratiche e poetiche del cinema italiano periferico 2001–2008*, ed. Roy Menarini (Gorizia: Transmedia, 2008), pp. 77–8.
2 On the generous hospitality extended to the actors and crew by members of the local community of Valle Maira, see Sara Martin, "Storia di una vita dimenticata," *Italiana OFF*, pp. 81–2. Martin notes that such generosity is especially admirable given the film's jaundiced view of local mores.
3 See Past, *Italian Ecocinema*, p. 102. According to Morandini ("... prima o poi ritorna," p. 33), there are 180,000 speakers of Occitan in 120 Italian municipalities of Piedmont and Liguria, and in one zone in Calabria!
4 See Past, *Italian Ecocinema*, p. 108.
5 Quoted in Gherardi, "L'anomala ventata," p. 78.
6 See Martin, "Storia di una vita dimenticata," p. 82.
7 Strikingly, the film operates on three different linguistic registers: Occitan, standard Italian, and French, necessitating the use of subtitles even for domestic audiences, and providing one of the several reasons why mainstream distributors refused to promote it. See Gherardi, "L'anomala ventata," pp. 75, 77.

8 See Morandini, "... e prima o poi ritorna," p. 33.
9 Gherardi makes the insightful comparison between Philippe's character and that of the iconic hero of the Western: "the hero in flight from civilization with his own pride or individualism" who brandishes "a certain energetic rhetoric of life in contact with the wilderness." Gherardi goes on to note that the bar where Philippe first meets some of the local residents "is precisely a saloon"! See "L'anomala ventata," p. 77.
10 See Martin, "Storia di una vita dimenticata," p. 83.
11 On Philippe's insensitivity to his wife's plight, see Martin, "Storia di una vita dimenticata," p. 83.
12 On the animalization of the family, see Past, *Italian Ecocinema*, p. 96.
13 Past focuses extensively on the characterization of Roberto within the human-animal spectrum in ibid., pp. 100–1.
14 Past also sees the slaughter of the goats as the occurrence that marks the plot's tragic denouement, and muses about the relevance of the etymology of tragedy in "goat-song." See *Italian Ecocinema*, p. 113.
15 As Past puts it, "the end of the film deconstructs the memory of the *rueido*, as well as the 'anthropocelebrative' ... promotional film being created to advertise Chersogno as a tourist destination." See *Italian Ecocinema*, p. 116.
16 César Vallejo, "Mass," 1939, trans. Paul O'Prey, https://war-poetry .livejournal.com/317625.html.
17 On the role of Massimo in the film's concluding frames, see Past, *Italian Ecocinema*, p. 113.
18 For his seminal theory of folkloric time, see Mikhail Bakhtin, "Forms of Time and of the Chronotope in the Novel," in *The Dialogic Imagination*, ed. Michael Holquist, trans. Caryl Emerson and Michael Holquist (Austin: University of Texas Press), pp. 146–151 and 206ff.

Chapter 6

1 Though Marzabotto is only one of the municipalities in the zone of Monte Sole whose populations were exterminated by the Nazis between 29 September and 5 October 1944, it was the largest and has therefore come to stand, by antonomasia, for all the areas included in the Nazi round-up and slaughter during those days. The other municipalities that were struck included Grizzana and Monzuno, all in the area of Monte Sole.
2 See Roberto Chiesi, "Un film 'inattuale': *L'uomo che verrà* di Giorgio Diritti," *Cinemasessanta* 303 (January–March 2010): p. 8.
3 Excerpted from Daniela Basso, "L'uomo che verrà? Intervista a Giorgio Diritti," in *Uomini d'ogni tempo*, ed. Daniela Basso (Milan: Feltrinelli, 2010), p. 30. See also Alessandra De Luca and Giorgio Diritti, "Sul Set," *Ciak* (January 2010): p. 111; and Goffredo Fofi, "Prima e dopo la strage," in Basso,

Uomini d'ogni tempo, p. 13. The focus on *quotidianità* is a constant in Diritti's self-commentary. See, for example, Diritti, "*L'uomo che verrà*: Un film su Monte Sole," p. 10, and Basso, "L'uomo che verrà?" pp. 22, 23, both in Basso, *Uomini d'ogni tempo*.
4 See, for example, Diritti, "*L'uomo che verrà*," p. 11; and Basso, "L'uomo che verrà?" pp. 23, 25, 29. See also Diritti and De Luca, "Sul Set," p. 109.
5 Diritti, "*L'uomo che verrà*," p. 23.
6 Quoted from the interview with Barbara Sorrentini on the Dolmen Home Video DVD.
7 See Fabio Ferzetti, "Tante emozioni per soffiar via la polvere della Storia," in Basso, *Uomini d'ogni tempo*, p. 55. For related observations, see Gianluca Arnone, "*L'uomo che verrà*: Rigore stilistico e morale per raccontare la strage di Marzabotto: Film civile, non politico," *Rivista del cinematografo*, nos. 1–2 (January–February, 2010): p. 68.
8 Diritti's non-ideological treatment of the victim's plight in *L'uomo che verrà* comes in for particular praise in Giacomo Lichtner's *Fascism in Italian Cinema since 1945: The Politics and Aesthetics of Memory* (London: Palgrave Macmillan, 2013), pp. 39–40, as the antidote to films made during the Berlusconi era that exploited the "blood of the victims" in the interests of a right-wing, revisionist history of atrocities committed during and shortly after the end of the Second World War in Italy and Yugoslavia.
9 See Basso, "L'uomo che verrà?," p. 31.
10 On the need to therapeutically overcome historical trauma through a collective mourning process in order to build a healthy, cohesive, and forward-moving social identity, see the previously mentioned essay by Eric Santner, "History beyond the Pleasure Principle: Some Thoughts on the Representation of Trauma," in *Probing the Limits of Representation: Nazism and the "Final Solution,"* ed. Saul Friedlander (Cambridge, MA: Harvard University Press, 1992), pp. 123–54.
11 On Diritti's apt use of music in the film, see Fofi, "Prima e dopo la strage," p. 14.
12 Though several critics have taken issue with this "happy ending" as a concession to sentimentality, I find it essential to Diritti's testimonial purpose in making L'uomo che verrà, as does Attilio Coco in "La trasparenza della Storia," *Segnocinema* 30 (March–April 2010): p. 34. For another cogent defence of the ending, see Eliana Elia's review, *Segnocinema* 30 (September–October 2010): p. 74. Among the ending's detractors, see Roberto Chiesi, "Un film 'inattuale,'" p. 8, and again in "*L'uomo che verrà*," *Segnocinema* 30 (March–April 2010): p. 34.
13 Quote from Paolo D'Agostini's "Cronaca di una strage per non dimenticare" in Basso, *Uomini d'ogni tempo*, p. 46.
14 For Diritti's comments on the "collateral damage" caused by war, and on the scarce media attention to it, see Basso, "L'uomo che verrà?," p. 26.

15 See the review by Arnone in *Rivista del cinematografo*, p. 68.
16 D'Agostini, "Cronaca di una strage per non dimenticare," p. 46.
17 Giorgio Diritti, "*L'uomo che verrà*: Un film su Monte Sole," in *Uomini d'ogni tempo*, p. 10.
18 Karl Schoonover, *Brutal Vision: The Neorealist Body in Postwar Italian Cinema* (Minneapolis: University of Minnesota Press, 2012), p. 110.
19 Ibid., p. 6.

Chapter 7

1 Quoted in Sonia Cincinelli, *Senza frontiere: L'immigrazione nel cinema italiano* (Rome: Kappa, 2012), p. 451.
2 Dialogues, in particular, were basically transcriptions of conversations between the elderly woman and her *badante* documented in the copious notes that Bondi had made during his visits with his grandmother. See Nuccio Lodato, "Una struttura musicale: Intervista a Federico Bondi," *Cineforum* 49 (March 2009): p. 20.
3 On the strategic timing of this scene, set on the eve of Romania's accession to the European Union on 1 January 2007, see Áine O'Healy, *Migrant Anxieties: Italian Cinema in a Transnational Frame* (Bloomington: Indiana University Press, 2019), pp. 69, 70.
4 On the parallelism between the protagonists' desires to sacrifice for the good of their offspring, see the review by Laura Ricci in Cincinelli, *Senza frontiere*, p. 458.
5 For his canonical formulation of the free indirect subjective technique, see Pier Paolo Pasolini, "Il cinema di poesia," *Empirismo eretico* (Milan: Garzanti, 1981), pp. 175–83. For the English translation, see "The Cinema of Poetry," in *Heretical Empiricism*, ed. Louise K. Barnett, trans. Ben Lawton (Bloomington: Indiana University Press, 1988), pp. 167–86.
6 O'Healy makes the astute observation that the Italian term *romeni* (Romanians) is closely related to *rom* (Romani or gypsies) and that the categories are sometimes collapsed in ordinary parlance. See *Migrant Anxieties*, p. 69.
7 The eroticizing of Angela by these downstairs neighbours exemplifies what O'Healy sees as the culture's general tendency to mark the Eastern European woman "as a sexually exploitable commodity." See *Migrant Anxieties*, p. 70.
8 In fact, the Black Sea is never represented in the film. On its absence, see Bondi's comments in Mauro Donadelli, "Intervista a Federico Bondi," in *Accadde domani: Nuovo cinema italiano* 54 (Comune di Reggio Emilia: Assessorato cultura, 2009), p. 37.
9 See the review by Silvio Alovisio in *Segnocinema* (March–April 2009): p. 43.

10 Curiously, Angela slowly picks up Gemma's Tuscan inflection as their relationship evolves. For this observation, see Cincinelli, *Senza frontiere*, p. 455.
11 Significantly, as O'Healy observes, in the Romanian part of the film there is a marked shift in focalization (*Migrant Anxieties*, p. 70). Angela's centrality to the narrative gradually gives way to Gemma's, and by the end of the film "the young woman's fate is no longer a driving concern" (p. 71).
12 Ilaria Occhini makes pointed reference to this fact on the supplementary material of the DVD.
13 On the analogy between the Romania of today, "poor and degraded," and the "ragged Italy of the postwar period," see Silvio Alovisio's review in *Segnocinema*, p. 44. Alovisio pushes the analogy even further, comparing the Danube to the Po, "both welcoming and mysterious river-nations that traverse landscapes oblivious to their identity" (ibid.).
14 Bondi's explanation of his filming technique is highly informative in this regard. Rather than impose a prefabricated vision on his protagonists, he chose to film scenes in extended shot sequences that would allow the actresses to interpret their roles freely. "I wanted to wait and let myself be surprised by them, to be guided by the actresses, without imposing myself on them invasively, respecting the intimacy that they were establishing. To eliminate the shot/counter-shot, the change of lighting and of sets allowed them a freer performance." See Mauro Donadelli "Intervista a Federico Bondi," *Accade domani: Nuovo cinema italiano* (Comune di Reggio Emilia: Assessorato cultura, 2009): p. 37.
15 See Pasolini, "Il cinema di poesia," pp. 168–75. For the English translation, see *Heretical Empiricism*, pp. 168–75 (coincidentally, the same page spread as in the original Italian text).
16 Pasolini, "Il cinema di poesia," p. 173, and in the English translation *Heretical Empiricism*, p. 172.

Chapter 8

1 Quoted from the Extra Features of the DVD, 01Distribution, 2016. Unless otherwise noted, the quotes from Rosi come from this source.
2 Rosi was born in Eritrea and lived there for his first twelve years – a biographical fact that could explain, in part, his personal stake in the mass migrations from Africa.
3 In Rosi's words, "My film is not political, but the political valence is inseparable from it." Quoted in Arianna Finos, "Berlino, applausi per *Fuocoammare*: Raccontiamo l'Olocausto di oggi," www.repubblica.it/spettacoli/cinema /2016/02/13/news/berlino_applausi_per_fuocoammare_-133340575/.
4 The decision to juxtapose Samuele's story with that of the migrant crisis has led to the charge that the film is essentially two in one. See, for

example, Goffredo Fofi, "*Fuocoammare* racconta Lampedusa con pudore e rispetto," https://www.internazionale.it/opinione/goffredo-fofi/2016/02/22/fuocoammare-rosi-lampedusa-recensione. This criticism misses the crucial point of Rosi's decision to implicate viewers in the clash between the film's two major narrative currents.

5 On the non-connectivity between these two adjacent worlds, see Áine O'Healy, *Migrant Anxieties: Italian Cinema in a Transnational Frame* (Bloomington: Indiana University Press, 2019), p. 162.

6 A number of reviewers have remarked on the figurative meaning of this optical condition. See, for example, the reviews by Alessandra Levantesi Kezich in *La Stampa*, 18 February 2016, and by Paolo Mereghetti in *Il Corriere della Sera*, 14 February 2016.

7 O'Healy notes the metaphoric link between Samuele's "restricted vision ... [and] the islanders' inability to see." Significantly, however, she absolves the local populace from any willed indifference to the migrants' plight, blaming instead the "increasing militarization of the borderscape" for separating the islanders from the tragedy playing out on their shores. See *Migrant Anxieties*, p. 165.

8 O'Healy finds these images especially problematic, raising "ethical questions regarding the symbolic violation of the dignity of the dead for the purpose of provoking spectatorial involvement." See *Migrant Anxieties*, p. 163. On the filming of this episode in particular, and all of the footage dedicated to rescue efforts in general, Rosi's extended commentary warrants quoting: "I spent a month on a military ship. For three weeks, nothing happened, I filmed what seemed to be a phantom ship. Then I discovered that this was a kind of test on the part of the commander and crew: they wanted to understand what type of person I was. Having disembarked, I requested to leave with them again, and this time, on the second trip, I encountered a tragedy. The most difficult moment was when I filmed that terrible scene on the [migrants'] boat. There I understood that the film was complete and I wouldn't be able to film anything more. I wouldn't have been able to add one more photogram. I still have many nightmares about this experience. Having mounted onto that boat, having seen and breathed. To feel those bodies. Filming death was something harsh and difficult. However, there's a moment in which you find yourself confronted with a choice. You must decide whether to film or not. And I remember the words of the ship's commander, who said, 'It's necessary. Like finding oneself in front of a gas chamber during the Holocaust and not filming it because it's too strong.' However, that was a moment that marked me. For a long time during the editing I couldn't manage to see the images, to treat [the footage] like material to edit ... Still today I have difficulty in facing that moment." Quoted in Arianna Finos, "Berlino, applausi per *Fuocoammare*."

9 See Mereghetti's review in *Il Corriere della Sera*, 14 February 2016.
10 In commenting on this episode, Rosi wryly compared the boys' exercise to those of European politicians, whose actions only serve to create problems that then necessitate considerable efforts to repair.

Chapter 9

1 A note on nomenclature: From here on, the text will refer to the main character as "Giulio" to maintain the distinction between Sorrentino's fictional construction of the character and his "real-life" referent.
2 *Grande dizionario della lingua italiana*, vol. 8, ed. Salvatore Battaglia (Turin: UTET, 1973).
3 See the introduction to Pierpaolo Antonello and Florian Mussgnug, *Postmodern Impegno: Ethics and Commitment in Contemporary Italian Culture* (Oxford: Peter Lang, 2009), pp. 1–26. As indicated in this book's introduction, Antonello and Mussgnung's groundbreaking volume has played a crucial role in my overall conception of Italian engagé cinema in the contemporary age.
4 On *Il Divo*'s position in relation to the genre of Italian committed cinema, see Guido Bonsaver's comments in the introduction to his interview with Sorrentino, p. 326, as well as the director's own direct statements of indebtedness to the tradition on p. 331–2, in "Dall'uomo al divo: Un intervista con Paolo Sorrentino," *The Italianist* 29, no. 2 (2009): pp. 325–37.
5 On the inherently anti-cinematic nature of Sorrentino's subject matter, see Stanley Kaufmann's review in *The New Republic*, 20 May 2009, p. 27. See Sorrentino's own comments on the "staticità," the "assenza di dinamicità" of the Andreotti story in his interview with Adriano Piccardi: "Fare buio per vedere: Intervista a Paolo Sorrentino," *Cineforum* 476 (2008): p. 13. For Servillo's comments on the difficulty of filming *La vita spettacolare di Giulio Andreotti* given the unspectacular nature of the subject matter, see Bonsaver, "Dall'uomo al divo," p. 334.
6 Andreotti served seven terms as prime minister, eight as minister of defence, five as minister of foreign affairs, and multiple terms in numerous other cabinet positions. He was elected for his seventh and final term as prime minister in 1992.
7 Lydia Tuan notes the frequency of walking scenes in Sorrentino's works, citing such moments as prime examples of the stylistic excess that characterizes his authorial method. For her acute analysis of the function of walking within Sorrentino's lexicon, see "Paolo Sorrentino's Cinematic Excess," *Journal of Italian Cinema & Media Studies* 7 (2019): p. 434.
8 On the music in this scene, and throughout *Il Divo*, see Chiara Borroni, "Le ritmiche del grottesco," *Cineforum* 476 (2008): pp. 9–10.
9 Cossiga was a fellow Christian Democrat who, like Andreotti, held numerous positions of power within the party throughout the post-war years.

10 See V.I. Pudovkin, "The Plastic Material," in *Film: A Montage of Theories*, ed. Richard Dyer MacCann (New York: Dutton, 1966); and T.S. Eliot, "Hamlet and His Problems," in *The Sacred Wood: Essays on Poetry and Criticism* (London: Methuen, 1920), pp. 95–103.
11 See Luca Malavasi, "Studio cubista di Andreotti," *Cineforum* 476, pp. 2–3.
12 Sorrentino set the household scenes in the Turinese apartment of a woman of the protagonist's generation where "c'era una serie di soprammobili, di materiale umano che mi riconduceva alla vita di Andreotti. E così curiosavamo continuamente per cercare oggetti che arricchissero la messa in scena." See the Bonsaver, "Dall'uomo al divo," p. 10.
13 In staging the arrival of Giulio's henchmen, Sorrentino's choices involve recalls of the spaghetti western (Ennio Morricone's iconic soundtrack for *The Good, the Bad, and the Ugly* featuring human whistles) and Quentin Tarantino's slow-motion march of the criminal band during the credit sequence of *Reservoir Dogs*.
14 See Bonsaver, "Dall'uomo al divo," p. 333.
15 Hence Stephen Holden calls *Il Divo* a "biographical fantasy.'" See his review "Out of Fellini and into the Godfather: A Politician's Life," *New York Times*, 24 April 2009, p. C10. A number of reviewers locate the film's vision between the grotesque and the surreal.
16 On his reluctance to pronounce overtly on Andreotti's culpability, see Sorrentino's own statement in the interview with Adriano Piccardi, "Fare buio per vedere," p. 13.
17 Sorrentino explains that the film's Giulio shows much more contrition than Andreotti himself did in the filmmaker's encounter with him. "Questo [la sua estrema sensibilità emotiva nei confronti dell'affaire Moro] è qualcosa che non ho riscontrato in Andreotti. Al contrario, l'Andreotti che ho incontrato personalmente in questo senso è stato molto gelido e scettico riguardo a Moro." Bonsaver, "Dall'uomo al divo," p. 331.
18 I am indebted to my student Mattia Acetoso for this insight, included in his paper "The Double-Sided Portrait of Power in *Il Divo*," presented at the annual conference of the American Association of Italian Studies, New York, 9 May 2009.

Chapter 10

1 Roberto Andò, *Il trono vuoto* (Milan: Bompiani, 2012), p. 40. All quotes from the novel will be from this edition, and page numbers will be included in the text. All translations are mine.
2 On this background, see the reviews of the film by Franco Colombo in *L'Eco di Bergamo*, 19 February 2013, and by Eliana Lo Castro Napoli in *Il Giornale di Sicilia*, 15 February 2013.

3 Significantly, Matteo Renzi was among those who comment on Giovanni's recourse to humanist culture to cut through the tired rhetoric and petty power games of contemporary political practice. See "L'imprevisto ci può salvare," Renzi's review of *Il trono vuoto* first published in *Panorama* (29 March 2012). For a review by a more seasoned politician at the time of the novel's release, see Walter Veltroni's "Il nostro nemico è il cliché," published in the same issue of *Panorama*. Both reviews can be found at https://www.dagospia.com/rubrica-6/cafonalino/cafonalino-regista-roberto-ando-che-fu-assistente-francesco-37839.htm.
4 In his review of *Il trono vuoto* Andrea Camilleri credits Giovanni with implementing "l'agire comunicativo di Habermas, quello dove i progetti d'azione politica non si basano su egocentrici calcoli di successo bensì su atti dell'intendersi reciproco." *Il sole 24 ore*, 8 April 2012.
5 On the prehensile performance of Toni Servillo as both brothers, see Marco Olivieri, *La memoria degli altri: Il cinema di Roberto Andò* (Turin: Edizioni Kaplan, 2013), p. 99.
6 Peter Bondanella and Federico Pacchioni claim that it was Giovanni's "radical thinking [that] led him to be labeled as crazy and to be held in a clinic for many years." See *A History of Italian Cinema*, 2nd ed. (New York: Bloomsbury, 2017), p. 589.
7 Marco Olivieri offers an ingenious reading of this scene, based on Giovanni's quip "se l'Europa è una miserabile bottega." The critic sees this as a commentary on the reduction of the world to a globalized marketplace, where economic concerns have trumped all issues of human rights and the needs of the downtrodden. See *La memoria degli altri*, p. 98.
8 Marco Olivieri devotes much insightful commentary on the "recomposizione di un'unica personalità" that marks the narrative resolution. See *La memoria degli altri*, p. 103.
9 In Marco Olivieri's reading, the ambiguity of the secretary's identity in this last scene is anticipated by the montage of the twins as young boys, which "dimostra quanto l'ambiguità sia connaturata con la loro origine." See *La memoria degli altri*, p. 101.
10 In his review of the film, Paolo Mereghetti sees *Viva la libertà* as a revival of the *cinema politico* genre, but with a decided shift in tone. Andò, according to Mereghetti, has chosen "una strada più leggera e 'laterale'in certi momenti, quasi favolistica." See "Servillo si sdoppia per le elezioni e la politica sembra una favola," *Corriere della sera*, 11 February 2013. The strategic scheduling of the film's opening in the run-up to the 24–25 February parliamentary elections could be understood as an indication of an activist political agenda on the part of the film's promoters. See, for example, the review by Emiliano Morreale, *Il Sole 24 Ore*, 3 March 2013.

Chapter 11

1 About the prescience of his film, Moretti modestly replied, "What am I supposed to say? Every now and then cinema manages to anticipate reality." Quoted in Catherine Hornby, "Pope Benedict – A Resignation Foretold, If You Knew Where to Look," https://www.reuters.com/article/us-pope-resignation-film-idUSBRE91C1DS20130213.
2 Michael O'Sullivan comments on this aspect of the film in "A Sense of Self in a Leap of Faith," *Washington Post*, 27 April 2012, p. 35.
3 According to Giancarlo Zappoli, "We smile and we certainly laugh at their weaknesses but they remain [fully fleshed-out] people." See "Il ritratto ironico di un papa umano, al di sopra di ogni sospetto," *MYmovies*, 16 April 2011, https://www.mymovies.it/film/2011/habemuspapam/. Instead, Alessandro Cappabianca finds Moretti's satire too sweet "to truly attack *filmically* the conclave and its surprising consequences" (emphasis in the original). See "Il no del papa/attore," *Filmcritica* 61 (June–July 2011): p. 220.
4 I have devoted considerable attention to this issue in "*Caro diario* and the Cinematic Body of Nanni Moretti," in *After Fellini: National Cinema in the Postmodern Age* (Baltimore: Johns Hopkins University Press), pp. 285–99.
5 It is worth noting that the film could not be shot in Vatican interiors. The Sistine Chapel was replicated, with a 10 per cent reduction in scale, at Cinecittà studios. Other Vatican scenes were set in various sixteenth- and seventeenth-century palaces, including the Palazzo Farnese (seat of the French Embassy), Villa Medici at the Spanish Steps, Palazzo Muccioli, and Palazzo Sacchetti, the latter chosen for its original frescoes. See the review by Franco Montini in *Vivilcinema*, 24 February 2011.
6 Regarding the idealized representation of the theatre troupe, see the review by Flavio De Bernardinis in *Segnocinema* 31 (May–June 2011): p. 36.
7 On Melville's election because he is a "nobody," and therefore a perfect candidate to play the part of a pope, see the review by Flavio De Bernardinis, ibid.
8 The name also alludes to the French filmmaker Jean-Pierre Melville, who adopted this pseudonym in homage to his favourite American author. Shortly before making *We Have a Pope*, Moretti curated a retrospective of Melville's films.
9 Reviewers who cite the relevance of this Melville short story to the film include Bruno Fornara in "????????," *Cineforum* 51 (April 2011): p. 9; Edoardo Bruno, "Segni e allegorie," *Filmcritica* 61 (June–July, 2011): p. 216; and Alessandro Cappabianca, "Il no del papa/attore," ibid., p. 218.
10 "He is not a coward, but a humble [man]," writes Giancarlo Zappoli in "Il ritratto ironico di un papa umano al di sopra di ogni sospetto," https://www.mymovies.it/film/2011/habemuspapam/.

11 On the grandeur of Michel Piccoli's performance, and particularly his mastery of facial nuance, see Eliana Elia, "Il mondo è tutto un palcoscenico," *Segnocinema* 31 (May–June 2011): p. 36.
12 Béla Balázs, "Insegnamenti," *Cinema* no. 175/176 (25 November 1943): p. 139.
13 Ibid.
14 See Noa Steimatsky, *The Face on Film* (New York: Oxford, 2017), p. 13. I am heavily indebted to this groundbreaking work for my thinking about the function of the facial close-up in *We Have a Pope*.
15 Steimatsky, *The Face on Film*, p. 38.
16 See Pier Paolo Pasolini, "Il 'Cinema di poesia,'" *Empirismo eretico* (Milan: Garzanti, 1981), pp. 175–83. For the English translation of the essay, see *Heretical Empiricism*, ed. Louise K. Barnett, trans. Ben Lawton (Bloomington: Indiana University Press, 1988), pp. 167–86.
17 For Steimatsky's extended discussion of facial depictions as objects of veneration and sources of revelation, see the section entitled "An Ur-Image" in *The Face on Film*, pp. 5–11.
18 Steimatsky, *The Face on Film*, p. 38
19 On the primacy of the image of the empty balcony, see Eliana Elia, "Il mondo è tutto un palcoscenico e uomini e donne, tutti, sono attori," *Segnocinema* 31 (May–June, 2011): p. 36. See also Paolo Mereghetti, "Nanni senza certezze (non basta l'idea geniale): L'impatto emotivo schiacciato delle scenette cardinalizie," *Il Corriere della Sera*, 15 April 2011.
20 In "Nanni senza certezze," Mereghetti argues that by centring his film on the church, "the last great Power today in Italy, the most compact, the most solid, the most true," Moretti generalizes his critique to include "the scarce sense of responsibility of [all] those who wield other powers in Italy."

Chapter 12

1 The film's representation of Naples has garnered much critical attention, and not always of a complimentary sort. Claudia Karagoz critiques the film's depiction of Naples as "devitalized" and lacking in "individuality" ("Motherhood Revisited in Francesca Comencini's *Lo spazio bianco*," in *Italian Women Filmmakers and the Gendered Screen*, ed. Maristella Cantini [New York: Palgrave Macmillan 2013], p. 108). In a similar vein, Fabio Ferzetti notes that the film is set against a background of a "Napoli quasi astratta" (*Il Messaggero*, 16 October 2009); Valerio Caprara complains of "una Napoli presepiale, cullata da un folklore alternativo quantomeno dattata" (*Il Mattino*, 17 October 2009); and Enrica Re characterizes the city as "affascinante ma nello stesso tempo insostenibile" (*Film* TV 2009-41-7). Shedding a far

more positive light on the film's representation of Naples, Micaela Veronesi calls the city "la vera co-protagonista ... con la sua presenza imperante, la sua contradditoria bellezza." See her review of the film in *Segnocinema* 30 (January–February 2010): p. 51.

2 Valeria Parrella, *Lo spazio bianco* (Turin: Einaudi, 2008). Page references can be found in the body of this chapter. One of the discrepancies between the novel and the film is the amount of time that the infant remains in intensive care. While the novel specifies forty days, the film extends the period to fifty.

3 For a detailed account of this tradition, see my essay "The Italian Body Politic Is a Woman: Feminized National Identity in Postwar Italian Film," in *Sparks and Seeds: Medieval Literature and Its Afterlife: Essays in Honor of John Freccero*, ed. Dana E. Stewart and Alison Cornish (Turnhout: Brepols, 2000), pp. 329–47.

4 In an interview with Comencini included in the extra material on the DVD, the filmmaker stated that the story could have been set anywhere, yet "c'è stata qualcosa di prepotente. Napoli tirava il film a sé perchè quest'idea di una sopravvivenza, di una resistenza, resistenza a tutto, è di una bellezza struggente. È magnifica che questa città continua, malgrado tutto, a buttare alla faccia del mondo. È qualcosa che ha molto a che fare col senso nudo e profondo della vita e della sopravvivenza. E quindi mi sembrava sbagliato tirar fuori questa storia da Napoli, che ci stava un po' dentro con dei legami forti."

5 Karagoz, in keeping with her critique of the film's Naples as "devitalized," takes Maria's comment as another example of the city's portrayal "as infected by chaos and decay" ("Motherhood Revisited," p. 107), whereas I see it as linked to the fertility topos described above.

6 According to Maria Letizia Bellocchio, Naples is so transformed in the film as to seem almost unrecognizable: "Naples is a deserted and silent city, characterized by cool colors that make it more like a northern city than a Mediterranean one." See "Francesca Comencini's Single Moms and Italian Family Law," in *Italian Motherhood on Screen*, ed. Giovanna Faleschini Lerner and Maria Elena D'Amelio (New York: Palgrave Macmillan, 2017), p. 163.

7 For her acute insights about the use and interpretive significance of this editorial device, see Karagoz, "Motherhood Revisited," p. 111.

8 See ibid.

9 Of considerable sociological importance is the way in which Maria's acceptance of her solo motherhood reflects the radical transformation of family structure in the current age. Maria Letizia Bellocchio focuses on this dimension of the film, and the larger societal debate that played a role in the 2012 law to acknowledge the legitimacy of children born out of wedlock. See Bellocchio, "Francesca Comencini's Single Moms," p. 166.

10 Walter Benjamin, "The Work of Art in the Age of Mechanical Reproduction," in *Illuminations*, ed. Hannah Arendt, trans. Harry Zohn (New York: Schocken Books, 1969), pp. 248, 234 respectively. I am grateful to Megan Crognale for pointing out the relevance of Benjamin's analogy to my study.
11 This surrealistic dance scene has occasioned considerable critical commentary. See, for example, Micaela Veronesi, *Segnocinema* 30 (January–February 2010): p. 51, and Valerio Caprara, "Brava Buy in una Napoli da folklore alternativo," *Il Mattino*, 17 October 2009.
12 On Maria's increased engagement with the glimpses of domestic life in the second sequence, see Karagoz, "Motherhood Revisited," p. 114.
13 The model for this judge is the activist magistrate Ilda Boccassini. See Maria Letizia Bellocchio, "Francesca Comencini's Single Moms," pp. 163, 170n15. This character comes in for sharp criticism as being "figura scontata e convenzionale" by Micaela Veronesi. See her review in *Segnocinema* 30 (January–February 2010): p. 51.
14 See Frank Kermode, *The Sense of an Ending: Studies in the Theory of Fiction* (New York: Oxford University Press, 1975).

Chapter 13

1 See the interview with Arianna Finos, "Paola Cortellesi: 'Puniremo i bulli con una risata,'" https://rep.repubblica.it/pwa/intervista/2019/04/19/news/paola_cortellesi-224468605/.
2 These quotes come from an interview with Claudia Catalli, "Riccardo Milani e la nuova commedia sociale 'Tutti sanno tutto,'" https://news.cinecitta.com/IT/it-it/news/54/76182/riccardo-milani-e-la-nuova-commedia-sociale-tutti-sanno-tutto.aspx.
3 The film's joking treatment of work in the government bureaucracy follows up on the blockbuster satire of Cecco Zalone's *Quo Vado* (2016), which targets the Italian dream of state employment as a sinecure.
4 See Linda Hutcheon, *A Theory of Parody: The Teachings of Twentieth-Century Art Forms* (New York: Methuen, 1985), p. 26.
5 Ibid., p. 34.
6 For streamlining purposes, I will limit my focus on *Alias* to its first episode, which sets the operational groundwork for the show's six-season run.
7 See Andrea Fornasiero, "Tra spy story e parodia, Paola Cortellesi dichiara guerra al degrado," 17 April 2019, https://www.mymovies.it/film/2019/ci-penso-io/.
8 Ibid.
9 For a cultural history of the body politic trope, see my essay "The Italian Body Politic Is a Woman: Feminized National Identity in Postwar Italian

Film," in *Sparks and Seeds: Medieval Literature and Its Afterlife*, ed. Dana E. Stewart and Allison Cornish (Turnhout: Brepols, 2000), pp. 329–47.
10 These are the words of actress Paola Cortellesi. Her comments can be found on the extra material of the Wildside DVD.
11 See Hutcheon, *A Theory of Parody*, p. 43.
12 By making Roberto's obesity the occasion for a sight gag in this scene, the film introduces an unfortunate element of fat shaming. While later scenes will add nuance to the public reception of his size, making it an object lesson in the kind of incivility that the film condemns, this does not offset the disturbing effect of his initial presentation on screen.
13 As previously discussed in connection with Linda Hutcheon's *A Theory of Parody*, p. 34.

Chapter 14

1 Nanni Delbecchi, *Il fatto quotidiano* (29 May 2013) and Paolo Mereghetti, *Il corriere della sera* (21 May 2013) respectively.
2 Monica Facchini further expands the thrust of this critique to encompass the "society of spectacle" (Guy Débord's resonant term) as a whole. For her acute analysis of the film, see "A Journey from Death to Life: Spectacular Realism and the 'Unamendability' of Reality in Paolo Sorrrentino's *The Great Beauty*," in *Encountering the Real in Italian Literature and Cinema*, ed. Loredana Di Martino and Pasquale Verdicchio (Newcastle upon Tyne: Cambridge Scholars Publishing, 2017).
3 Accordingly, "*The Great Beauty* is at its core a film about the nature of the creative process," writes Gary Crowdus in his essay "In Search of *The Great Beauty*," *Cineaste* (Spring 2014): p. 10.
4 Roland Barthes, "The Third Meaning: Research Notes on Some Eisenstein Stills," in *Image-Music-Text*, trans. Stephen Heath (New York: Noonday, 1988), p. 65.
5 Ibid., p. 67.
6 The recurrent use of aquatic imagery is fraught with symbolic significance, as Facchini argues in her analysis of the film; see in particular "Journey from Death to Life," p. 195. Building on the variegated meanings that Mircea Eliade attributes to water, Facchini brings its immersive, dissolutive, and regenerative functions to bear on Jep's aquatic encounters throughout the film.
7 Susan Sontag, *On Photography* (New York: Dell, 1977), p. 15.
8 Erwin Panofsky, "Style and Medium in the Motion Pictures," in *Film: An Anthology*, ed. Daniel Talbot (Berkeley: University of California Press, 1972), p. 18.

9 For her seminal work on this vast subject, see Noa Steimatsky, *The Face on Film* (New York: Oxford University Press, 2017). I made detailed reference to Steimatsky's study in chapter 11 on Moretti's *Habemus Papam*.
10 Béla Balázs, *Early Film Theory: Visible Man* and *The Spirit of Film*, ed. Erica Carter, trans. Rodney Livingstone (New York: Berghahn Books, 2010), especially p. 37. I referenced Balázs's work on the facial close-up in chapter 11.
11 Sontag, *On Photography*, p. 70.
12 A great deal of ink has been spilled on the topic, much of it by critics who mistake the time-honoured technique of creative *imitatio* with uninspired rehashings of earlier works. Gary Crowdus charges such critics with the inability "to appreciate both the original qualities, distinctive style, and substantial themes" of Sorrentino's film. See "In Search of *The Great Beauty*," p. 10. Among those critics who see Sorrentino's debt to Fellini as the younger filmmaker's self-imposed challenge to forge a distinctive authorial signature in the shadow of the *maestro*, see Lydia Tuan, "Paolo Sorrentino's Cinematic Excess," *Journal of Italian Cinema & Media Studies* 7 (2019): p. 427.
13 Here it's tempting to consider the autobiographical parallels which the two filmmakers have inscribed in their main characters. Like the Marcello, the young Fellini came from Rimini and relocated to Rome at a formative time in his own career, much as Jep, like Sorrentino, left Naples for the Eternal City as a young artist on the rise.
14 Specific echoes of *8½* in *The Great Beauty* include: a random shot of an anonymous behatted dowager sitting on a park bench, recalling her counterpart perched on a bench waiting to take the waters of the spa; the line-up of customers at the Botox clinic, who are called forth by number to submit to the doctor's injections, harking back to the procession of toga-clad clients called forth by number to undergo the various rejuvenating services offered at the spa; the grotesque image of the sleeping Suor Maria echoing the young Guido's glimpse of a dead nun's effigy.
15 "At the end of the film," Facchini notes, "we realize that we are at the beginning of the novel, or better, at Jep's initial conception of it." See "A Journey from Death to Life," p. 197.

Bibliography

Alovisio, Silvio. Review of *Mar nero*. *Segnocinema* (March–April 2009): pp. 43–4.
Andò, Roberto. *Il trono vuoto*. Milan: Bompiani, 2012.
Antonello, Pierpaolo. "Dispatches from Hell: Matteo Garrone's *Gomorrah*." In *Mafia Movies: A Reader*, 2nd ed., edited by Dana Renga, pp. 294–9. Toronto: University of Toronto Press, 2019.
Antonello, Pierpaolo, and Florian Mussgnug, eds. *Postmodern Impegno: Ethics and Commitment in Contemporary Italian Culture*. Oxford: Peter Lang, 2009.
Argentieri, Mino. "Pasquale Scimeca e il mondo contadino del dopoguerra." *Cinemasessanta* 42 (March–April 2002): pp. 6–7.
Arnone, Gianluca. "*L'uomo che verrà*: Rigore stilistico e morale per raccontare la strage di Marzabotto: Film civile, non politico." *Rivista del cinematografo*, nos. 1–2 (January–February 2010): p. 68.
Bakhtin, Mikhail. "Epic and Novel: Toward a Methodology for the Study of the Novel." In *The Dialogic Imagination: Four Essays*, edited by Michael Holquist, translated by Caryl Emerson and Michael Holquist, pp. 3–40. Austin: University of Texas Press, 1981.
– "Forms of Time and of the Chronotope in the Novel." In *The Dialogic Imagination*, edited by Michael Holquist, translated by Caryl Emerson and Michael Holquist, pp. 84–258. Austin: University of Texas Press, 1981.
Balázs, Béla. *Early Film Theory: Visible Man* and *The Spirit of Film*. Edited by Erica Carter, translated by Rodney Livingstone. New York: Berghahn Books, 2010.
– "Insegnamenti." *Cinema*, no. 175/176 (25 November 1943): p. 13.
Basso, Daniela. "L'uomo che verrà? Intervista a Giorgio Diritti." In Basso, *Uomini d'ogni tempo*, pp. 22–33.
Basso, Daniela, ed. *Uomini d'ogni tempo*. Milan: Feltrinelli, 2010.
Baudrillard, Jean. *Simulations*. Translated by Paul Foss, Paul Patton, and Philip Beitchman. New York: Semiotext(e), 1983.

Bellocchio, Maria Letizia. "Francesca Comencini's Single Moms and Italian Family Law." In *Italian Motherhood on Screen*, edited by Giovanna Faleschini Lerner and Maria Elena D'Amelio, pp. 157–73. New York: Palgrave Macmillan, 2017.
Benjamin, Walter. "The Work of Art in the Age of Mechanical Reproduction." In *Illuminations*, edited by Hannah Arendt, translated by Harry Zohn, pp. 217–52. New York: Schocken Books, 1969.
Bernardi, Sandro. *Il paesaggio nel cinema italiano*. Venice: Marsilio, 2002.
Bertozzi, Marco. "Di alcune tendenze del documentario italiano nel terzo millennio." In *Il reale allo specchio: Il documentario italiano contemporaneo*, edited by Giovanni Spagnoletti, pp. 17–32. Venice: Marsilio, 2012.
Bini, Andrea. *Male Anxiety and Psychopathology in Film: Comedy Italian Style*. New York: Palgrave Macmillan, 2015.
Bini, Daniela. *Portrait of the Artist and His Mother in Twentieth-Century Italian Culture*. Madison: Fairleigh Dickinson University Press, 2021.
Bondanella, Peter, and Federico Pacchioni. *A History of Italian Cinema*, 2nd ed. New York: Bloomsbury, 2017.
Bondavalli, Simona. "Waste Management: Garbage Displacement and the Ethics of Mafia Representation in Matteo Garrone's *Gomorrah*." *California Italian Studies* 2, no. 1 (2011): pp. 1–16.
Boni, Marta. "Mapping *Crime Novel*: An Epic Narrative Ecosystem?" *Series* 1, no. 1 (2015): pp. 77–88.
– *Romanzo criminale: Transmedia and Beyond*. Venice: Ca' Foscari University Press, 2013.
Bonsaver, Guido. "Dall'uomo al divo: Un intervista con Paolo Sorrentino." *The Italianist* 29, no. 2 (2009): pp. 325–37.
Borroni, Chiara. "Le ritmiche del grottesco." *Cineforum* 476 (2008): pp. 9–10.
Braucci, Maurizio. "*Gomorra*, il film: Conversazione con Matteo Garrone." In De Sanctis, Monetti, and Pallanch, *Non solo* Gomorra, pp. 65–76.
Brizio-Skov, Flavia, ed. *Popular Italian Cinema: Culture and Politics in a Postwar Society*. London: I.B. Gauris, 2011.
Brunetta, Gian Piero. *Il cinema italiano contemporaneo: Da "La dolce vita" a "Cento chiodi."* Bari: Laterza, 2007.
Bruno, Edoardo. "Segni e allegorie." *Filmcritica* 61 (June–July 2011): pp. 216–17.
Buccheri, Vincenzo. "Gli anni '70, la politica, l'immaginario." *Segnocinema* 25, no. 136 (November–December 2005): p. 35.
Buell, Lawrence. "Introduction: In Pursuit of Ethics." *PMLA* 114, no. 1 (January 1999): pp. 7–19.
Camilleri, Andrea. Review of *Il trono vuoto*. *Il sole 24 ore* (8 April 2012).
Canova, Gianni. *Cinemania: 10 anni 100 film: Il cinema italiano del nuovo millennio*. Venice: Marsilio, 2010.

Cappabianca, Alessandro. "Il no del papa/attore." *Filmcritica* 61 (June–July 2011): pp. 218–20.
Caprara, Valerio. "Brava Buy in una Napoli da folklore alternativo." Review of *Lo spazio bianco*. *Il Mattino*, 17 October 2009.
Carlorosi, Silvia. "Epilogue: Neorealism, Cinema of Poetry, and Italian Contemporary Cinema." In *Global Neorealism: The Transnational History of a Film Style*, edited by Saverio Giovacchini and Robert Sklar, pp. 240–56. Jackson: University of Mississippi, 2012.
Catalli, Claudia. "Riccardo Milani e la nuova commedia sociale 'Tutti sanno tutto.'" https://news.cinecitta.com/IT/it-it/news/54/76182/riccardo-milani-e-la-nuova-commedia-sociale-tutti-sanno-tutto.aspx.
Catanea, Ofelia. "Perdersi: Geografie e spazi del nuovo cinema italiano." In *Gli invisibili: Esordi italiani del nuovo millennio*, edited by Vito Zagarrio, pp. 81–7. Turin: Kaplan, 2009.
Cattaneo, Francesco. "L'insostenibile quotidianità del degrado." *Cineforum* 475 (1 June 2008): pp. 9–11.
Cervini, Alessia, ed. *Il cinema del nuovo millennio: Geografie, forme, autori*. Rome: Carocci editore, 2020.
– "Il cinema politico." In Cervini, *Il cinema del nuovo millennio*, pp. 19–36.
– "Premessa." In Cervini, *Il cinema del nuovo millennio*, pp. 15–16.
Chiesi, Roberto. Review of *L'uomo che verrà*. *Segnocinema* 30 (March–April 2010): pp. 33–4.
– "Un film 'inattuale': *L'uomo che verrà* di Giorgio Diritti." *Cinemasessanta* 303 (January–March 2010): pp. 6–8.
Cincinelli, Sonia. *Senza frontiere: L'immigrazione nel cinema italiano*. Rome: Kappa, 2012.
Coco, Attilio. "La trasparenza della Storia." *Segnocinema* 30 (March–April 2010): p. 34.
Colombo, Franco. Review of *Viva la libertà*. *L'Eco di Bergamo*, 19 February 2013.
Colombo, Silvia. Review of *I cento passi*: *Panoramiche/Panoramiques: Rivista di cinema* 27 (Fall 2000): p. 24.
Cooper, Allison. "*Romanzo criminale*: Roma Caput Violandi." In "Italy's Other Mafias in Italian Film and Television: A Roundtable," edited by Alan O'Leary. *The Italianist Film Issue* 33, no. 2 (2013): pp. 204–6.
Coviello, Massimiliano. "Nuova serialità." In Cervini, *Il cinema del nuovo millennio*, 107–23.
Cozzi, Emilio. "La forma è sostanza: Intervista a Matteo Garrone." *Cineforum* 475 (1 June 2008): 14–17.
Crespi, Alberto. "Il miracolo di Pif, una commedia grottesca sulla mafia." Review of *La Mafia uccide solo d'estate*. *L'Unità* (25 November 2013).
Crowdus, Gary. "In Search of *The Great Beauty*." *Cineaste* (Spring 2014): pp. 8–13.

Cucco, Marco, and Giuseppe Richeri. *Il mercato delle location cinematografiche*. Venice: Marsilio, 2013.
D'Agostini, Paolo. "Cronaca di una strage per non dimenticare." In Basso, *Uomini d'ogni tempo*, pp. 45–6.
– "Gli attori e la recitazione." In *La meglio gioventù: Nuovo cinema italiano 2000– 2006*, edited by Vito Zagarrio, pp. 62–8. Venice: Marsilio, 2006.
De Bernardinis, Flavio. "*Habemus Papam.*" *Segnocinema* 31 (May–June, 2011): pp. 35–37.
– "*Romanzo criminale.*" *Segnocinema* 25 (November–December 2005): pp. 35–6.
De Cataldo, Giancarlo. *Romanzo criminale*. Turin: Einaudi, 2002.
De Gaetano, Roberto. "Prefazione: L'immagine documentaria come domanda di senso." In *Per un cinema del reale: Forme e pratiche del documentario italiano contemporaneo*," edited by Daniele Dottorini, pp. 9–11. Udine: Forum, 2013.
Delbecchi, Nanni. "*La grande bellezza* come *La dolce vita*? Ma per favore." Review of *La grande bellezza*. *Il fatto quotidiano* (29 May 2013).
Deleuze, Gilles. *Cinema I: The Movement Image*. Translated by Barbara Habberjam and Hugh Tomlinson. Minneapolis: University of Minnesota Press, 1997.
Delfino, Massimiliano. "A Cinematic Anti-Monument against Mafia Violence: P. Diliberto's *La mafia uccide solo d'estate*. *Annali d'italianistica* 35 (2017): pp. 385–401.
De Luca, Alessandra, and Giorgio Diritti. "Sul Set." *Ciak* (January 2010): pp. 108–13.
de Luca, Tigo, and Nuno Barradas Jorge, eds. *Slow Cinema*. Edinburgh: Edinburgh University Press, 2016.
De Sanctis, Pierpaolo. "Da Saviano a Garrone." In De Sanctis, Monetti, and Pallanch, *Non solo* Gomorra, pp. 35–44.
– "Il crepuscolo della bellezza: Lo sguardo e il metodo di Matteo Garrone." In De Sanctis, Monetti, and Pallanch, *Non solo* Gomorra, pp. 9–18.
De Sanctis, Pierpaolo, Domenico Monetti, and Luca Pallanch, eds. *Non solo Gomorra: Tutto il cinema di Matteo Garrone*. Cantalupo in Sabina: Edizioni Sabinae, 2008.
Dinoi, Marco. *Lo sguardo e l'evento: I media, la memoria, il cinema*. Florence: Le Lettere, 2008.
Diritti, Giorgio. "*L'uomo che verrà*: Un film su Monte Sole." In Basso, *Uomini d'ogni tempo*, pp. 9–12.
Donadelli, Mauro. "Intervista a Federico Bondi." *Accadde domani: Nuovo cinema italiano* 54 (Comune di Reggio Emilia: Assessorato cultura, 2009): pp. 35–41.
D'Onofrio, Emanuele. *Film music, nazione e identità narrativa: Il cinema italiano contemporaneo rivisita gli anni settanta*. Reggio Calabria: Città del Sole, 2013.
Dottorini, Daniele. "Il 'cinema-senza-nome': Lo sguardo documentario del nuovo millennio." In Cervini, *Il cinema del nuovo millennio*, pp. 89–106.

- "Per un cinema del reale: Il documentario come laboratorio aperto." In *Per un cinema del reale: Forme e pratiche del documentario italiano contemporaneo,*" edited by Daniele Dottorini, pp. 13–24. Udine: Forum, 2013.
Eco, Umberto. *Apocalypse Postponed*. Edited by Robert Lumley. Bloomington and Indianapolis: Indiana University Press, 1994.
Elia, Eliana. "Il mondo è tutto un palcoscenico." *Segnocinema* 31 (May–June 2011): pp. 36.
- "*L'uomo che verrà.*" *Segnocinema* 30 (September–October 2010): pp. 74–5.
Eliot, Thomas Stearns. "Hamlet and His Problems." In *The Sacred Wood: Essays on Poetry and Criticism*, pp. 95–103. London: Methuen, 1920.
Facchini, Monica. "A Journey from Death to Life: Spectacular Realism and the 'Unamendability' of Reality in Paolo Sorrentino's *The Great Beauty*." In *Encountering the Real in Italian Literature and Cinema*, edited by Loredana Di Martino and Pasquale Verdicchio, pp. 181–204. Newcastle upon Tyne: Cambridge Scholars Publishing, 2017.
Fantuzzi, Vittorio, "Intervista a Paolo Benvenuti." In Paola Baroni and Paolo Benvenuti, *Segreti di Stato*: Dai documenti al film," edited by Nicola Tranfaglia, p. 104. Rome: Fandango, 2003.
Ferzetti, Fabio. Review of *Lo spazio bianco*. *Il Messaggero*, 16 October 2009.
- "Tante emozioni per soffiar via la polvere della Storia." In Basso, *Uomini d'ogni tempo*, pp. 55–6.
Finos, Arianna. "Berlino, applausi per *Fuocoammare*: Raccontiamo l'Olocausto di oggi." www.repubblica.it/spettacoli/cinema/2016/02/13/news/berlino_applausi_per_fuocoammare_-133340575/.
- "Paola Cortellesi: "Puniremo i bulli con una risata." https://rep.repubblica.it/pwa/intervista/2019/04/19/news/paola_cortellesi-224468605/.
Fofi, Goffredo. "*Fuocoammare* racconta Lampedusa con pudore e rispetto." *Internazionale* 22 (February 2016). https://www.internazionale.it/opinione/goffredo-fofi/2016/02/22/fuocoammare-rosi-lampedusa-recensione.
- "Prima e dopo la strage." In Basso, *Uomini d'ogni tempo*, pp. 13–15.
Fornara, Bruno. "????????." *Cineforum* 51 (April 2011): pp. 8–10.
Fornasiero, Andrea. "Tra spy story e parodia, Paola Cortellesi dichiara guerra al degrado." https://www.mymovies.it/film/2019/ci-penso-io/.
Foucault, Michel. *Discipline and Punish: The Birth of the Prison*. Translated by Alan Sheridan. New York: Random House, 1977.
Fournier Lanzoni, Rémi. *Comedy Italian Style: The Golden Age of Italian Film Comedies*. New York: Continuum, 2008.
Gandolfi, Marzia. Review of *La mafia uccide solo d'estate*. www.mymovies.it/film/2013/solodestate.
Gaudioso, Massimo. "L'uomo delle storie: Conversazione con Massimo Gaudioso a cura di Pierpaolo De Sanctis." In De Sanctis, Monetti, and Pallanch, *Non solo Gomorra*, pp. 97–128.

Gherardi, Davide, "Giorgio Diritti e *Il vento fa il suo giro* (2007)." In *Italiana OFF: Pratiche e poetiche del cinema italiano periferico 2001–2008*, edited by Roy Menarini, pp. 75–8. Gorizia: Transmedia, 2008.

Grande dizionario della lingua italiana. Volumes 8 and 17, edited by Salvatore Battaglia. Turin, UTET, 1973, 1994.

Guerrini, Riccardo, Giacomo Taglianti, and Francesco Zucconi, eds. *Lo spazio del reale nel cinema italiano contemporaneo*. Genoa: Le Mani, 2009.

Holden, Stephen. "Out of Fellini and into the Godfather: A Politician's Life." *New York Times*, 24 April 2009, p. C10.

Hornby, Catherine. "Pope Benedict – A Resignation Foretold, If You Knew Where to Look." https://www.reuters.com/article/us-pope-resignation-film-idUSBRE91C1DS20130213.

Hutcheon, Linda. *A Theory of Parody: The Teachings of Twentieth-Century Art Forms*. New York: Methuen, 1985.

Iovino, Serenella. *Ecocriticism and Italy: Ecology, Resistance, and Liberation*. London: Bloomsbury, 2016.

Isola, Simone. "Intervista all'autore." In *Cinegomorra: Luci e ombre sul nuovo cinema italiano*, edited by Simone Isola, pp. 96–103. Rome: Sovera, 2010.

Jaffe, Ira. *Slow Movies: Countering the Cinema of Action*. London: Wallflower, 2014.

Jurgensen, John. "An Inside Look at the Real Wiseguys." *Wall Street Journal*, 6 February 2009, p. W4.

Karagoz, Claudia. "Motherhood Revisited in Francesca Comencini's *Lo spazio bianco*." In *Italian Women Filmmakers and the Gendered Screen*, edited by Maristella Cantini, pp. 103–19. New York: Palgrave Macmillan, 2013.

Kauffmann, Stanley. Review of *Il Divo*. *New Republic*, 20 May 2009, pp. 26–7.

Kermode, Frank. *The Sense of an Ending: Studies in the Theory of Fiction*. New York: Oxford University Press, 1975.

Kezich, Alessandra Levantesi. Review of *Fuocoammare*. *La Stampa*, 18 February 2016.

Landy, Marcia. *Italian Film*. Cambridge: Cambridge University Press, 2000.

Lane, Anthony. "Gritty Cities." *The New Yorker*, 23 February 2009: pp. 81–2.

Leopardi, Giacomo. *I canti di Giacomo Leopardi nelle traduzioni inglesi*. Edited by G. Singh. Recanati: Centro Nazionale di Studi Leopardiani, 1990.

Lichtner, Giacomo. *Fascism in Italian Cinema since 1945*. London: Palgrave Macmillan, 2013.

Lodato, Nuccio. "Una struttura musicale: Intervista a Federico Bondi," *Cineforum* 49, no. 482 (March 2009): pp. 20–1.

Lydia Tuan, Lydia. "Paolo Sorrentino's Cinematic Excess." *Journal of Italian Cinema & Media Studies* 7 (2019): pp. 425–42.

Malavasi, Luca. "Studio cubista di Andreotti." *Cineforum* 476 (2008): pp. 2–3.

Mancino, Anton Giulio. "Da Rosi a Garrone: L'ombra delle vele di Scampia." *Cineforum* 475, no. 1 (June 2008): pp. 12–14.
Marcus, Millicent. "*Caro diario* and the Cinematic Body of Nanni Moretti." In *After Fellini: National Cinema in the Postmodern Age*, pp. 285–99. Baltimore: Johns Hopkins University Press, 2002.
– "The Italian Body Politic Is a Woman: Feminized National Identity in Postwar Italian Film." *Sparks and Seeds: Medieval Literature and Its Afterlife: Essays in Honor of John Freccero*, edited by Dana E. Stewart and Alison Cornish, pp. 329–47. Turnhout: Brepols, 2000.
Marrone, Gaetana. *The Cinema of Francesco Rosi*. New York: Oxford University Press, 2020.
Martin, Sara. "Storia di una vita dimenticata." In *Italiana OFF: Pratiche e poetiche del cinema italiano periferico 2001–2008*, edited by Roy Menarini, pp. 81–4. Gorizia: Transmedia, 2008.
Masoni, Tullio. "La Mafia, Pasolini, i Procol Harum." *Cineforum* 40 (November 2000): pp. 60–2.
– "Traccia di pietà nel regno del male: Matteo Garrone: *Gomorra*." *Cineforum*, no. 475 (2008): pp. 6–8.
Mereghetti, Paolo. "Servillo si sdoppia per le elezioni e la politica sembra una favola." *Corriere della sera*, 11 February 2013.
– Review of *Fuocoammare*. *Il Corriere della Sera*, 14 February 2016.
– "Nanni senza certezze (non basta l'idea geniale): L'impatto emotivo schiacciato delle scenette cardinalizie." Review of *Habemus Papam*. *Il Corriere della Sera*, 15 April 2011.
– "Il ritratto di Roma volgare sbadiato da troppe ambizioni." Review of *La grande bellezza*. *Il corriere della sera*, 21 May 2013.
Miccichè, Lino. "Il lungo decennio grigio." In *Schermi opachi: Il cinema italiano degli anni '80*, edited by Lino Miccichè, pp. 3–16. Venice: Marsilio, 1998.
Miceli, Salvatore Salviano. "Il cinema antropocentrico di Matteo Garrone." In *Cinegomorra: Luci e ombre sul nuovo cinema italiano*, edited by Simone Isola, pp. 85–96. Rome: Sovera, 2010.
Mitry, Jean. *Aesthetics and Psychology in the Cinema*. Translated by Christopher King. Bloomington: Indiana University Press, 1997.
Modonesi, Chiara. "Cento passi verso la libertà." *Acting* 1 (September 2000): p. 18.
Montini, Franco. Review of *Habemus Papam*. *Vivilcinema*, 24 February 2011.
– "Una nuova generazione." In *La meglio gioventù: Nuovo cinema italiano 2000–2006*, edited by Vito Zagarrio, pp. 23–32. Venice: Marsilio, 2006.
Morandini, Morando. "... e prima o poi ritorna." *Cineforum* 465 (June 2007): pp. 32–3.
Morreale, Emiliano. Review of *Viva la libertà*. *Il Sole 24 Ore* (3 March 2013).

Napoli, Eliana Lo Castro. Review of *Viva la libertà*. *Il Giornale di Sicilia*, 15 February 2013.
Newman, Michael Z. "Intermediality and Transmedia Storytelling." https://www.c21uwm.com/2012/09/17/intermediality-and-transmedia-storytelling/.
O'Healy, Áine. *Migrant Anxieties: Italian Cinema in a Transnational Frame*. Bloomington: Indiana University Press, 2019.
O'Leary, Alan. *Fenomenologia del cinepanettone*. Soveria Mannelli: Rubbettino, 2013.
O'Leary, Alan, and Pierpaolo Antonello. "Sotto il segno della metafora: Una conversazione con Giancarlo De Cataldo," *The Italianist* 29 (2009): pp. 350–65.
Olivieri, Marco. *La memoria degli altri: Il cinema di Roberto Andò*. Turin: Edizioni Kaplan, 2013.
Olivieri, Marco, and Anna Paparcone. *Marco Tullio Giordana: Una poetica civile in forma di cinema*. Soveria Mannelli: Rubbettino, 2017.
Olivucci, Anna. "Una lupa distratta e venti gemelli affamati: Tra Stato centrale e politiche regionali di settore." In *Territori del cinema italiano: Produzione, diffusione, alfabetizzazione*, edited by Marco Maria Gazzano, Stefania Parigi, and Vito Zagarrio, pp. 83–7. Udine: Forum, 2013.
O'Sullivan, Michael. "A Sense of Self in a Leap of Faith." *Washington Post*, 27 April 2012, p. 35.
Panofsky, Erwin. "Style and Medium in the Motion Pictures." In *Film: An Anthology*, edited by Daniel Talbot, pp. 15–32. Berkeley: University of California Press, 1972.
Parrella, Valeria. *Lo spazio bianco*. Turin: Einaudi, 2008.
Pasolini, Pierpaolo. "Il 'Cinema di poesia.'" In *Empirismo eretico*, pp. 175–83. Milan: Garzanti, 1981,
– "The Cinema of Poetry." In *Heretical Empiricism*, edited by Louise K. Barnett, translated by Ben Lawton, pp. 167–86. Bloomington: Indiana University Press, 1988.
– *Poesie*. Milan: Garzanti, 1970.
Past, Elena, *Italian Ecocinema: Beyond the Human*. Bloomington: Indiana University Press, 2019.
Pesce, Alberto. *Cinema italiano duemila: Primo decennio tra crisi e trasformazione*. Brescia: Liberedizione, 2013.
Pettierre, Antonio. "*La mafia uccide solo d'estate* di Pierfrancesco Diliberto." www.ondacinema.it/film/recensione/Mafia_uccide_solo_estate.html.
Piccardi, Adriano. "Fare buio per vedere: Intervista a Paolo Sorrentino." *Cineforum* 476 (2008): pp. 13–14.
Pudovkin, Vsevolod. "The Plastic Material." In *Film: A Montage of Theories*, edited by Richard Dyer MacCann, pp. 23–33. New York: Dutton, 1966.

Quilici, Gianni. "I cento passi." *La linea dell'occhio* 39 (Spring 2001): p. 5.
Re, Enrica. Review of *Lo spazio bianco*. Film TV 2009-41-7.
Renga, Dana. *Unfinished Business: Screening the Italian Mafia in the New Millennium*. Toronto: University of Toronto Press, 2013.
Renzi, Matteo. "L'imprevisto ci può salvare." *Panorama*, 29 March 2012. https://www.dagospia.com/rubrica-6/cafonalino/cafonalino-regista-roberto-ando-che-fu-assistente-francesco-37839.htm.
Ricci, Laura. Review of *Mar nero*. In Sonia Cincinelli, *Senza frontiere*, pp. 457–8.
Roberti, Bruno, and Daniela Turco. "Oltre lo schermo: Conversazione con Michele Placido." *Filmcritica* 561/562 (January/February 2006): pp. 35–44.
Roland Barthes, "The Third Meaning: Research Notes on Some Eisenstein Stills." In *Image-Music-Text*, translated by Stephen Heath, pp. 52–68. New York: Noonday, 1988.
Romagnoli, Gabriele. "Siamo morti anche noi." In Basso, *Uomini d'ogni tempo*, pp. 36–42.
Santner, Eric. "History beyond the Pleasure Principle: Some Thoughts on the Representation of Trauma." In *Probing the Limits of Representation: Nazism and the Final Solution*, edited by Saul Friedlander, pp. 143–54. Cambridge, MA: Harvard University Press, 1992.
Saviano, Roberto. *Gomorra*. Milan: Mondadori, 2006.
– *Gomorrah*. Translated by Virginia Jewiss. New York: Picador, 2007.
Schoonover, Karl. *Brutal Vision: The Neorealist Body in Postwar Italian Cinema*. Minneapolis: University of Minnesota Press, 2012.
Sesti, Mario. *Nuovo cinema italiano: Gli autori, i film, le idee*. Rome: Teoria, 1994.
Sisto, Antonella. "*Gomorra*, a.k.a. *Gomorrah*: Italian Transnational Cinema." Paper presented at the American Association of Italian Studies, New York, 2009.
Sobchack, Vivian. *Carnal Thoughts: Embodiment and Moving Image Culture*. Berkeley: University of California Press, 2004.
Sontag, Susan. *On Photography*. New York: Dell, 1977.
Sorrentini, Barbara. Interview. Dolmen Home Video DVD, 2010.
Steimatsky, Noa. *The Face on Film*. New York: Oxford, 2017.
Torri, Bruno. "Ricambi generazionali (1943–2009)." In *Esordi italiani: Gli anni Dieci al cinema (2010–2015)*, edited by Pedro Armocida, pp. 19–40. Venice: Marsilio, 2015.
Uva, Christian. "I misteri d'Italia nel cinema: Strategie narrative e trame estetiche tra documento e finzione." In *Strane storie: Il cinema e i misteri d'Italia*, edited by Christian Uva, pp. 9–34. Soveria Mannelli: Rubbettino, 2011.
– "Nuovo cinema Italia: Per una mappa della produzione contemporanea, tra tendenze, formule e linguaggi." *The Italianist* 29 (2009): pp. 306–24.
–, ed. *Strane storie: Il cinema e i misteri d'Italia*. Soveria Mannelli: Rubbettino, 2011.

Veltroni, Walter. "Il nostro nemico è il cliché." *Panorama*, 29 March 2012. https://www.dagospia.com/rubrica-6/cafonalino/cafonalino-regista-roberto-ando-che-fu-assistente-francesco-37839.htm.

Veronesi, Micaela. "*Lo spazio bianco.*" *Segnocinema* 30 (January–February 2010): p. 51.

Viganò, Aldo. *Storia del cinema: Commedia italiana in cento film*. Genoa: Le Mani, 1995.

Villani, Simone. "Garrone, *Gomorra*: Un nuovo modello di 'visibilità' per il cinema italiano?" In *Gli invisibili: Esordi italiani del nuovo millennio*, edited by Vito Zagarrio, pp. 88–91. Rome: Kaplan, 2009.

Wood, Mary. *Italian Cinema*. Oxford: Berg, 2005.

Wu Ming. *New Italian Epic: Letteratura, sguardo obliquo, ritorno al futuro, Wu Ming I, New Italian Epic 3.0, Memorandum 1993–2008*. Turin: Einaudi, 2009.

Zagarrio, Vito. "Benvenuto al Nord: L'immaginario delle Film Commission del settentrione." In *Territori del cinema italiano: Produzione, diffusione, alfabetizzazione*, edited by Marco Maria Gazzano, Stefania Parigi, and Vito Zagarrio, pp. 155–65. Udine: Forum, 2013.

– "Il genere nel nuovo cinema italiano." In *Istantanee sul cinema italiano: Film, volti, idee del nuovo millennio*, edited by Franco Montini and Vito Zagarrio, pp. 51–60. Soveria Mannelli: Rubbettino, 2012.

– *La meglio gioventù: Nuovo cinema italiano 2000–2006*. Venice: Marsilio, 2006.

– "La rivoluzione documentaria." In *Istantanee sul cinema italiano: Film, volti, idee del nuovo millennio*, edited by Franco Montini and Vito Zagarrio, pp. 161–74. Soveria Mannelli: Rubbettino, 2012.

Zappoli, Giancarlo. "Il ritratto ironico di un papa umano, al di sopra di ogni sospetto." Review of *Habemus Papam*. *MYmovies*, 16 April 2011. https://www.mymovies.it/film/2011/habemuspapam/.

Zavattini, Cesare. "Some Ideas on the Cinema." In *Film: A Montage of Theories*, edited by Richard Dyer MacCann, pp. 216–28. New York: Dutton, 1966.

– "A Thesis on Neo-Realism." In *Springtime in Italy: A Reader on Neo-Realism*, edited by David Overbey, pp. 67–78. Hamden, CT: Archon Books, 1978.

Index

8 ½ (Fellini), 221–2
1968: and Moretti, 167, 168; and revolutionary enthusiasm, 28; and *Romanzo Criminale*, 48

Accattone (Pasolini), 26, 50
activism, 7; anti-Mafia, 8, 20, 31–2, 34, 137; anti-Mafia martyr film, 36–7; and *I cento passi*, 20, 25, 31–2, 34; of the resistance in *L'uomo che verrà*, 98
Aeneid (Virgil), 127
albero degli zoccoli, L' (Olmi), 103
Alias (TV series), 196–7
Alighieri, Dante: *Divina Commedia*, 31–2; *Inferno*, 30–1, 50, 171, 172, 190
Alla luce del sole (Faenza), 9
allegory: of the body politic in *Mar Nero*, 129; optical in *Fuocoammare*, 129, 132–3; in *Viva la libertà*, 163
alterity, 93. *See also* other, the
Altman, Robert: *Nashville*, 66; *Short Cuts*, 66
Ambrosoli, Giorgio, 137, 148
Amenta, Marco: *Diario di una siciliana ribelle*, 9; *La ragazza siciliana*, 9
Ammaniti, Niccolò, 211
Andò, Roberto: *Il trono vuoto*, 152, 153–4; *Viva la libertà*, 16, 152–64

Andreotti, Giulio, 16; and *Il Divo*, 8, 137–8, 142, 147–8, 149, 151, 245nn5–6, 246nn16–17; and *La Mafia uccide solo d'estate*, 36, 42, 44
Angela (Torre), 8
Angelini, Fiorenzo (cardinal), 144
anti-Mafia martyr film, 36–7
Antonello, Pierpaolo, and Florian Mussgnug, 5, 139, 226n12, 245n3
Antonioni, Michelangelo, 4
Archibugi, Francesca, 13
Ardent, Fanny, 137, 143
Atria, Rita, 9
Augustus (emperor), 54
aura, 187
auteurism, 4, 7, 13, 14, 15; and *I cento passi*, 33–4; and *Il Divo*, 138, 146–8; and Fellini, 146; and *Gomorra*, 7–8, 62; and *Romanzo criminale*, 59

Babel (Iñárritu), 66
Bakhtin, Mikhail, 50, 234n9
Balázs, Béla, 173, 219
"Ballroom Blitz" (Sweet), 52, 53
Banda della Magliana: and *Romanzo criminale*, 48, 50, 233n4
Barthes, Roland, 214
"Bartleby, the Scrivener: A Story of Wall Street" (Melville), 171–2

266   Index

Bartolo, Pietro, 125–6, 131
Basilica di Sant'Agostino, 55, 57, 58
Battle of Algiers, The (Pontecorvo), 229
Bellocchio, Marco, 229n1
Bellocchio, Maria Letizia, 250n6, 250n9
Benedict XVI (pope), 16, 166
Benigni, Roberto: *Life Is Beautiful*, 95
Benjamin, Walter, 187
Bentham, Jeremy, 70
Berlusconi, Silvio, 4, 16
Bizet, Georges, 220
body, the: aging, 111; of Andreotti
    in *Il Divo*, 141, 143–4, 145, 146–7;
    the body beautiful in *Gomorra*, 63;
    as cinematic sign in *Caro diario*, 4;
    corporate, 85; of dead protagonist
    in *Romanzo criminale*, 58; maternal,
    180–2, 187; and memory, 54; of
    migrant victims in *Fuocoammare*, 130,
    131, 244n8; of Moretti on screen, 167;
    of scapegoat, 88; social, 202–3; of
    spectator, 61–2. *See also* body politic
body politic: as aging and in need
    of care, 111, 117; as enlivened, 158;
    as feminized and maternal, 180–1;
    history of the trope, 251n9; and
    Mafia power, 41; as maimed, 202–3
Bondanella, Peter, 247n6
Bondavalli, Simona, 238n34
Bondi, Frederico: *Mar nero*, 13, 14,
    109–20, 242n2, 243n14
Boni, Marta, 226n21, 233n7
Borsellino, Paolo, 8, 36, 38, 44
Brecht, Bertolt, 157
Breton, André, 211
Brizzi, Fausto: *La note prima degli
    esami*, 14

Caimano, Il (Moretti), 147, 167, 175
Calvi, Robert, 137, 147, 148
camerawork: in *I Cento Passi*, 33;
    close-up in *Habemus Papam*, 172–4,
175; in *Il Divo*, 140, 142, 144–5, 147,
149–50; free indirect subjective,
69–70, 113; in *Fuocoammare*, 123–5,
128, 129–30, 13; in *Gomorra*, 62, 67,
68–71, 72–4; in *La grande bellezza*,
212, 218–9; in *La Mafia uccide solo
d'estate*, 39, 40; in *Mar nero*, 113,
117, 118–19; in *Romanzo criminale*,
52, 54, 55–6; in *Lo spazio bianco*,
186–7; in *L'uomo che verrà*, 96,
99–100, 101, 104; in *Il vento fa il suo
giro*, 79, 80–1, 82, 84, 87–8, 89; in
Viva la libertà, 159, 161–3
Camorra, 7, 9, 42, 60–74, 189–90,
236n10
Canova, Gianni, 14
Cappabianca, Alessandro, 248n3
Caravaggio: *Madonna of the Pilgrims*,
55–6, 58
Carlorosi, Silvia, 236n10, 237n22
Caro diario (Moretti), 4
Cassius, 145
Castel Sant'Angelo, 57
Cavani, Liliana, 13
Cavataio, Michele, 41
Celestine V (pope), 171, 172
cento passi, I (Giordana), 3, 8, 15,
    19–34, 36–7; and activism, 20, 25,
    31–2, 34; and anti-Mafia martyr
    film, 36–7; camerawork in, 33;
    credits, 19; and epitaph, 20–1,
    32–4, 36–7; and literature, 29–32;
    and *La Mafia uccide solo d'estate*,
    36–7, 45–6; and music, 21, 27–8,
    230n13; and Oedipal scenario, 21–
    3; portraiture in, 23, 25; and radio,
    26–7; synopsis, 19–20
Cervantes, Miguel de: *Don Quixote*, 30
Cervini, Alessia, 15
Chekov, Anton: *The Seagull*, 166,
    170, 172
Chiesi, Roberto, 93, 241n12

China Is Near (Bellocchio), 229n1
Chinnici, Rocco, 35, 37, 40, 44
Christian Democratic Party, 4, 137–8, 149
Chuck Berry, 155
Ciarrapico, Giuseppe, 144
Cimatti, Roberto, 80
cinema al femminile, 13, 16
cinema politico: and *I cento passi*, 21, 23, 25, 230n3; and *Il Divo*, 140, 147; and neorealism, 36, 229n1; and *Viva la libertà*, 247n10
cinematography. *See* camerawork
Cirasola, Nicola: *Focaccia Blues*, 10, 12
Citti, Sergio, 50
Cohen, Leonard: "Suzanne," 28
Cold War, 4, 58
Colosseum, the, 211
comedy: conventions of, 37–8, 197, 205; Italian film comedy, 7, 13, 14, 16, 205, 228n39; mask of, 163; romantic comedy, 37–8, 205
Comencini, Christina, 13
Comencini, Francesca: *Lo spazio bianco*, 13, 16, 179–92
Come un gatto in tangenziale (Milani), 194
commedia dell'arte, 13
commedia italiana, 16
consequenze dell'amore, Le (Sorrentino), 8
Coppola, Francis Ford: *Godfather* trilogy, 48
Corriere della sera, 155
Cortellesi, Paola, 193, 194, 198–9
Cossiga, Francesco, 142–3, 245n9
Cozzi, Emilio, 61, 238n39
Crash (Haggis), 66
crime film: and *Gomorra*, 63–4; and *Romanzo criminale*, 48–9, 50, 53, 58
Crowdus, Gary, 252n3, 253n12

D'Agostini, Paolo, 104
Dalla Chiesa, Carlo Alberto: and *Il Divo*, 137, 148; and *La Mafia uccide solo d'estate*, 35, 36, 40, 42, 43, 46
D'Annunzio, Gabriele, 211
Decameron (Pasolini), 26
De Cataldo, Giancarlo: *Romanzo criminale*, 49–50, 54, 234n12
De Gaetano, Roberto, 12
Deleuze, Gilles, 69
Delfino, Massimiliano, 231nn2–3
Del Volgo, Peppino, 122
Democrazia Proletaria, 20, 28
De Palma, Brian: *Scarface*, 48, 60, 64–5, 74
De Sica, Christian, 14
De Sica, Vittorio, 3, 4, 151, 181; *Yesterday, Today and Tomorrow*, 181
destiny, 51, 73, 174, 230n6, 234n14
Diario di una siciliana ribelle (Amenta), 9
Diliberto, Pierfrancesco: *La Mafia uccide solo d'estate*, 15, 35–46; television celebrity of, 37, 46
Diritti, Giorgio: influence of Olmi on, 103; *L'uomo che verrà*, 92–105; *Il vento fa il suo giro*, 11, 77–91
di Robilant, Alessandro: *Il giudice ragazzino*, 8
Divina Commedia (Dante), 31–2
Divo, Il (Sorrentino), 7, 8, 16, 137–51; camerawork in, 140, 142, 144–5, 147, 149–50; and caricature, 146–7; credits, 137; and documentary, 147; and form, 142, 144, 146; and irony, 138–9, 140–1, 142, 143, 146, 149–51; and Italian cinema of engagement, 139–40, 151; montage in, 137–8, 145, 148–9; music in, 141, 142, 145–6; satire in, 141, 147, 148; and spectacle, 140, 144; and spectator, 147, 150–1; staging in, 144–5; synopsis, 137–8

documentary: and *Caro diario*, 4; definition of, 228n37; and *Il Divo*, 147; and *Fuocoammare*, 121, 122–3, 125–6; and *Gomorra*, 62; and *Habemus Papam*, 165; and *La Mafia uccide solo d'estate*, 43–4, 46; and migration, 12; and peasant life, 103; simulated in *I cento passi*, 33, 45–6; types of, 12; and witnessing history in *L'uomo che verrà*, 94
dolce vita, La (Fellini), 220–1
D'Onofrio, Emanuele, 27, 28, 230n13
Don Quixote (Cervantes), 30
Dostoevsky, Fyodor, 211
Durtain, Luc, 187

Eco, Umberto, 26
eco-cinema, 11, 227n33
economic miracle, Italian, 28, 181
ecphrasis, 55
Elia, Eliana, 241n12, 249n11
Eliot, T.S., 144
Enea, Signora, 137, 143–4, 149
engagement, Italian cinema of: 5, 7, 10; and *I cento passi*, 21; and *Il Divo*, 139–40, 151, 245n4; and *Fuocoammare*, 122; and *Ma cosa ci dice il cervello*, 194; and *La Mafia uccide solo d'estate*, 37. See also *impegno*
Evangelisti, Franco, 142
Evola, Julius, 48

Faenza, Roberto: *Alla luce del sole*, 9
Falcone, Giovanni, 8; and *Il Divo*, 137, 145, 146, 148; and *La Mafia uccide solo d'estate*, 36, 37, 38
Fauré, Gabriel, 141, 145
Fellini, Frederico, 4; *8 ½*, 221–2, 253n14; *La dolce vita*, 220; influence on Sorrentino, 146, 220–2, 253nn12–14
film commissions, 9–10

Fine pena mai (Barletti and Conte), 8
First Republic, 4, 58, 139
flashback: in *Romanzo criminale*, 58–9
Flaubert, Gustave, 211
Focaccia Blues (Cirasola), 10, 12
fornarina, La (Raphael), 220
Fornasiero, Andrea, 197–8
Fort'apasc (Risi), 9
forza del destino, La (Verdi), 152, 154–5, 156, 157, 162–3
Frammartino, Michelangelo: *Le quattro volte*, 11
Frazzi, Andrea and Antonio: *The Sky Is Falling*, 95
free indirect subjective camerawork: in *Gomorra*, 69–70; in *Mar nero*, 113
Freud, Sigmund, 189
Fukuyama, Francis, 6
Fuocoammare (Rosi), 12, 121–33; camerawork in, 123–5, 128, 129–30, 13; credits, 121; documentary, 12, 121, 122–3, 125–6; intermediality in, 124–6; making of, 122–3; and migrant crisis, 122, 123, 126, 128, 133; music in, 124–5, 127; optical allegory in, 129, 132–3, 244nn6–7; reception, 122, 243n4; and spectator, 122, 125, 128, 130, 133, 243n4; synopsis, 121; theme of weaponry in, 131–2

Gadot, Gal, 196
Garibaldi, Giuseppe, 57
Garner, Jennifer, 196
Garrone, Matteo: *Gomorra*, 6, 7, 8, 15, 60–74
Gassman, Mary, 143
Gaudioso, Massimo, 236n17, 237n25
gaze: of camera in *Gomorra*, 67, 70–1, 72; of filmmaker in *Il vento fa il suo giro*, 88; in *Fuocoammare*, 130, 131; in *La grande bellezza*, 219, 220, 223;

interpretive, 34; in *Mar nero*, 110; mobilized in *Lo spazio bianco*, 189; of photographer, 219; in *Romanzo criminale*, 50, 52–3, 56; of spectator in *Lo spazio bianco*, 191; and spectatorship in *L'uomo che verrà*, 93, 95–6. *See also* spectator, the
Gelli, Licio, 148
genre: anti-Mafia martyr film, 36–7; *cinema politico* (see *cinema politico*); comedy, 37–8, 163, 197, 205; *commedia italiana*, 16; crime film (*see* crime film); documentary (*see* documentary); Italian film comedy, 7, 13–14, 16, 205, 228n39, 229n45; the novel, 49–50, 153–4, 234n9; poetry (*see* poetry); *poliziesco*, 50, 53, 55; romance (*see* romance); thriller, 13, 198, 205; travelogue, 20, 198; *See also* pastiche
Gherardi, Davide, 239n7, 240n9
Giordana, Marco Tullio: *I cento passi*, 3, 8, 15, 19–34, 36, 45
Giuliano, Boris, 35, 40, 148
Godfather trilogy (Coppola), 48
Gomorra (Garrone), 6, 7, 8, 15, 60–74; camerawork in, 62, 67, 68–71, 72–4, 238n34; compared to Saviano's novel, 65–7, 72, 73, 236nn18–20; credits, 60; and documentary, 62–3, 65–6; and embodied spectatorship, 61–2; and free indirect subjective cinematography, 69–70; and genre (crime film), 63–4; image of mobster in, 64–5; manhood in, 71; and music, 61; narrative structure in, 64, 66, 237n25; synopsis, 60–1; Le Vele di Scampia as image of mob rule in, 67, 68, 71, 72, 73, 74
Gomorra (Saviano), 65–7, 72, 73, 236nn18–20

Goodfellas (Scorsese), 48
Gospel According to Matthew, The (Pasolini), 26
Grand Canyon (Kasdan), 66
grande bellezza, La (Sorrentino), 16, 209–24; camerawork in, 212, 218–19; credits, 209; and debt to Fellini, 220–2, 253nn12–14; and literature, 210–12, 215, 217, 222; mise-en-scène, 214; and music, 216, 218, 220, 223; reception, 211, 214, 253n12; and satire, 211; synopsis, 209–10
Guzzanti, Sabrina, 13

Habemus Papam (Moretti), 16, 165–76; and the church, 165–6, 168–9, 170–1, 172, 174, 176, 249n20; close-up in, 172–4, 175; credits, 165; and literature, 171–2; and music, 176; reception, 248n3; satire of psychoanalysis in, 166–7; and the self, 168–70, 172, 173–5; synopsis, 165–6; and theatre, 166, 169–71, 172
Hadrian (emperor), 54
Haggis, Paul: *Crash*, 66
Hamlet (Shakespeare), 159
Hegel, 155
Hitler, Adolf, 54
Hollywood, 13, 14, 36, 64
humanism: and *Habemus Papum*, 174; and *Ma cosa ci dice il cervello*, 203–4; and *Viva la libertà*, 152, 153, 154, 164, 247n3
Hutcheon, Linda, 196, 197, 202, 231n21

Idea Socialista, 26
image: of the community, 88; and documentary, 43, 123, 126, 128, 129–30, 131; of empty balcony in *Habemus Papam*, 176; and

facial close-up, 174; of Falcone's incinerated vehicle in *Il Divo*, 145; and *Gomorra*, 64–5, 67, 237n20; and *La grande bellezza*, 210–11, 214–15, 217, 223, 224; of *homo politicus*, 163; of horse-drawn cart in *Mar nero*, 117; of infant in *Lo spazio bianco*, 182, 185, 186–7, 191; of inner thoughts, 161; and mass media, 122; of mirror in *Viva la libertà*, 160–1; and music in *Il Divo*, 145–6; Pasolinian image-signs in *Mar nero*, 119–20; of prisoner in *Il Divo*, 149; testimonial force of, 3
Impastato, Peppino, 19–34, 46
impegno, 225n3; and *I cento passi*, 29, 225n3; and *Il Divo*, 139–40, 151, 245n4; and *Gomorra*, 65; and *La Mafia uccide solo d'estate*, 40, 46; postmodern, 5, 139–40, 226n12. *See also* engagement: Italian cinema of
Iñárritu, Alejandro González: *Babel*, 66
Inferno (Dante), 30–1, 50, 171, 190
intermediality, 6; in *Fuocoammare*, 124–6
Investigation of a Citizen above Suspicion (Petri), 229n1
"Io ho in mente te" (Equipe 84), 51
Istituto Luce, 122
Italian Communist Party, 4
Italian Socialist Party, 4, 138

Jesus, 26, 86, 89
John Paul II (pope), 16, 165
Joplin, Janis: "Summertime," 28
Journey to Italy (Rossellini), 181
Judah, 145

Kant, Immanuel, 203–4
Karagoz, Claudia, 249n1, 250n5
Kasdan, Lawrence: *Grand Canyon*, 66
Kermode, Frank, 190

Labate, Wilma, 13
Largo Argentina, 57
Last Supper, The, 145
La Torre, Pio, 35
Lazarus, 89
Lega Nord, 10
Leopardi, Giacomo: "L'infinito," 29–31
Life Is Beautiful (Benigni), 95
Ligabue, Luciano, 26
Lima, Salvatore, 36, 142, 148–9
"L'infinito" (Leopardi), 29–31, 231n19
Lippok, Robert, 145
literature: and *La grande bellezza*, 210–12, 215, 217, 222; and the novel, 234n9, 49–50, 153–4; and pastoral in *Il vento fa il suo giro*, 81–2, 83–4; and politics in *I cento passi*, 29–32; and *Viva la libertà*, 153–4, 156–7, 159, 164. *See also* poetry
litotes, 122
Livatino, Rosario, 36
Lo Cascio, Luigi, 33

Ma cosa ci dice il cervello (Milani), 13, 16, 193–205; and the body politic, 202–3; credits, 193; and genre, 194–8; and media, analogue vs. digital, 200–1; and parody, 196–9, 202, 205; reception, 197–9; and satire, 194, 202–3; synopsis, 193–4
Madonna: *Madonna of the Pilgrims* (Caravaggio), 55; pregnant, 97, 103; statue of, 125
Mafia: anti-Mafia martyr film, 36–7; Camorra, 7, 9, 42, 60–74, 189–90, 236n10; and *I cento passi*, 19–21, 28, 30–2, 34; and *Il Divo*, 137–8, 145–6, 148; and *La Mafia uccide solo d'estate*, 35–46; 'Ndrangheta, 42; and *Romanzo criminale*, 48, 52, 54

Mafia uccide solo d'estate, La (Diliberto), 15, 35–46; as anti-Mafia martyr film, 37–8; camerawork in, 39, 40; civic monuments in, 38–41, 231nn2–3; and collective trauma, 44; and credits, 35; documentary, 43–4, 46; and genre (romantic comedy), 37–8; historical pedagogy in, 39–40; as homage to *I cento passi*, 45–6; *impegno*, 40, 46; montage in, 39–40, 46; and news archive, 41, 43–4; and *La notte di San Lorenzo*, 40; synopsis, 35–6; and television, 37, 46

Mahler, Gustav, 28

Mama roma (Pasolini), 50

mani pulite (clean hands) campaign, 4

mani sulla città, Le (Rosi), 21, 34

Marazzi, Alina, 13

Mar nero (Bondi), 13, 15, 109–20; and autobiography, 110–11, 242n2; and the body politic, 111, 117; camerawork in, 113, 117, 118–19; credits, 109; and the filmic unconscious, 119–20; and the geographic imaginary, 113–16, 118–19, 120; the immigrant other in, 111–12, 113; and migration, 110, 117; montage in, 118–19; poetic vs. prosaic language in, 114, 119–20; and subjectivity, 111–12, 116–18; synopsis, 109–10

marriage: and comedy, 197, 205; and *Journey to Italy*, 181; and *Ma cosa ci dice il cervello*, 197, 205; and *La Mafia uccide solo d'estate*, 37; and *Mar nero*, 112–13; and *La messa è finita*, 167–8; and *Il vento fa il suo giro*, 84

Marrone, Gaetana, 229–30

Martino, Bruno, 145

Marx, Karl, 145

Marxism, 5, 98, 209

Masoni, Tullio, 230

"Mass" (Vallejo), 89

mass media, 44, 64, 117, 122, 133, 200–1, 214

Mayakovsky, Vladimir, 25–6, 29, 32

Melville, Herman, 171–2

Menaechmi (Plautus), 154

Mereghetti, Paolo, 130, 247n10, 249n20

messa è finita, La (Moretti), 167–8, 174–6

metaphor: in *I cento passi*, 25; of the chambers of the mind in *L'uomo che verrà*, 104; of dancing in *Il Divo*, 141; of life as theatre, 170; of the scapegoat in *Il vento fa il suo giro*, 87; of the body politic, 180–1, 202–3 (*see also* body politic)

Micciché, Lino, 5

Milani, Ricardo: *Come un gatto in tangenziale*, 194; *Ma cosa ci dice il cervello*, 13, 16, 193–205

"Minor Swing" (Reinhardt), 28

Mitry, Jean, 69

Modonesi, Chiara, 34

Modugno, Domenico: "Volare," 27

montage: in *I cento passi*, 33; in *Il Divo*, 137, 138, 145, 148–9; in *Ma cosa ci dice il cervello*, 202; in *La Mafia uccide solo d'estate*, 40, 46, 51; in *Romanzo criminale*, 52–3, 55; in *Lo spazio bianco*, 189; in *Il vento fa il suo giro*, 80, 82, 84–5; in *Viva la libertà*, 160, 162, 247n9

Montini, Franco, 5

Morandini, Morando, 239n1, 239n3

Moretti, Nanni: and *Il Caimano*, 147, 167, 175; and *Caro diario*, 4; and *Habemus Papam*, 16, 165–76; and *La messa è finita*, 167–8, 174–6

Morgenstern, Barbara, 145

Moro, Aldo: and *I cento passi*, 20; and *Il Divo*, 137, 138, 150–1; and *Romanzo criminale*, 55
Mosè in Egitto (Rossini), 125
Moses, 127
music: in *I cento passi*, 21, 27–8, 230n13; in *Il Divo*, 141, 142, 145–6; in *Fuocoammare*, 124–5, 127; in *Gomorra*, 61; in *La grande bellezza*, 216, 218, 220, 223; in *Habemus Papam*, 176; in *Romanzo criminale*, 51, 52, 57; in *L'uomo che verrà*, 96, 99–100, 101, 104; in *Il vento fa il suo giro*, 81; in *Viva la libertà*, 154, 155, 156, 157, 159–60, 162–3
Mussolini, Benito, 16, 54

Nashville (Altman), 66
national identity: and collective consciousness, 148; and Italian film comedy, 13; and the Italian national self, 105; and the Italian national story, 151; and the Italian New Man, 97
Nazi occupation of/killing in Italy, 93, 94–5, 97, 98–101
'Ndrangheta, 42
neorealism, 3; and anti-Mafia martyr film, 36–7; influence on new Italian cinema, 3, 139–40; memorialist strain in, 20–1, 37; and Rossellini, 62; and Zavattini, 64. See also *pedinamento*; Zavattini, Cesare
neo-regionalism: and films of Diritti, 11–12, 15; and regional film commissions, 9, 227n26
new Italian cinema: debt to neorealism, 3, 139–40; and documentary filmmaking, 12, 62; and *impegno*, 103; and neo-regionalism, 9–10; and New Italian Epic, 6; the novelistic turn in, 5–6. See also anti-Mafia martyr film; engagement, Italian cinema of; *impegno*; neo-regionalism
New Italian Epic, 6
Nicchiarelli, Susanna, 13
Night of the Shooting Stars (Paolo and Vittorio Taviani), 95
notte di San Lorenzo, La (Paolo and Vittorio Taviani), 40
notte prima degli esami, La (Brizzi), 14
novel, the. See under literature

Occhini, Ilaria, 117, 118
Odyssey, 127
O'Healy, Áine, 244nn7–8
Olivieri, Marco, 231n19, 247n5, 247nn7–9
Olmi, Ermanno, 103
other, the: immigrant in *Mar nero*, 111–12, 113; specular in *Viva la libertà*, 160–1; in *Il vento fa il suo giro*, 80, 88, 91

Pacchioni, Frederico, 247n6
Pacino, Al, 74
Padre padrone (Paolo and Vittorio Taviani), 229n1
Padre Pio, 125
Paisà, 237n25
Paisan (Rossellini), 20
Panofsky, Erwin, 218
panopticon, 70
Paparcone, Anna, 231n19
Parenti, Neri, 14
parody: of Dante's *Inferno* in *I cento passi*, 30–2, 231n21; in *Ma cosa ci dice il cervello*, 196–9, 202, 205; and postmodernism, 4
Parrella, Valeria (*Lo spazio bianco*, novel), 16, 179, 180, 184, 189, 190, 192

partisans: portrayal in *L'uomo che verrà*, 93, 96, 97–101
Pasolini, Pier Paolo, 4; *Accattone*, 26, 50; and *I cento passi*, 22–4, 29, 31; *Che cosa sono le nuvole*, 238n39; "Cinema di poesia," 174; *Decameron*, 26; and free indirect subjective cinematography, 69–70, 113; *The Gospel According to Matthew*, 26; and image-signs in *Mar nero*, 119–20; influence on *Romanzo criminale*, 50–1, 55, 58, 59; *Mamma Roma*, 50; *Ragazzi di vita*, 50–1; *Una vita violenta*, 50
Past, Elena, 235n7, 237n27, 239n1
pastiche: and *Il Divo*, 139; in *Ma cosa ci dice il cervello*, 194, 198; and postmodernism, 4
pastoral: and *Il vento fa il suo giro*, 81–2, 83–4
Pavane pour Orchestra Op. 50 (Fauré), 141
Pecorelli, Carmine, 137, 138, 148
pedagogy: in *Fuocoammare*, 128–9; in *Gomorra*, 66, 68; and *Ma cosa ci dice il cervello*, 203; of Mafia history in *La Mafia uccide solo d'estate*, 39–40
pedinamento: in *Gomorra*, 66, 68; in *Mar nero*, 113
Petri, Elio, 140, 147, 229n1
phenomenology: and the spectator, 11; and *Gomorra*, 62, 65
photography, 217–19
physiognomy: and *I cento passi*, 23–5; film as, 173, 218–19
Piazzale Michelangelo, 115
Piazza San Pietro, 176
Piccoli, Michel, 249n11
Pieraccioni, Leonardo, 14
Pirandello, Luigi, 170, 211
Pisciotta, Gaspare, 148

Placido, Michele: *Romanzo criminale*, 6, 8, 15, 47–59
Placido Rizzotto (Scimeca), 3, 8, 225n3
Plautus, 154
poetry: in *I cento passi*, 22–3, 29; in *Il vento fa il suo giro*, 89; in *Viva la libertà*, 157, 164
poliziesco, 50, 53, 55. See also crime film
Pomicino, Paolo, 137, 140, 144–5
Pontecorvo, Gillo: *The Battle of Algiers*, 229
portraiture in *I cento passi*, 23, 25
postmodern *impegno*. See *impegno*
postmodernism, 4–5
Procol Harum: "A Whiter Shade of Pale," 28
Propaganda Due (P2), 148
Proust, Marcel, 211
psychoanalysis: Freudian slip, 189; satire of, 165–7; and Oedipal scenario in *I cento passi*, 21–3, 230n4; and primal scene, 93
Pudovkin, Vsevolod, 144

Quatriglio, Costanza, 13
quattro volte, Le (Frammartino), 11

radio: in *I cento passi*, 26–7, 31–2; in *Fuocoammare*, 124–5, 127
Radio Aut: in *I cento passi*, 20, 26–7, 30, 32
Radiofreccia (Ligabue), 26
ragazza siciliana, La (Amenta), 9
Ragazzi di vita (Pasolini), 50–1
Raphael (*La fornarina*), 220
reception: of *I cento passi*, 27, 230n5; of *Fuocoammare*, 122, 243n4; of *La grande bellezza*, 211, 214, 253n12; of *Ma cosa ci dice il cervello*, 197–8; of *Romanzo criminale*, 48–9, 233n6; of

L'uomo che verrà, 94, 104–5, 241n8, 241n12. *See also* spectator, the
Red Brigades, 20, 138, 149
Reinhardt, Django: "Minor Swing," 28
Renaissance, the: and Florence, 115
Renga, Dana, 44, 237n25, 238n30, 238n38
Renzi, Matteo, 247n3
Repubblica, La, 138
Riina, Salvatore: and *Il Divo*, 138, 145–6, 148; and *La Mafia solo uccide d'estate*, 35, 41–2
Ripa, Cesare, 180
Risi, Marco (*Fort'apasc*), 9
Rohracher, Alice, 13
romance: conventions of, 183, 185, 191, 192; and parody, 198, 205
romanzo cavalleresco, 50
Romanzo criminale (De Cataldo), 49–50, 54
Romanzo criminale (Placido), 6, 8, 15, 47–59; aesthetics in, 55–6, 58; camerawork in, 52, 54, 55–6; and civic condemnation, 58; credits, 47; flashback in, 58–9; freedom in, 54, 55, 59; and genre (crime film), 48–9, 50, 53, 58; influence of Pasolini on, 50–1, 55, 58, 59; montage in, 51, 52–3, 55; music in, 51, 52, 57; and the novel, 49–50, 54; reception, 48–9, 233n6; synopsis, 47–8; theme of destiny in, 51; transmedia life of, 49
Rome, Open City (Rossellini), 20
Rosi, Francesco: and *cinema politico*, 139–40, 229n1; influence on *Il Divo*, 151; and *Le mani sulla città*, 21, 34, 229nn2–3
Rosi, Gianfranco: *Fuocoammare*, 12, 15, 122–33, 243nn2–3, 244n8, 245n10

Rossellini, Roberto, 3, 4, 37, 62, 151; *Journey to Italy*, 181; *Paisan*, 20; *Rome, Open City*, 20
Rossini, Gioachino (*Mosè in Egitto*), 125

Saint-Saëns, Camille, 145
Salvini, Matteo, 10
Santa Maria di Trastevere, 57
Santner, Eric, 232n13, 241n10
Saviano, Roberto, 7, 65–7, 72, 73, 236n18, 236n20
Sbardella, Vittorio, 137, 138, 144
Scalfari, Eugenio, 137, 138, 148
Scamarcio, Riccardo, 14
Scarface (De Palma), 48, 60, 64–5, 74
Schiavone, Walter, 64, 65
Schubert, Franz, 155
Sciascia, Leonard, 147
Scimeca, Pasquale (*Placido Rizzotto*), 3, 8
Scorsese, Martin (*Goodfellas*), 48, 62
Scotti, Vincenzo, 137, 142
Seagull, The (Chekov), 166, 170, 172
self, the: Italian collective, 14; and role in *Habemus Papam*, 168–70, 172, 173–5; self-absorption in *Mar nero*, 111, 116; self-distancing in *Il Divo*, 146, 151; and *Viva la libertà*, 160–1
Servillo, Toni, 16; and *Il Divo*, 137, 147; and *Viva la libertà*, 152, 155, 157–8, 247n5
Sesti, Mario, 5
"Shake Your Booty" (KC and the Sunshine Band), 57
Short Cuts (Altman), 66, 237n25
Siani, Giancarlo, 9
Simone, Nina, 192
Sindona, Michele, 137, 147, 148
Sistine Chapel, the, 169, 248n5
sitcom: and *Ma cosa ci dice il cervello*, 195, 198, 205

Sky Is Falling, The (Andrea and Antonio Frazzi), 95
Slow Cinema, 11
Sobchack, Vivian, 62
Sonata in A major (Schubert), 155
Sontag, Susan, 217
Sorrentino, Paolo: *Le consequenze dell'amore*, 8; *Il Divo*, 7, 8, 16, 42, 137–51; *La grande bellezza*, 16, 209–24
Spanish Steps, the, 57
spazio bianco, Lo (Comencini), 13, 16, 179–92; and blank space, motif of, 183, 184–5, 188, 191, 192; and camerawork, 186–7; and cinema, theme of, 182–3; credits, 179; and montage, 189; and motherhood, 183, 188–9, 190–1, 192, 250n9; and music, 192; and Naples as topos, 180–2, 183–4, 188–9, 192, 249n1, 250nn5–6; and the novel (Parrella), 16, 179, 180, 184, 189, 190, 192, 250n2; reception, 249n1, 250nn5–6; and romance, 183, 185, 191, 192; synopsis, 179–80; and technology, 181–2, 183, 185–8; and time, 184, 190–1
spazio bianco, Lo (Parrella), 16, 179, 180, 184, 189, 190, 192, 250n2
spectacle: and *cinema politico*, 139–40; and *Il Divo*, 8, 140, 144; and *Fuocoammare*, 129; and *La grande bellezza*, 217, 218, 219; of mainstream media, 117; of *Romanzo criminale*, 58; and slow cinema, 11; and *Lo spazio bianco*, 186–7, 191; and *Il vento fa il suo giro*, 86, 87, 88; and *Viva la libertà*, 155
spectator, the: of *Il Divo*, 147, 150–1; and facial close-up, 174; of *Fuocoammare*, 122, 125, 128, 130, 133; of *Gomorra*, 61–2, 65; of *La grande bellezza*, 214, 216, 223–4; of *La Mafia uccide solo d'estate*, 44; as moral onlooker, 105; and phenomenology, 11, 62, 65; and *Romanzo criminale*, 55, 59; as second-order witness in *L'uomo che verrà*, 95–6, 101, 104; of *Lo spazio bianco*, 180, 191; of *Il vento fa il suo giro*, 81, 85, 90; of *Viva la libertà*, 157–8, 162. See also witness
spy film: and *Ma cosa ci dice il cervello*, 195–9
Stalin, Joseph, 54
Stazione di Santa Maria Novella, 113, 114, 115
Steimatsky, Noa, 174, 249n14, 249n17
Stella Rossa Brigade, 94, 98, 99, 100
"Summertime" (Gershwin): as performed by Janis Joplin, 28
"Suzanne" (Cohen), 28
Symphony No. 2 (*Resurrection*) (Mahler), 28

Tangentopoli, 138, 148
Taviani, Paolo and Vittorio: and *cinema politico*, 139–40, 229n1; *Night of the Shooting Stars*, 95; *La note di San Lorenzo*, 40
television: aesthetics of, 37, 62; and celebrity, 37, 117; and film in *La Mafia uccide solo d'estate*, 37–8, 46; as mass medium, 5; in *Il vento fa il suo giro*, 87, 88
testimony, 25, 41; in *Fuocoammare*, 125–6; in *Mar nero*, 111; in *L'uomo che verrà*, 94, 97, 102, 103–4
theatre: in *Habemus Papam*, 166, 169–71, 172; as mass spectacle, 117; and politics in *I cento passi*, 26, 27
Three Brothers (Rosi), 229n1

thriller, 13, 198, 205
Titus (emperor), 54
Todo modo (Petri), 147
"To One Who Hesitates" (Brecht), 157
Tore delle Milizie, the, 57
Torre, Roberta, 8, 13
Trajan's market, 57
transmedia storytelling: as field of scholarship, 6; in *La Mafia uccide solo d'estate*, 46; of *Romanzo criminale*, 49, 233n7
trauma: collective, 44, 238n30; historical, 6, 97, 241n10; and muteness, 95; of premature birth, 13, 185; of the Years of Lead, 49
travelogue, 198, 20
Trio, 145
Tuan, Lydia, 245n7, 253n12
Turgenev, Ivan, 211

Una vita violenta (Pasolini), 50
uomo che verrà, L' (Diritti), 15, 92–105; bearing witness to history in, 93–5, 97–102, 103–5, 241n12; camerawork in, 96, 99–100, 101, 104; credits, 92; editing in, 101, 104; influence of Olmi on, 103; and the Italian New Man, 94, 97; and memory, 104; and music, 93, 101–3; and partisans, 93, 96, 97–101; reception, 241n8, 241n12; and regional identity, 98; and spectator, 93, 95–6, 101, 104–5; synopsis, 92–3
Uva, Christian, 4, 13, 14, 43

Vallejo, César: "Mass," 89
Vele di Scampia, Le: as image of Camorra rule in *Gomorra*, 67, 71, 72, 73, 74, 237n27

vento fa il suo giro, Il (Diritti), 11, 15, 77–91; camerawork in, 79, 80–1, 82, 83, 87–8, 89; credits, 77; flashback in, 79, 91; landscape in, 80–1, 83, 87; and language, 78, 79, 80, 90, 239n7; making of, 78, 239n1; montage in, 80, 82, 84; music in, 81; and neo-regionalism, 11, 15; regional identity in, 78–80, 82, 84–6, 87, 88, 90–1; spectacle in, 86, 87, 88; and spectator, 81, 85, 90; synopsis, 77–8; temporality in, 79, 81, 87, 90–1; theme of resurrection in, 89–90
Verdi, Giuseppe: *La forza del destino*, 152, 154–5, 156, 157, 162–3
Verdone, Carlo, 14
Veronesi, Micaela, 251n11, 251n13
Victor Emmanuel II, 57
Villani, Simone, 237
Virgil (poet), 32, 180
Visconti, Luchino, 3, 4, 151
Viva la libertà (Andò), 16, 152–64; allegory in, 163; camerawork in, 159, 161–3; and cinema of engagement (*impegno*), 154, 159, 163–4; credits, 152; and humanism, 152, 153, 154, 164; and literature, 153–4, 156–7, 159, 164; montage in, 162; music in, 154, 155, 156, 157, 159–60, 162–3; and the spectator, 157–8, 162; synopsis, 152–3; and *Il trono vuoto*, 153–4, 155–6, 159, 160, 163, 164
Vivaldi, Antonio, 145
"Volare" (Modugno), 28

Wertmuller, Lina, 13
"Whiter Shade of Pale, A" (Procol Harum), 28
witness: to art, 155, 220; and documentary, 33, 44, 62; in *Gomorra*, 65; to history, 40, 44, 94, 97, 99,

101, 102, 103, 104, 127; to migrant crisis in *Fuocoammare*, 122, 126, 133; spectator as, 51, 124, 130, 133, 222; in *L'uomo che verrà*, 95, 97, 99, 101, 102, 103. *See also* spectator; testimony
Wonder Woman (Jenkins), 196
"The Work of Art in the Age of Mechanical Reproduction" (Benjamin), 187
Wu Ming, 6, 226n17, 234n12

Years of Lead: *Romanzo criminale* as critique of, 49, 53
Yesterday, Today and Tomorrow (De Sica), 181

Zagarrio, Vito, 10, 13
Zappoli, Giancarlo, 248n3
Zavattini, Cesare, 64, 65–6, 236n15
Zero, Renato, 142, 145

Milton Keynes UK
Ingram Content Group UK Ltd.
UKHW022211040324
438897UK00023B/182